The Metaphysics of World Order

Oliur Hearse.

The Metaphysics of World Order

A Synthesis of Philosophy, Theology, and Politics

Studied mathematics and social sciences
in University of La Verne, California

NICOLAS LAOS

Dr Nicolas
Laos

works as a philosopher and neopolitical
which is politics through reforming
social aspects such as the media. In
addition, he is associated with private
intelligence companies as a consultant
internationally. He previously worked
in investment services recieving
professional training in political,
economic and cultural-psychological
analysis

⌒**PICKWICK** *Publications* • Eugene, Oregon

THE METAPHYSICS OF WORLD ORDER
A Synthesis of Philosophy, Theology, and Politics

Pickwick Publications
An Imprint of Wipf and Stock Publishers
199 W. 8th Ave., Suite 3
Eugene, OR 97401

www.wipfandstock.com

ISBN 13: 978-1-4982-0101-8

Cataloguing-in-Publication Data

Laos, Nicolas K., 1974–.

    The metaphysics of world order : a synthesis of philosophy, theology, and politics / Nicolas Laos

    X + Y p. ; 23 cm. Includes bibliographical references.

    ISBN 13: 978-1-4982-0101-8

    1. Metaphysics. 2. Theology. 3. Political science—philosophy. 4. World politics. 5. Geopolitics. I. Title.

JA71 L36 2015

Manufactured in the U.S.A.

CONTENTS

CONTENTS

ACKNOWLEDGEMENTS

I WOULD LIKE TO dedicate this book to the following persons and communities: Roman Vladimirovich Romachev, President and Founder of the R-Techno group of companies (Moscow); Professor Themistocles M. Rassias, who introduced me in advanced mathematical analysis and logic during my mathematical studies at the University of La Verne (California); the Dean and the Faculty of the Academia Teológica de San Andrés (Mexico), from which I earned my Doctoral Degree in Christian Philosophy; the Executive Board of the University of Indianapolis (Athens Campus), where I have taught the postgraduate course "Theory of International Relations"; Professor Alexander Dugin, Faculty of Sociology, State University of Moscow; Professor Conor Cunningham, Department of Theology and Religious Studies, University of Nottingham; my editors, especially Dr. Robin Parry and Mr. Matthew Wimer, who helped me to improve the clarity of my case.

INTRODUCTION

[handwritten margin note: A political situation in which the countries of th world are no longer divided because of their support for either the US or Soviet Union.]

THE EXTENSIVE USE OF the expression 'world order' by scholars, policy-makers, journalists, political commentators, and newswatchers cultivates an illusion of understanding, while it leaves the outline of the above expression blurred, and, furthermore, it preserves the ambiguity of the terms 'world' and 'order.' Every meaningful enquiry into a 'world order' must be able to clarify what transforms a formless group of actors into a 'world' (i.e., into a meaningful whole) and, also, which are the fundamental organizing principles (i.e., which is the 'order') of the world under consideration. In addition, World Order Studies should investigate the reality status of its object, the moral dimension of each world order model, and the wider issues of meaning and interpretation generated by the methodical study of world order models.

[handwritten margin note: any study that describes or analyzes methods in literature]

In the present book, based on the aforementioned remarks, I try to articulate a unified theory of world order, i.e., a theory that combines philosophy, political theory, and theology. The reason why the previous three scholarly disciplines should be combined together into a unified theory of world order is that, due to its very nature, the study of a world order has philosophical, political, and theological aspects. Therefore, if World Order Studies ignores any of the previous three aspects of a world order, then it is profoundly incomplete and misguided. Furthermore, one can better understand the interdisciplinary character of World Order Studies by contemplating the purposes of philosophy, political theory, and theology.

The term 'philosophy' comes from the Greek word *philosophia*, which means love of wisdom. Philosophy is primarily a way of thinking and asking questions about the big problems of humanity. The main areas of philosophy are the following: (i) ontology or metaphysics, which is concerned

[handwritten margin note: Relating to more than one branch of knowledge]

[handwritten margin note: branch of metaphysics dealing with the nature of being.]

ix

with questions about the nature of the world and the existence of God; (ii) epistemology, which is concerned with questions about the validity of knowledge, and it investigates how we know what we think we know; and (iii) ethics, which investigates how we discern right from wrong.

theory of Knowledge

In the natural sciences, the distinctive way of thinking is 'explanation,' which consists in an attempt to reduce phenomena to their causes and to general laws. Apart from explanation, there is another way of thinking which is called 'understanding.' Understanding is concerned with the human space, and it consists in a methodical study of the meanings and the significances that underpin the creation of civilization. Furthermore, one may attempt to understand the world at large, i.e., he may seek to find the meaning or the significance of the world. Philosophy is concerned with the elucidation of the entire spiritual activity of the human being. Thus, philosophy aims at elucidating both explanation (e.g., it aims at comprehending the concepts of causality and law) and understanding (e.g., it aims at understanding what exactly one means by stating that he understands a civilization).

Philosophy is much deeper than science, because philosophy aims at continually evaluating itself and its achievements as a whole. At the conclusion of the nineteenth century, science started developing in depth (whereas, until that historical period, it had been developing almost exclusively in breadth), but, with this, begins the crisis of the positivists' scientific world-conception; this is when scholars started noticing a certain incongruity and a type of artificiality of the doctrines on which the growth of positivism persisted for approximately two centuries. In the beginning of the twentieth century, the Austrian mathematician and logician Kurt Gödel proved, mathematically, that logic can organize/formalize everything but itself, and, therefore, truth transcends logico-mathematical formalism. Additionally, in the beginning of the twentieth century, quantum physics proved that the axioms and the theorems of the natural sciences are structurally related to human consciousness, and, therefore, the scientific world-conception is a 'conception' (i.e., something created by human consciousness) at least as much as it is a 'world,' (i.e., something objective).

Political theory is widely regarded as a subfield of the academic discipline of political science. From this perspective, political theory exists alongside other subfields of political science, such as American government, European politics, comparative politics, international relations, etc. However, from another perspective, political theory is concerned with fundamental problems and fundamental categories of politics, and, therefore, political theory is not simply a subfield of the academic discipline of political science, but it is the foundation of the entire scholarly discipline of politics. In order to understand politics, one must understand the foundation of politics, and, therefore, he must know history of political theory. Furthermore, a student studying the history of political theory is obliged to delve into difficult ontological, epistemological, and ethical questions, and, soon enough, he realizes that he is working in the realm of philosophy.

Theology, as the highly influential British theologian and philosopher Conor Cunningham has argued, is what makes the existence of all other scholarly subjects possible.[1] Cunningham's theological research emphasizes that the central topic of theology is not simply an 'object,' but it is the 'Person' (namely, God), regardless of particular religions. Due to the unity of the divine essence and due to the perfection of God's way of being, God is the only ontologically stable mirror in which one can see and evaluate oneself. Thus, God is the source of the values and the measures by means of which humanity creates civilizations and 'world orders.' In other words, the manner in which humanity understands God determines the manner in which humanity acts in history. As Cunningham has pointedly argued, every meaningful act is ultimately theological.[2] Moreover, the book *Faith-Based Diplomacy: Trumping Realpolitik*, edited by Douglas Johnston, is a methodical investigation of the religious underpinnings of political action, and it highlights the role that religious or spiritual factors can play in preventing or resolving conflict.[3]

The present book tells a coherent story, and, therefore, one should start at the beginning and work through to the end. Chapter 1 interweaves a story about *logos* and myth with a story about the ancient Greek *polis*, the origins of politics, and the meaning of civilization in the context of classical Greek philosophy. In chapter 1, Plato is taken to be the first great thinker to realize the need for a full characterization of political philosophy as not simply concerning the relations of human beings with historical entities, but as equally concerned with eternity, *logos*, and humanity taken as a whole. Moreover, this completeness is situated within the context of Plato's wider philosophy and is comprehensible only in

1 Cunningham, *Darwin's Pious Idea*; Cunningham and Candler, *Belief and Metaphysics*.

2 Cunningham, *Darwin's Pious Idea*.

3 Johnston, *Faith-Based Diplomacy*.

this context. In chapter 1, my interpretation of Plato's philosophy often diverges from mainstream Western approaches to Plato's thought, since I argue that Plato's philosophy is substantially different from the entire Western philosophical tradition.

In chapter 2, I study the spiritual division of Europe into a Greek East and a Latino-Frankish West. More specifically, in chapter 2, I study early Christianity and the apologists, emphasizing the cultural differences between the Greek church fathers and the Latin church fathers, the history of scholasticism and its departure from the Greek philosophical tradition, and the clash between scholasticism and Hesychasm. Thus, I elucidate the intellectual context within which the West has articulated its own ways of interpreting classical Greek philosophers and of thinking about God, man, the natural world, politics, and civilization.

Chapter 3 is a thought-provoking and intellectually challenging survey of modern Western philosophy (including Descartes, Spinoza, Leibniz, Locke, Berkeley, Hume, Rousseau, Kant, Hegel, Kierkegaard, Husserl, and Heidegger) and of Nietzsche's and the postmodernists' criticism of modernity. This chapter is more than just a summary of the views of others, since I evaluate the achievements of the philosophies under investigation; additionally, I compare and contrast modern and postmodern philosophers with one another and, also, with ancient and medieval Greek philosophical and theological tradition.

In chapter 4, I study the history and the arguments of the three basic political theories of modernity; namely, Liberalism (including right-wing/conservative liberalism and left-wing/'progressive'/social liberalism), Communism (including Marxism, socialist schools of thought, and social democracy), and Fascism (including Mussolini's fascist model, National-socialism, Franco's National Syndicalism, Perón's ideology of Social Justice, Salazar's regime, etc.). Moreover, I elucidate the philosophical foundations and 'pedigree' of each of the three basic political theories of modernity, and I evaluate their outcomes.

Chapter 5 is devoted to the study of the three basic theoretical debates in International Relations; namely, the idealism/utopianism versus political realism debate, the behavioralism versus traditionalism debate, and the so-called triple inter-paradigm debate among political realism, pluralism/interdependence, and Marxism/radicalism. In chapter 5, I elucidate the philosophical foundations and 'pedigree' of each of the previous schools of thought, I study their historical development, and I evaluate their outcomes.

Chapter 6 examines the different types of political power and the different geopolitical 'schools,' and it aims at placing geopolitics within a philosophical framework which helps one to understand the dynamic interplay among geography, culture, and politics. Geopolitical preponderance can yield important benefits, but, if one conquers space without conquering the hearts and minds of the people who live in that space, even the most ingenious geopolitical calculations eventually lead to failure. For instance, in the fifth century A.D., Attila the Hun (died 453) created the Hunic Empire, which stretched from the Ural River to the Rhine River and from the Danube River to the Baltic Sea. The Hunic Empire was relatively disorganized and uncultured, even compared to the Germanic tribes, and Roman historians, such as Priscus, Procopius of Caesarea, Jordanes, and Marcellinus Comes, describe Attila the Hun as a destroyer rather than a builder of civilizations. Because Attila the Hun was unable to achieve the spiritual unification of his empire, and because his European subjects were always seeing him as a barbarian ruler, the Hunic Empire was dissolved almost immediately after Attila the Hun's death. In 454, the Huns were defeated at the Battle of Nedao, and soon afterward they disappear from European history.

Chapter 7 is devoted to the study of noopolitics and of the different levels at which noopolitics can be conducted; namely, cyberspace, infosphere, and noosphere. Noopolitics is the conduct of politics in the information field that is created by the communication among conscious beings. In a sense, noopolitics is an explicitly philosophical type of political struggle. In chapter 7, I study cyberwar, netwar, cultural warfare, 'human terrain systems,' political crime, propaganda, and the international economic system within a coherent noopolitical framework.

In chapter 8, I study the problem of the 'fourth political theory,' i.e., the quest for a new political theory, substantially different from liberalism, communism, and fascism. I review and evaluate the major attempts that have been made until now in the area of the 'fourth political theory.' Building upon the arguments that I put forward in chapters 1–7, I propose a 'fourth political theory' that I call 'metaphysical republicanism,' and, in this context, I study what I call 'cosmogenetic systems' (i.e., archetypal forms of humanity and society, from which different civilization zones are derived).

1

LOGOS AND ANCIENT PHILOSOPHY

LOGOS AND MYTH

The ancient Greek *polis* (city-state) has a unique characteristic on the basis of which and due to which the institution of *polis* has been differentiated from other forms of organized collective behavior, and, furthermore, it has given rise to the notions of 'political art,' 'political virtue,' and 'political science.' This unique characteristic of the ancient Greek *polis* consists in a collective attempt to institute a community whose *telos*, or existential purpose, is not exhausted in the management of needs, but it is an attempt to live in harmony with the principle of truth.[1]

From the aforementioned philosophical perspective, we can talk meaningfully about 'politics' and 'civilization' only when the organization and management of collective life does not aspire merely to the maximization of a utility function. We can talk meaningfully about 'politics' and 'civilization' only when the *telos* (i.e., the ultimate goal) of collective life is the 'truth,' which, according to Plato and Aristotle, consists in the imitation of true being, i.e., of that mode of existence which is free from corruption, alterations, and annihilation.[2]

In the context of Plato's and Aristotle's philosophical works, politics is, in essence, an existential goal of the human being, a collective struggle that transcends the logic of individual and/or collective utility, and it aims at the truthfulness of human existence. In other words, the *telos* of politics is to help humanity to exist authentically through and

1. Aristotle, *Nicomachean Ethics*, X.
2. Plato, *Republic*, II, IV, VII, and X. Aristotle, *Nicomachean Ethics*, II–VI.

1

within a social system. This aspiration is the core of classical Greek political thought.

In order to clarify the arguments that politics consists in the pursuit of truth and that truth consists in the imitation of true being, we should, first of all, turn to the semantics of the Greek words *aletheia*, meaning 'truth,' and *logos*, which means word, speech, a ground, a plea, an expectation, account, and reason.[3]

The Greek word *aletheia* is a combination of the prefix a- (signifying lack) and the Greek word *lethe*, meaning forgetfulness. Therefore, for the ancient Greeks, truth means un-forgetfulness, un-concealment, and disclosure. In the early- to mid-twentieth century, the German philosopher Martin Heidegger interpreted the Greek term *aletheia* by relating it to the notion of disclosure, or the way in which things appear as entities in the world.[4] Hence, *aletheia* is distinct from both the correspondence theory[5] of truth and the coherence theory[6] of truth. In terms of the Greek word *aletheia*, everything that exists appears as an entity in the world, and 'existence' corresponds to 'disclosure.' The term that the ancient Greeks used in order to refer to the event of disclosure was *logos*. Disclosure speaks about and declares the existence of an entity in the world, and, additionally, it refers to a conscious being that is aware of the event of disclosure. Hence, from the perspective of the Greeks' notion of *aletheia*, truth emerges from the relationship between a disclosed entity and the viewer of this disclosure.

As a result of the above arguments, *logos* is the event of disclosure and the elucidation of the way in which disclosure takes place. That which exists is disclosed through its form, or species (i.e., through its distinctive way of being). For instance, the form of a pot 'says' to its viewer that the given object is a pot. However, *logos* is not only the individual form of beings, but also their overall formation (i.e., the way in which they relate to each other). Furthermore, according to ancient Greek aesthetics,

---

3. Liddell and Scott, *Greek-English Lexicon*, 'aletheia' (truth), and 'logos.'

4. Heidegger, *Being and Time*.

5. According to the correspondence theory of truth, the truth or falsity of a statement is determined only by how it relates to the world and whether it accurately describes (i.e., corresponds with) that world. Hanna and Harrison, *Word and World*.

6. According to the coherence theory of truth, the truth or falsity of a statement is determined by its relations to other statements rather than its relation to the world (i.e., it regards truth as some specified set of sentences, propositions, or beliefs). Benjamin, "Coherence Theory."

the overall formation of the entities that exist in the word has *kāllos*, which means beauty.[7] The Greek noun *kāllos* is semantically related to the Greek verb *kalō*, meaning attract and invite. By viewing and contemplating the way of the overall formation of the entities in the world, the ancient Greeks recognized the harmony and, hence, the beauty of the world. Therefore, the ancient Greeks called the universe *cosmos*, which, in Greek, is semantically related to the Greek noun *cōsmema*, meaning jewel, ornament, and embellishment.

The *logos* of the entities that exist in the world consists in the way in which they participate in the corresponding species/form and, also, in the way in which they relate to each other in the context of the cosmic harmony and order. The *logos* of the cosmic entities that belong to the same species is common to all of them, and, furthermore, it is unchangeable and eternal, independent of the characteristics of particular entities. For instance, every particular rose and every particular lion will perish, and, eventually, they will be annihilated. But the form of a rose, i.e., its *logos*, or the way of its participation in existence, which makes it what it is (the given plant), and the form of a lion, i.e., its *logos*, or the way of its participation in existence, which makes it what it is (the given animal), are not susceptible to corruption, but they are unchangeable and eternal. Moreover, the set of the relations in which every particular plant and every particular animal participate (e.g., the way of a plant's sowing, vegetation, and blossoming, and the way of an animal's birth, development, and reproduction) is an integrated, unchangeable, and eternal whole.

As a result of the aforementioned awarenesses, from ancient Greeks' viewpoint, *logos* (i.e., the way in which beings exist, or the disclosure of true being) is the only true existential given, in that it is unchangeable, perfect, and eternal. That which exists actually, authentically, and, hence, free from corruption, change, and death is exclusively contained in the *logos*. In other words, in the context of classical Greek philosophy, *logos* means that relationship of participation in the corresponding (eternal and unchangeable) form which makes existents what they are and, additionally, the relationship of participation in the formation of the entire cosmos.

True being (i.e., the way of eternity and immortality) is the participation in the *logos*, and, therefore, according to Plato, it is clear what a

---

7. Plato, *Timaeus* 29a–d, 47b–c, *Republic*, 443d, 500c, *Phaedrus*, 246–251, 247c–d, *Laws*, 734a–741a. Aristotle, *Physics*, 265a25 *ff.*, *Politics*, 1289b25, *Nicomachean Ethics*, 1181b21 *ff.*

human being must do if he "seeks . . . to be immortal"[8]: he must imitate the *logos* of the relations of participation in the formation of the cosmos; for instance, he must understand and organize society as an event of participation in the order, harmony, and decency of the relations that constitute the eternal cosmic beauty. This is the essence of politics and the way of the ancient Greek *polis* (city-state).

The aforementioned unified and universal criterion of truth unifies all aspects of the Greeks' life into a common species, and, thus, it constitutes the distinctive characteristic (the cultural identity) of the Greek way of life. Since this way of life can be primarily attained in the city, it is a product of the city (*polis*), and, therefore, it is called civilization (in Greek, *politismōs*).

In general, by the term 'civilization,' we should understand a way of life. Civilization is a structure that consists of institutions and technologies, and, from a broad perspective, it includes culture. Culture is the result of man's reflection on his life, and it is historically objectified through artistic creation, philosophy, religion, and science. Culture is embodied in civilization and underpins civilization; additionally, civilization underpins the integration of culture into history. Thus, culture, corresponding to spiritual 'creation,' and civilization, corresponding to technological 'construction,' are inextricably and dialectically related to each other, regarding both their essences and their manifestations.[9]

Culture is a reflective attitude toward institutions and an attempt to transcend institutions through myth. Myth's complex structure reflects the structure of institutions, and it is the center of culture. Myth translates experienced reality into a symbolic language, and, in this way, it is conductive to the participation of a society as a whole in the same experience of reality, since myth integrates all areas of conscious and unconscious life into a common experience of reality.[10]

There is a strong relation between myth and *logos*. In the context of myth, knowledge is not the result of a static representation, but, due to myth's plot, it is an itinerary toward *logos*. Myth does not serve ideas in a passive way, but, due to its plot, it endows ideas with inner life. Thus, myth is not an allegory, which is something intrinsically static; myth is actually a symbol.

---

8. Plato, *Symposium*, 207d1–2.
9. Lévi-Strauss, *Raw and Cooked*.
10. Jung, "Ego and Unconscious."

A symbol is something different from an image or visual icon. In case of an image, the signified is absent. On the contrary, a symbol discloses the signified. For instance, a pair of scales does not simply mean counterbalance, but it also means the administration of justice. Instead of simply referring to something external, a symbol shows within itself what is the symbolized object. In other words, a symbol is not an outward, formalistic reproduction of the symbolized object, but it participates in the spiritual reality (significance) of the symbolized object, without, however, encompassing the entire reality of the symbolized object. Thus, the knowledge that derives from symbols is always combined with a person's faith and intuition.[11]

PLATO'S MYTH OF THE CAVE

In the seventh book of the *Republic*, Plato narrates a myth that is known as the 'myth of the cave,' and it symbolizes humanity's relationship with the Good as a process of education and psychological remolding.[12]

In the depths of a gloomy, underground chamber like a cave, are men who have been prisoners there since they were children. They are fastened in such a way that they cannot turn their heads. Some way off, behind and higher up, a fire is burning. Between the fire and the prisoners and above them runs a road, in front of which a curtain-wall has been built, like the screen at puppet shows between the operators and their audience. Furthermore, there are men carrying all sorts of gear along behind the curtain-wall, projecting above it. Hence, due to the way in which the prisoners' legs and necks are fastened, the only things that the prisoners can see are the shadows of the objects carried along the road (these shadows are thrown by the fire on the wall of the cave opposite them). Suppose that one of these prisoners were let loose, suddenly compelled to stand up and turn his head and look and walk toward the fire and that, ultimately, he were forcibly dragged up the steep and rugged ascent and not let go until he had dragged out into the sunlight. The previous process would be a painful one, to which the prisoner would much object. However, during his march toward the sun, the prisoner would realize that, apart from the shadows, there were other things, too, such as a burning torch and several objects carried along the road, and, when, at

11. Biedermann, *Symbolism*.
12. Plato, *Republic*, 514a *ff.*

last, he would manage to get out of the cave, he would see things in the upper world outside the cave, and, finally, he would manage to look at the sun itself. Later on, he would come to the conclusion that, when he was in the cave, he was looking at the shadows of things and not at things themselves. Finally, according to Plato's narration, this ex-prisoner would think of the gloom of the cave, and he would decide to descend again into the cave in order to bring the good news to his ex-fellow prisoners, even though he was aware that they would not believe his word and they would react aggressively.

After the narration of the myth of the cave, Plato makes interpretive comments about it. The space of the cave corresponds to an unilluminated sensuous world, and it can be properly understood only if one bears in mind the ancient Greek philosophy of optics. In the context of ancient Greek philosophy, 'sight' and 'intellect' are essentially united with each other.

According to Plato's *Timaeus* (where Plato uses the expression "light-bearing eyes"[13]), 'seeing' means that the light of one's eyes coalesces with the light of the seen body, which, according to Plato's *Meno*, "is an effluence of figures, commensurate with sight and sensible."[14] However, the encounter between the previous two lights takes place in the context of a third light: the daylight. In other words, Plato argues, sight is possible due to a slim stream of light which has the same essence with sunlight, it is emitted from the eyes, and it is interwoven with daylight. Thus, in *Timaeus*, Plato argues the following: "owing to the fire of the reflected face coalescing with the fire of the vision on the smooth and bright surface."[15]

Even though Aristotle,[16] in his works *On Senses and the Sensible* and *On the Soul*, criticizes Plato's optics and argues that the eye's light is not fire, since the eye's major component is liquid, Aristotle's optics does not substantially contradict Plato's optics. Both Plato and Aristotle argue that we see through the soul by means of the organ of sight and that intellect is inextricably linked to sensation, and, more specifically, that intellect is the deepest layer of sensation and not a totally different process.

In his works *On Senses and the Sensible* and *On the Soul*, Aristotle agrees with Plato's thesis that we see through the soul. In particular,

13. Plato, *Timaeus*, 45b.
14. Plato, *Meno*, 76d.
15. Plato, *Timaeus*, 46b.
16. Aristotle, *Senses and the Sensible*, 437b11 *ff.*, and *On the Soul*, II.

in *Timaeus*, Plato argues the following: "distributes the motions of every object it touches, or whereby it is touched, throughout all the body even unto the soul, and brings about the sensation which we now term 'seeing.'"[17] But, because, *contra* Plato, in Aristotle's philosophy, the soul is united with the body as its form and entelechy (actuality), Aristotle proposes the theory of the 'transparent.' By the term 'transparent,' Aristotle means that which is between the sense organ and the sensible; it receives the information about the species of the sensible and transfers this information to the sense organ. Thus, in the second book of his work *On the Soul*, Aristotle maintains that, by the term 'transparent,' he means what is visible, but not visible in itself, since it owes its visibility to the color of something else; of this character are air, water, and aether. According to Aristotle's *On the Soul*, sight is the entelechy, or energy, of what is transparent, and, therefore, both the soul and the body participate in the process of knowledge.[18]

In his work *On Senses and the Sensible*, Aristotle describes sight as a potential and an actual sense, and he explains the difference between the potential and the actual (e.g., it is owing to this difference that we do not actually see its ten-thousandth part in a grain of millet).[19] Moreover, in his work *On Senses and the Sensible*, Aristotle describes the soul *qua* exercising sight.[20] Since the soul perceives, and especially during the process of seeing, it is the center of the senses (each faculty of sense perception is connected with the soul), it operates within the eye[21], and it needs an inner light, while the eye needs an external light. Thus, from Aristotle's perspective, the cause of sight is light and not the fire of the eyes. Additionally, according to Aristotle, light is the entelechy of what is transparent.[22] As a conclusion, according to Aristotle, when some light actualizes what is transparent, we perceive the mental reality of the visible bodies.

From the perspective of Aristotle's optics, the eye is not light in itself, but it becomes the organ of sight through and due to the actualization of what is transparent. When we receive light, what is transparent inside and outside the eye is immediately actualized (in other words, it becomes

---

17. Plato, *Timaeus*, 45d.
18. Johansen, *Aristotle*.
19. Aristotle, *On Senses and the Sensible*, 438b22–23.
20. Ibid., 439a15.
21. Ibid., 438b10.
22. Aristotle, *On the Soul*, 419a11.

light, too), and, therefore, it transfers the information about the species of the visible object to the eye, enabling us to see. Hence, Aristotle has adopted Plato's notion of the third light. In his *Republic*, Plato writes about the significance of the third light: "he will see nothing and the colors will remain invisible unless a third element is present which is specifically and naturally adapted for the purpose. . . . What you call light."[23] In his work *On Senses and the Sensible*, Aristotle adds that sight, which is the entelechy of the eye, and light, which is the entelechy of what is transparent, presuppose a common power (i.e., a light that generally exists in what is transparent and is actualized in the colored figure of the visible object as light sense).[24]

In the context of Plato's and Aristotle's optics, 'shadow' is understood as an unilluminated object, an object that is deprived of light, and it is treated as a negative substance. Shadow is lack of light due to the presence of an opaque object, which hinders the progress of the rays of the source of light and thus causes lack of light. Therefore, a shadow cannot be seen, not because we cannot identify its figure, but because a shadow does not 'look at' us, in the sense that our eyes' light cannot meet a light deriving from a shadow. In other words, 'shadow' means lack of communication, lack of society, and an entity that remains closed toward the rays of the source of light.

The fire that burns in the Platonic Cave corresponds to the sun of the Good (i.e., to the ultimate source of goodness). The liberated prisoner's ascent toward the view of the sun corresponds to the mind's ascent from the sensible world to the intelligible world. The previous correspondences imply that, at the edge of the sensible world (i.e., at the borderline between the sensible world and the intelligible world) the mind just starts seeing the sunlight (i.e., the idea of the Good). When the liberated prisoner is in a condition to gaze at the 'sun' (i.e., the absolute Good), he manages to realize that the 'sun' is the universal cause of goodness and beauty. The sun, which is outside the cave, is the source of light; it provides the necessary condition under which things can be disclosed (known) in the sensible world, and it is the necessary presupposition under which we can understand which of the things we see are true and which are not, since it makes us capable of discerning the intelligible reality of things. Thus, Plato argues that everyone who intends to act wisely,

23. Plato, *Republic*, 507d–e.
24. Aristotle, *On Senses and the Sensible*, 439a15–23.

either in public or in private life, must gaze at the sun; in other words, he must be in a position to discern one thing from another guided by the idea of the Good.

From the aforementioned Platonic arguments, it follows that, contrary to what the sophists and the empiricists maintain, knowledge does not consist in the accumulation of experiences, or of data from the sensible world, but it can be achieved inside the soul; therefore, the *telos* of theorizing and education is to turn one's mind away from darkness until he can bear to gaze at the 'sun,' which symbolizes the idea of the Good. The *telos* of Plato's philosophy is psychotherapy, which, for the ancient Greeks, consists in psychic order, harmony, and beauty. Plato made this point clear in most of his works.[25] There are several treatments for the various corporal illnesses, but, according to Plato, 'cleansing' is the essence of psychotherapy, and education, consisting in a spiritual orientation toward the truth, is the treatment for spiritual illnesses.

The soul suffers because it is mixed with the body and its appetites, and it can be cured with psychic cleansing. Plato understands psychic cleansing as "purification and purgations,"[26] and, from this viewpoint, he speaks about the acquisition of "a pure mind"[27] and about "making a man pure in body and soul."[28] Hence, when Plato writes that "they expel the lot and leave the soul of their victim swept clean, ready for the great initiation,"[29] he means that the soul must be liberated from the corporeal passions; additionally, when he writes that "true philosophers practice dying," since "they desire to have the soul apart by itself alone,"[30] he means that the soul must be liberated from the senses because a soul that is enslaved to the senses cannot sense the truth.[31]

The issue of philosophical cleansing was methodically studied by Plato in his book *Phaedo*. In *Phaedo*, Plato made the first presentation of his theory of ideas as autonomous entities and as the archetypal reality of beings.[32] Additionally, in *Phaedo*, Plato studies the problem of the

---

25. Plato, *Republic*, 580d, *Laws*, 650b, *Cratylus*, 440c, *Charmides*, 157b, *Laches*, 185e, *Protagoras*, 312c, *Gorgias*, 513e, *Timaeus*, 87c.

26. Plato, *Cratylus*, 405a.

27. Ibid., 396c.

28. Ibid., 405b.

29. Plato, *Republic*, 560e.

30. Plato, *Phaedo*, 67e.

31. Ibid., 114c.

32. Ibid., 74a–c.

knowledge of ideas, since he argues that "he who prepares himself most carefully to understand the true essence of each thing that he examines would come nearest to the knowledge of it" and that this would be done most perfectly by employing "pure, absolute reason" and by removing oneself "so far as possible, from eyes and ears, and, in a word, from his whole body."[33] In this way, Plato integrated the Orphic Mysteries' tradition of cleansing into philosophy.

According to ancient Greek mythology, Orpheus founded the Orphic Mysteries. The rites of those mysteries were based on the myth of Dionysus Zagreus, the son of Zeus and Persephone. When Zeus proposed to make Zagreus the ruler of the universe, the Titans disagreed, and they dismembered the boy and devoured him. Athena saved Zagreus's heart and gave it to Zeus, who swallowed the heart, from which was born the second Dionysus Zagreus. Moreover, Zeus destroyed the Titans with lightning. From the ashes of the Titans sprang the human race, who were part divine (Dionysus) and part evil (Titan). This double aspect of human nature, the Dionysian and the Titanic, plays a key role in Orphism. The Orphics affirmed the divine origin of the soul, but they believed that the soul could be liberated from its Titanic inheritance and could achieve eternal bliss through initiation into the Orphic Mysteries.[34]

Plato's theory of ideas transformed Orphism's tradition of mystical cleansing into an integrated philosophical system. If Platonic ideas were not ontologically autonomous, they would be reduced to categories of understanding, or abstractions. Moreover, without Plato's principle of philosophical cleansing, the inner journey of the soul toward the world of ideas would be impossible. In Plato's philosophy, the knowledge of truth leads us to psychic cleansing. In order to understand how and why this happens, we must understand Plato's theory of ideas.

Plato was not familiar with abstract thinking. Abstraction was invented by Aristotle. Hence, Platonic ideas were not abstract concepts. An abstract concept is an abstraction of genus.[35] An idea, in its original

33. Ibid., 65e–66a.

34. Guthrie, *Orpheus and Greek Religion*.

35. By the term 'genus' (or family), we mean a pre-defined term that includes the species defined as a subtype. In other words, genus is that part of a definition which is also predicable of other things different from the *definiendum*. Abstraction is a process by which just part of an existing definition is used itself as a new definition; the new definition is called abstraction, and it is said to have been 'abstracted away from' the existing definition. Copi and Cohen, *Logic*.

Platonic sense, is the conception of one out of many. Thus, in *Phaedrus*, Plato maintains that the process of knowing an idea consists in taking "a synoptic view of many scattered particulars" and collecting them "under a single generic term."[36] Moreover, in his *Republic*, Plato argues that "the only way to acquire lasting knowledge" is to "bring together the disconnected subjects . . . and take a comprehensive view of their relationship with each other and with the nature of reality."[37] In Plato's philosophy, idea and species display the visible rational form of the life-giving universal One, and the theory of, or contemplation on, the life-giving universal One leads us to the conclusion that the truth of the world of ideas is identical with the essence of reality. Thus, according to Plato, a dialectical philosopher is 'synoptic'[38]; that is, he reduces a multitude of phenomena to the archetypal 'one,' instead of analyzing phenomena.

The sixth book of Plato's *Republic* makes it amply clear that, in Plato's philosophy, the term 'idea' should not be identified with the term 'concept' for two reasons. First, in Plato's *Republic*, the Good itself is not determined by its essence (namely, it is free from every essential determination), since it is beyond and above the world of ideas, and it is the ultimate, absolutely transcendent, cause of the existence of ideas and of man's cognitive capacity. Second, because in Plato's *Republic*, the Good has the same meaning with the terms truth and idea.[39] Under the light of the Good, truth is the disclosure of being in its perfection (in ideational terms), as opposed to its imperfect empirical reality ('phenomenon'). The Good is absolutely transcendent, and, therefore, external to human consciousness, but it embraces the human being from the inside; that is, it is available to be known by the psyche which decides to turn toward the Good. According to Plato's *Republic* (476b) and *Phaedrus*, the relationship between the philosopher and the Good is not only a cognitive one, but also an erotic one. Within the framework of Plato's philosophy, man becomes aware of his existential otherness (and, hence, individuated) through his *personal* (namely, free from every rational necessity) relationship with the Good.[40]

36. Plato, *Phaedrus*, 265d.

37. Plato, *Republic*, 537c.

38. The term 'synoptic' is derived from the Greek words *syn*, meaning together, and *opsis*, meaning view, and it describes observations that give a broad view of something/someone.

39. Plato, *Republic*, 508d.

40. McCabe, *Plato's Individuals*.

Contrary to what the German idealist Edward Zeller[41] has argued, in Platonic philosophy, the 'individual' is neither absorbed nor nullified by the 'universal,' since Platonic 'ideas' are not 'concepts,' and, therefore, the knowledge of Platonic ideas is not based on a leveling principle of logical coercion, but it is a process of entering into true being rather than syllogistically going around it from the outside. In Plato's philosophy, 'truth' and 'reality' are inextricably linked to each other, whereas, from the viewpoint of the modern Western individual, they are different from each other, and, therefore, the imagination of the modern Western individual is unbridled and potentially destructive. The inseparability between 'truth' and 'reality' allows and motivates Plato to seek true being; Plato, *contra* modern philosophers, seeks the 'idea' *qua* 'reality' and not *qua* 'concept.'

Modernity has differentiated 'truth' from 'reality' and seeks truth *qua* 'concept' through abstract reasoning. However, even though Aristotle invented abstraction, there is a significant difference between Aristotle's philosophy and modernity. For both Aristotle and Plato, knowledge does not consist in abstraction, but it is a relationship with the universal, with the *logos* of the cosmos. In his *Categories*, Aristotle substituted Plato's transcendent ideas with immaterial species, arguing that forms are not apart from things, but inherent in them (matter combines with the form to constitute individual things, and each individual moves and changes, or evolves under the control and direction of its form). However, even though Aristotle brings Plato's ideas/forms down from heaven to earth, so to speak, he agrees with Plato that knowledge is a task of the mind and that the mind is transcendent. By retaining the transcendence of the mind, Aristotle's philosophy remains essentially Platonic, even though Aristotle rejects the transcendence of Plato's ideas (as a pointless doubling of the world) and subjects them to concepts. For both Plato and Aristotle, the immortality of the soul is the ontological presupposition and foundation of their theory of knowledge.

Plato extended his dialectical method far beyond Socrates's method of 'maieutics.'[42] In Plato's dialogue *Sophist*, it is shown that Plato developed

41. Zeller, *Greek Philosophy*.

42. Maieutics means midwifery, and it is a pedagogical method according to which the idea of truth is latent in the mind of every human being due to his innate reason, but it has to be 'given birth' through a form of enquiry and debate between individuals with opposing viewpoints based on asking and answering questions in order to stimulate critical thinking and thus illuminate ideas. Liddell and Scott, *Greek-English Lexicon*, 'maieutics.'

dialectic as a taxonomic method by which beings can be classified into genera and species in order to be elucidated in the light of ideas.[43] Before Plato, dialectic was a method of seeking truth through oppositional discussion and a negative method of hypothesis elimination in order to convince the opponent. In Plato's dialogue *Phaedo*, it is clear that Plato transformed dialectic into an art of reconciliation with one's spiritual self, and, in Plato's dialogues *Theaetetus*, *Charmides*, *Philebus*, *Sophist*, and *Laws*, we realize that Plato understood dialectic as a form of inner dialogue which presupposes that the philosopher's soul seeks truth in order to attain existential perfection.[44] Moreover, in his *Phaedo*, Plato argues that, without a method of correct reasoning ("belief without art"), every argument becomes an idol, an illusion, and it undermines every attempt to find the ontological foundation of phenomena.[45] In his *Philebus*, Plato shows that his method of classifying things into genera and species leads from one concept to another until the philosopher's mind conceives of the ultimate causes of things, and, therefore, the philosopher manages to know the truth of phenomena through their corresponding ideas.[46]

According to Plato, reducing a collection of phenomena to an idea is equivalent to understanding their unity into a 'whole' which is a universal signification or value (idea). In other words, the *telos* of the mind's movement from impressions to the truth and from phenomena to ideas is a value. Hence, within the framework of Plato's philosophy, ideas are neither one's own concepts of things nor images of things, but they are the fundamental values of things, which hold universally, regardless of whether some persons (e.g., the prisoners in the Platonic myth of the cave) want to know them or not. Ideas hold universally because within their context life acquires an intrinsic value (i.e., a value beyond ephemeral conventions). Every other existential condition lacks intrinsic value, because it is conventional, and, hence, perilous, since it is self-overcoming and, thus, potentially self-destructive. For instance, the prisoners in the Platonic myth of the cave could establish an order of things based on their illusions, but such an order of things would be threatened with collapse immediately after the first expression of doubt about its merits, and the expression of doubt about its merits would be only a matter of

43. Plato, *Sophist*, 253c–d, 264c–265.

44. Plato, *Phaedo*, 90a–b, 100d–e, *Theaetetus*, 154d–e, *Charmides*, 166c–e, *Philebus*, 38c–e, *Sophist*, 263e, *Laws*, 893a.

45. Plato, *Phaedo*, 89d–90d.

46. Plato, *Philebus*, 57–58.

time, since illusions preclude the knowledge of truth *qua* universal value, which could underpin a real and ontologically stable order of things.

Plato's myth of the cave is intimately related to what Plato has described as the graph of knowledge in the sixth book of his *Republic*.[47] According to Plato, knowledge can be graphically represented by a divided line: (i) the first half of this divided line corresponds to the knowledge of the visible things, and it is further divided into two parts: the realm of shadows, and the realm of images (which are more visible than shadows); (ii) the second half of this divided line corresponds to the knowledge of the intelligible things, and it is further divided into two parts: the ideas of logical reasoning (the realm of logical reality), and the supersensuous reality (the realm of the Good). The myth of the cave transforms the previous graph of knowledge into a lively story, and, thus, it explains the manner in which the problem of knowledge is experienced by humans. By narrating the myth of the cave, Plato's graph of knowledge becomes a symbol of humanity's relationship with truth, the levels of knowledge become steps of spiritual life, and the divided line corresponds to the human condition. Thus, truth is not merely an object of abstract thinking, but it corresponds to an existential condition, to a way of life and to a struggle.

THE FOUR LEVELS OF KNOWLEDGE
ACCORDING TO PLATO

In his graph of knowledge and in his the myth of the cave, Plato discerns four different types of 'seeing,' which are four different types of knowledge and four different states of consciousness, or existential conditions: (i) illusion, or conjecture (*eikasia*), which provides only the most primitive and unreliable opinions; (ii) belief (*pistis*), being empirical knowledge which allows one to distinguish objects from their shadows, but it lacks epistemological and methodological rigor; (iii) rule-based reasoning, or logic (*dianoia*), with which one can achieve systematic knowledge of the objects of consciousness through a disciplined application of the understanding, and (iv) intelligence (*noesis*), which is the comprehension of the true nature of reality.

When a person is in the cognitive state of illusion, he sees things and events through the prism of his arbitrary assumptions, and he is sunk in a great confusion of emotions. Such a person is unable to distinguish

47. Plato, *Republic*, 510a–511e.

reality from what he himself would desire to be real. In other words, such a person cannot distinguish beings/things from their images. Illusions are often purposely cultivated, especially in the context of propaganda, advertizing, political rhetoric, and postmodern thought.

In the cognitive state that Plato calls 'belief,' a person transcends his illusions by processing sensible data. As mentioned by Plato in the seventh book of the *Republic*, at the stage of belief, man can distinguish the images of beings/things from their prototypes.[48] Whereas the cognitive stage of illusion is characterized by uncontrolled emotions and, hence, by spiritual chaos, which transforms everything into a shadow of itself, the cognitive stage of belief is characterized by the emergence and the operation of the principle of the mean and by the treatment of virtue as a kind of moderation inasmuch as it aims at the mean. In the second book of his *Nicomachean Ethics*, Aristotle defines the principle of the mean as a condition intermediate between two other states: excess and deficiency. Additionally, in the sixth chapter of the second book of Aristotle's *Nicomachean Ethics*, virtue is defined as "a state of character concerned with choice, lying in a mean" and, thus, "in respect of its substance and the definition which states its essence virtue is a mean." Without the ability to distinguish the image of a thing from the reality of this thing, the endorsement of the principle of the mean is impossible.

The cognitive stage that Plato calls rule-based reasoning, or logic, is that stage at which the liberated prisoner, in the Platonic myth of the cave, becomes aware that he is dragged out into the sunlight. In his myth of the cave, Plato writes that, as the liberated prisoner ascends toward the light, he observes the heavenly bodies and the sky. By making this remark, Plato means that the liberated prisoner starts comprehending the mathematical structure (order) of the world. Now, at the stage of rule-based reasoning, man can test and confirm the truth of the criteria by which he distinguishes shadows from reality, because now he is aware of the existence of physical entities through reasoning about their material substance and mathematical structure.

The knowledge that is achieved at the cognitive level of rule-based reasoning, or logic, recognizes reality in its most abstract, general form, but its coordinate system is determined by variables of the given, sensible reality, and, therefore, this type of knowledge is not sufficient in order to lead one to the ultimate heights of the mental (intelligible) world, where

48. Plato, *Republic*, 515d.

Plato's idea of the Good resides. From Plato's point of view, the knowledge that is achieved at the stage of rule-based reasoning, or logic, is restricted to scientific hypotheses which are related only to the logical form of reality, and, therefore, this type of knowledge cannot lead the philosopher to the first, absolute principle, namely, the Good.

The limits and the inherent weakness of the knowledge that is achieved at the stage of rule-based reasoning, or logic, have been exposed in a scientifically rigorous manner by the famous mathematician and logician Kurt Gödel (1906–78). In 1931, Gödel published his ground-breaking article "On Formally Undecidable Propositions of Principia Mathematica and Related Systems," in which he proved that, for any computable axiomatic system that contains the finitary arithmetic, the following theorems hold: (i) if the system is consistent, it cannot be complete, and (ii) the consistency of the axioms cannot be proven within the system.[49] In other words, in his previous scientific work, Gödel proved that truth transcends every possible formal (i.e., hypothetico-deductive) system. According to Gödel, who was philosophically a Platonist, human mind and thought processes are not merely algorithmic. Gödel established the following argument mathematically: "Either . . . the human mind (even within the realm of pure mathematics) infinitely surpasses any finite machine, or else there exist absolutely unsolvable Diophantine problems."[50] Thus, for Gödel, important epistemological questions require philosophical methods that transcend formal mathematical methods and necessarily lead scholars to the fields of metamathematics and metaphysics. Furthermore, the highly influential Dutch mathematician and philosopher L. E. J. Brouwer (1881–1966) has distinguished immanent truths, which are suggested by perception, from the transcendent truth, which is primarily approached by distinguishing oneself from the sensible world and breaking the cycle of fear and desire caused by our relationship with the sensible world.[51]

According to Plato, 'intelligence' is the most perfect and *ne plus ultra* level of knowledge, and it corresponds to the knowledge of the Good, which presupposes a different method of knowledge. Plato calls the method that leads to the knowledge of the Good "dialectic." This is a logical as well as meta-logical method of knowledge. The knowledge of the Good is logical, in the sense that it presupposes that the mind has progressed

49. Dawson, *Kurt Gödel*.
50. Gödel, "Basic Theorems," 310.
51. Brouwer, "Life, Art, and Mysticism."

from the first level of knowledge to the third level of knowledge, and, therefore, it has transcended illusions, empiricism, and anecdotal wisdom. Simultaneously, the knowledge of the Good is meta-logical, in the sense that it presupposes that the mind is aware of the limits of logic, and it has acquired a type of knowledge that is derived from an experience of enlightened intuition.

In Plato's philosophy, the 'idea' is not a historical entity, but it is a trans-historical, metaphysical entity (irreducible to practice), and it constitutes the *telos* and the guide of historical action. Hence, Plato's *Republic* is not an exposition of a coercive cornucopia, but it is a methodical study of the metaphysical idea that should inspire and guide an actual republic in the historical sphere. Plato's *Republic* is not a practical political model *per se*, but it is the transcendent *telos* of historical/political action. Those scholars who, like Karl R. Popper,[52] argue that Plato's *Republic* is a totalitarian political theory have failed to understand Plato's theory of ideas and to bear in mind that Plato's *Republic* is not an exposition of an actual republic *per se*, but it is an exposition of the *idea* of a republic. The essence of totalitarianism is the thesis that the end of practice (i.e., of historical action) is a necessary practical, historical, and quantifiable goal. On the other hand, if the end of historical action is not a historical goal but a metaphysical one of purely qualitative character, such as Plato's idea of the Good, historical action is based on freedom, for it is a matter of personal choice.

According to Plato's *Republic*, the 'idea' is a principle that guides practice, but the 'idea' itself is irreducible to practice, meaning it is not a practical, quantifiable goal *per se*. From Plato's perspective, ideas constitute the life of God's essence, and, therefore, the partaker of the world of ideas is a partaker of divinity. Given the level of existential perfection that one can attain by becoming a partaker of the world of ideas, the confinement of one's mind to the realm that Plato calls 'intellect' (i.e., logic) is equivalent to the "ancestral sin," because such a person is self-confined to his own logical structures and refuses to receive the light of the metaphysical 'sun' of the Good. Hence, in Plato's philosophy, the 'mind,' being receptive to the light of the metaphysical 'sun' of the Good, is differentiated from the 'intellect,' which is the rational function of consciousness. In other words, within the framework of Plato's philosophy, the mind is a spiritual entity in the image of God and knows through its participation in the Good (the divine), which is the ultimate meaning of existence.

52. Popper, *Open Society*.

2

"THE LOGOS BECAME FLESH"[1]
LOGOS-CHRIST AND MEDIEVAL PHILOSOPHY

EARLY CHRISTIANITY AND THE APOLOGISTS

As I ARGUED IN chapter 1, from the perspective of classical Greek philosophy, true being consists in a harmonious, meaningful, and decent order, in the common *logos*, which is manifest in the cosmos. Thus, ancient
Greeks managed to endow their life with a transcendent scope; namely,
the scope of harmonizing oneself with the cosmic *logos*, thus bridging
the gap between history and eternity. According to Plato's *Timaeus* and
Plotinus's *On Time and Eternity*, time is an image of eternity. This does
not mean that, for Plato and Plotinus, time consists in a deterministic
cycle of the world of becoming, but it means that the image (in this case,
time) refers and leads to the creative archetypal good. Plotinus argues
that we must release time from the shackles of the physical world (e.g.,
space) and seek the origin of time in the nature of the soul.

In his book *On Time and Eternity*, Plotinus describes 'eternity' as
the radiance of the substratum of the mental principle, and he argues
that it is in a state of unending, changeless timelessness, whereas, following Plato, he describes time as the activity of the soul in the world and
as an image of eternity. Furthermore, in the same essay, Plotinus argues
that 'being' is related to eternity and that real being in its absolute ideal
state is unmanifested, but 'existence' is the manifestation of being in the
world of becoming. Hence, time manifests a tendency toward perfection,

1. John 1:14 (in most English translations of the Bible, 'Word' is used for 'Logos,'
but, in theological discourse, the term 'Logos' is often left untranslated).

and eternity manifests the participation of beings in the state of the intelligible world, precisely in a state of ontological completeness.

As Aristotle maintains in his *Physics*, divinity is the direct object of the love (universal magnetism) of the eternal physical beings (i.e., of the celestial spheres), which imitate divinity's perfect life through their harmonious motion.[2] Thus, ancient Greek philosophers see the divine *logos* within the world. For this reason, according to classical Greek philosophy, it is only through his participation in the cosmos that one can actualize his divine potential. The Greek philosophy of participation in the cosmos has a dual impact on the ancient Greek person: it socializes the ancient Greek person by teaching him to be a member of the harmonious whole, and simultaneously it urges the ancient Greek person to seek and actualize his own divine potential; therefore, it is a process of individuation. As a result of the previous process of individuation, the ancient Greek person is gradually led to an existential crisis, because, at the zenith of Greek philosophy, Greeks encountered the tragedy of existence: the ancient Greek person does not know exactly how to preserve the divine justice that characterizes the cosmos (which is a presupposition of every being and reality) while simultaneously experiencing the divine element that lies within him and is manifested in the freedom of will.

The Greeks' philosophical achievements and ontological orientation led them to the following ultimate questions: Which are the specific criteria of the divine *Logos*' action? How exactly can a historical being (namely, man) know God and actualize his divine potential? Christianity offered answers to the previous ultimate questions of ancient Greek philosophy, thus giving new life to it and throwing a new light on the cultural heritage of ancient Greece.

Christianity shifted the ontological foundations of politics and generally of civilization away from the rationality of the relations that constitute the cosmic harmony and moved them toward the principle of a society of persons, whose archetype is the Holy Trinity. From Christianity's perspective, true being, which constitutes the measure of true life, is not the harmonious cosmic rationality *per se* (i.e., it is not the ancient Greeks' unmanifested common *logos*), but it is a personal *Logos*, who is God and reveals the personhood of God.

In the era of the early church councils, there was much confusion concerning the meaning of the Trinitarian formula. The doctrine of the

---

2. Aristotle, *Physics*, 265a25 *ff*.

Trinity was upsetting both to the Jewish monotheism and to the Greek philosophical tradition, according to which singleness and simplicity are preferable to multiplicity in defining divinity. The Cappadocian Fathers—namely, Basil the Great (330–79), who was Bishop of Caesarea, Gregory of Nyssa (c.332–95), who was Bishop of Nyssa, and Gregory of Nazianzus (329–89), who became Patriarch of Constantinople—made major contributions to the definition of the Holy Trinity finalized at the Second Ecumenical Council (convened in Constantinople, in 381 A.D.) and the final version of the Nicene Creed, finalized there. Thus, they are highly respected as saints in both Eastern and Western churches.

Following Platonic terminology, Basil the Great explains the important role of the Spirit in the Trinity in chapter 9 of his *On the Holy Spirit*, where he writes that the Paraclete (i.e., the Holy Spirit), "like the sun", "by the aid of your purified eye," "will show you in himself the image of the invisible," and, additionally, "in the blessed vision of the image," i.e., the Son (Logos/Word), "you will see the intelligible beauty of the archetype," i.e., the Father (Nous/Mind). Based on Basil's theological essays, Gregory of Nyssa stresses that the Three Persons are *hypostatic*, meaning essentially equal and the same, and the only way to tell them apart is their mutual relations.[3]

Gregory of Nyssa has emphasized the difference between the terms *ousia* (essence) and *hypostasis*. The distinction between essence and *hypostasis* corresponds to the distinction between what is common (*koinon*) and what is particular and proper (*idion*). Essence is related to *hypostasis* as the common is to the particular. Following the same reasoning, in his *Epistle* 236, Basil the Great writes that "there is the same difference between essence and hypostasis as between what is common and what is particular, for example between animal and a certain man."[4] In summary, the Cappadocian Fathers have developed the following conceptual correspondences:

Essence = common = species (according to Aristotle's terminology: universal or secondary substance)

Hypostasis = proper = individual (according to Aristotle's terminology: primary substance).

In order to understand God's hypostatic way of existence (i.e., the Trinitarian doctrine), let us consider a metaphor about the poet T. S. Eliot.

---

3. Meredith, *Gregory of Nyssa*, 40–41, 46.
4. Courtonne, *Saint Basil*, III, 53:1–3.

The poetry of T. S. Eliot is his 'logos,' or word, it proceeds from Eliot's 'nous' (mind), and it gives to those who read it the 'spirit' of Eliot, which is a special culture and a special feeling of participation in Eliot's personal world. The spirit of Eliot remains with us even if we do not have his poems in front of us. By analogy, God the Father is the Nous, or Mind, of God, God the Son is the Logos, or Word, of God, and the Holy Spirit is the Spirit of God. However, in the Holy Trinity, the Nous of God (Father), the Logos of God (Son), and the Holy Spirit are not attributes or functions of a being, but they are distinct Persons (*hypostases*) of the same Divine Nature/Essence. Therefore, God is a communion of three *hypostases*. According to the Nicene Creed, the relationship between the Father and the Son is called generation/birth: the *Logos* (i.e., the Son) of God is born from the Divine *Nous* (i.e., God the Father) "before all ages," that is, "before" creation, "before" the commencement of time, in an eternally timeless existence without beginning or end. Moreover, according to the Nicene Creed, the relationship between the Father and the Holy Spirit is called procession. Gregory of Nazianzus is the first to use the idea of procession to describe the relationship between the Holy Spirit and the Father/Godhead. In his *Fifth Theological Oration*, Gregory of Nazianzus writes that the Holy Spirit is truly Spirit and comes forth from the Father, but not after the manner of the Son, for it is not by 'generation' but by 'procession.'[5]

John of Damascus[6] (c.675/76–749), in his book entitled *The Exact Exposition of the Orthodox Faith*, defines 'nature' as the principle of motion and repose, and, on this ground, he identifies 'nature' with 'substance.' However, he endorses the Aristotelian distinction between primary substance and secondary substance. The distinction (central to Aristotle's *Categories*) between primary and secondary substances is reformulated by John of Damascus with the help of a non-Aristotelian concept, that of *hypostasis*. His originality with regard to Gregory of Nyssa lies in the priority given to the *hypostasis*. John of Damascus reinterprets the Cappadocian Fathers' distinction between essence and *hypostasis* from the perspective of the priority of primary substances in Aristotle's *Categories*.[7] In other words,

5. McGuckin, *St Gregory of Nazianzus*.

6. John of Damascus was a Syrian monk and priest, and one of the most influential Fathers of the Eastern Orthodox Church. He is venerated as a saint by the Eastern Orthodox churches, and the Roman Catholic Church regards him as a "Doctor of the Church."

7. Louth, *St John Damascene*.

according to John of Damascus, reality is fundamentally *hypostatic*: everything exists as, or in relation to, *hypostases*.

Hypostasis signifies an existential otherness, and John of Damascus defines individuality as numerical difference. John of Damascus defines *hypostasis* and, hence, individuality by following Porphyry's *Isagoge*, 7, 19–27, according to which one individual is distinct from other individuals of the same species due to its unique bundle of properties; these properties are not essential, and John of Damascus calls them "accidental."

John of Damascus emphasizes that *hypostasis* not only possesses common as well as individual characteristics of the subject, but also exists in itself, whereas nature does not exist in itself, but is to be found in hypostasis. Thus, the God of Christianity, existing in a *hypostatic* way, is not the same with the God of general, abstract 'monotheism.' Christianity stresses the personhood of God, whereas general, abstract monotheism stresses the unity of God's nature. Through the distinction between *hypostasis* and nature/essence, the church fathers managed to explain how God can assume the human nature without losing or degrading His divinity. In particular, in the case of Jesus Christ, the same *Hypostasis* of the Logos/Word became the *hypostasis* of divine and human natures.

The early Greek church fathers, such as the Cappadocian Fathers, emphasize the ontology of particularity and freedom. The *hypostatic* way of God's existence implies that God is not constrained by His nature and that the way of God's existence is freedom. In the second book of his *Answer to Eunomius*, Gregory of Nyssa wrote that "God has created everything by His will and without any difficulty and pain the divine will became nature."[8] In other words, the divine action does not admit any mediation, and the only 'raw material' that God used in order to create the world was His own free will. Hence, God is free from every logical determination, and the cosmos is a result of God's will, and not an emanation from God's nature (the nature of the cosmos is created, whereas God's nature is uncreated). This position has been methodically elucidated by Maximus the Confessor (c.580–662).[9]

8. *Patrologia Graeca*, 46, 124B.

9. Initially, Maximus the Confessor was an aide to the Byzantine Emperor Heraclius. However, he gave up his career as a senior civil servant in order to become a monk. He moved to Carthage, where he studied Greek philosophy and especially Neoplatonism, and he became a prominent author. He fought against the heresy of Monotheletism, by defending the Chalcedonian doctrine that Jesus Christ had both human and divine will. Maximus the Confessor is venerated as a saint in both Eastern and Western Christianity.

In his *Ambiguum*, 7, Maximus the Confessor writes that the act of bringing being out of non-being, which only a sovereign God can do, can only be understood in terms of a common *arche* (beginning) and *telos* of being in God, and, therefore, as the source and goal of all being, the *Logos* is in the *logoi* of his creation.[10] Moreover, in his *Ad Thalassium*, 64, Maximus the Confessor adds that both creation and Scripture contain the fullness of the Logos in their *logoi*, and, therefore, they function together, and they are mirror images of one another. However, in his *Ambiguum*, 7, he makes an important clarification: the *logos* of a created entity is not a substance, and, therefore, it does not subsist by itself, but it only exists potentially in the creative divine *Logos* as a yet unmanifested possibility. Furthermore, in his *Ambiguum*, 7, following Dionysios the Areopagite,[11] Maximus the Confessor names the *logoi* divine "wills" (*thelēmata*). Hence, God knows and treats the beings and things in the world as manifestations of His will, and He relates with them through love and not according to any logical/natural necessity (since God's way of being is freedom).

For Maximus the Confessor, the incarnation of the Logos in Jesus Christ reveals the *telos*, or the ultimate scope, of the cosmos. In his *Ad Thalassium*, 60, Maximus the Confessor argues that "the Logos, by essence God, became a messenger of this plan when he became a man and . . . established himself as the innermost depth of the Father's goodness while also displaying in himself the very goal for which his creatures manifestly received the beginning of their existence." Moreover, in his *Ambiguum*, 7, Maximus the Confessor writes that the *Logos* of God, who is God, wills always and in all his creatures to accomplish the mystery of his embodiment.

The Greek Apologists were mainly philosophy graduates, and, therefore, their Christian theology was articulated on the basis of Greek philosophical terms, and it was focused on the Greek philosophers' quest for true being or for a way of making life meaningful. On the other hand, the Latin Apologists were mainly law graduates, and, therefore, their

10. Blowers and Wilken, *Cosmic Mystery*, 54.

11. Dionysios the Areopagite was a judge of the Areopagus who, as related in the *Acts of the Apostles* (Acts 17:34), was converted to Christianity by the preaching of the Apostle Paul during the Areopagus Sermon. According to Dionysios of Corinth (Bishop of Corinth; died in 171), quoted by the Roman historian and exegete Eusebius of Caesarea, Dionysios the Areopagite then became the first Bishop of Athens. In the early 6th century, a series of famous writings, employing Neoplatonic language to elucidate Christian theology, was ascribed to Dionysios the Areopagite.

Christian theology was articulated on the basis of the terminology of Roman law, and it was focused on the goal of the Latin founders of Roman Law, who were primarily seeking a practical way of organizing life. As a result of the previous cultural difference between the Greek Apologists and the Latin Apologists, the theology of the first has a deeply philosophical character, whereas the theology of the latter is notably legalistic.

Justin Philosopher and Martyr (c.100–165), one of the most influential early Greek Apologists, is regarded as the foremost interpreter of the Logos Doctrine in the second century A.D., and he is venerated as a saint in both Eastern and Western Christianity. In his *Dialogue with Trypho*, II, 1, Justin argues that "philosophy is, in fact, the greatest possession, and most honorable before God, to whom it leads us and alone commends us; and these are truly holy men who have bestowed attention on philosophy." Moreover, Clement of Alexandria (c.150–215), another highly influential early Greek Apologist, articulated a philosophical approach to Christianity.[12] In particular, in his work *Stromata*, VI, 5–6, Clement of Alexandria argues that "the same God that furnished both the Covenants was the giver of Greek philosophy to the Greeks, by which the Almighty is glorified among the Greeks," and he adds that "as the proclamation [of the Gospel] has come now at the fit time, so also at the fit time were the Law and the Prophets given to the Barbarians, and Philosophy to the Greeks."

On the other hand, Tertullian (c.160–c.225), the first Christian author to produce an extensive corpus of Latin Christian literature, was suspicious toward Greek philosophy, because several heresies were based on Greek philosophical terms and methods. Tertullian preferred the terminology and the mentality of Roman law. In his work *De Praescriptione*, 7, Tertullian asked the following question: "What indeed has Athens to do with Jerusalem?" And to this he gave a negative answer. Thus, Tertullian's work signals a transition from a critique of Greek philosophy to a cultural clash.

Tertullian's legalistic theology is a characteristic example of the path that has been followed by the Western world. Many legal expressions and terms that were used by Tertullian in his treatise *Adversus Praxean* became permanent in Western theology and were used by several Western church fathers in debates about the Holy Trinity and Jesus Christ. Moreover, Tertullian articulated a legalistic approach to Christian ethics, and

12. He is venerated as a saint in Eastern Christianity and in Anglicanism. His name was removed from the Roman Martyrology in 1586 by Pope Sixtus V on the advice of the Italian Cardinal and ecclesiastical historian Cesare Baronio.

he argued that sin is a transgression of law and is punishable, whereas virtue obliges God to render benefits.

In contrast to Tertullian's approach to sin and soteriology, the Greek church fathers interpret Paradise as a symbol of that existential state in which the human mind is united with God; that is, it is in communion with the divine *Logos*. From this perspective, life in Paradise signifies a dynamic course toward existential perfection. The second-century Greek church fathers Theophilus of Antioch (Bishop of Antioch and Christian Apologist) and Irenaeus of Lyons (Bishop of Lugdunum), who are venerated as saints in both Eastern and Western Christianity, have argued that the forebears of humanity were not endowed from the start with actual perfection, but only with *potential* perfection, and, therefore, man was not made to remain in a static condition, but he was made to become perfect, or divinized. Man was made needing to acquire perfection and, hence, to develop himself beyond the state in which God originally made him, not because he was created morally or intellectually deficient, but because perfection, or divinization, presupposes freedom of choice.[13] From the perspective of the previous Greek church fathers, the fall of humanity (Gen 3:1–19) was not at all a judicial matter, but it should be interpreted as the failure of humanity to maintain its orientation toward the God-given goal of divinization. In other words, the fall of man means that man lost his existential *telos* and his direct communion with the *Logos* of God, and, thus, he substituted illusions for the true *logoi* of the beings and things in the world.

According to Tertullian and many other legalist Western theologians, the Genesis should be interpreted in accordance with the rationality of Roman law. On the other hand, the Greek church fathers interpret the Genesis as a story about man's struggle for existential perfection, and they teach that the incarnation of the *Logos* in Jesus Christ is the historical manifestation of the Archetypal Man; in other words, through Jesus Christ, humanity discovered the lost *Logos*/Word. Tertullian was so strongly committed to legalism that he even attempted to fight against heresies by putting forward legal arguments. In his *De Praescriptione*, 37, Tertullian argued that the Bible is the property of the church, and, therefore, the use of the Bible by people who are not members of the church constitutes intrusion and robbery, and the church should ask the government to forbid the free reading of the Bible!

13. Romanides, *Ancestral Sin*.

As a result of the cultural differences between the Greek Apologists and the Latin Apologists, Christian theology was already trapped in a cultural clash before the end of the second century A.D. A serious manifestation of this cultural division between the Greek East and the Latin West was the Easter controversy (i.e., a dispute over the celebration of Easter). In 192, under the bloodstained reign of Commodus, Victor, Bishop of Rome, caused a dispute over the celebration of Easter. In his *Church History*, V, 24, Eusebius of Caesarea (c.275–339), regarded as the "Father of Church History," writes the following about the Easter controversy: "Victor, who presided over the Church at Rome, immediately attempted to cut off from the communion unity the parishes of all Asia, with the Churches that agreed with them, as heterodox; and he wrote letters and declared all the brethren there wholly excommunicate." Thus, Victor, who was the first Bishop of Rome to use the Latin language instead of the Greek one, brought the Christian world to the brink of a schism, which was finally averted mainly due to an appeasement initiative launched by Irenaeus of Lyons.

The secularization of the church of Rome was continued in the third century, when the Roman Empire was in a period of decay and Pope Stephen I, who was the Bishop of Rome from 254 to his death in 257, proclaimed the so-called "Petrine theory," according to which Rome is the Chair of Saint Peter (*Cathedra Petri*), the supposed leader of Jesus Christ's church, and, therefore, the Bishop of Rome has primacy over the whole church. Cyprian of Carthage (c.200–258), who is venerated as a saint in both Eastern and Western Christianity, fought vigorously against the theory of the primacy of the Bishop of Rome, by pointing out that the Apostles were equal (nothing was withheld from any of the Apostles) and by emphasizing that all bishops have equal authority since they derived this from the equality of the Apostles.[14] Moreover, Von Campenhausen has argued that Cyprian of Carthage made an important contribution to the substitution of the original Christian idea of 'spiritual power' for the secular concept of 'authority.'[15] The aforementioned dispute faded after the death of Pope Stephen I and the martyrdom of Cyprian of Carthage, but it did not disappear completely, and the West continued following the path of legalism and secularization.

---

14. McCarthy, *Gospel*.

15. Von Campenhausen, *Ecclesiastical Authority and Spiritual Power*.

The essence of the Western church's secularization consists in a tendency of the Western church fathers to give priority to history itself over its *telos* and, hence, to give priority to essence over person. On the other hand, the Eastern church fathers give priority to person over essence. By the term 'person,' the Greek church fathers mean an existential-otherness-in-communion. Whereas the Greek East's vision is the divinization of humanity, the Latin West's vision is the most efficient adaptation to historical necessities possible. Thus, the Greek East has given rise to the theology of personhood, whereas the Latin West has given rise to the rationalist theology of scholasticism.

On May 11, 330, Emperor Constantine the Great dedicated the new capital of the Roman Empire, namely Constantinople, and transferred his seat of government there from Rome. This event gave an important boost to the Greek philosophical tradition. As a result of the change of the Roman Empire's capital from Rome to Constantinople, the church of Constantinople could utilize the best elements of the Roman legal tradition in order to create a successful system of law and order, while simultaneously remaining committed to the Greek philosophical tradition. In contrast, after the change of the Roman Empire's capital from Rome to Constantinople, the Latin West was compelled to develop without having a powerful authority center within its territory; additionally, it had to face the Barbarian hordes that were raiding the Western Roman Empire. The Roman Empire wanted to Christianize the Barbarians, to make them assimilate the social significance of law and, ultimately, to integrate them into a balanced system of international relations. The Seat of the Bishop of Constantinople was close to the Roman Emperor's Palace (*Sacrum Palatium*), which was located in the south-eastern end of Constantinople's Peninsula, but the Bishop of Rome was geographically detached from the Roman Empire's political center, and he had to deal with burdensome historical conditions. Furthermore, as I have already mentioned, the Bishop of Rome was heir to a tradition of legalism and secularization. The combination of the aforementioned geopolitical and cultural factors impelled the church of Rome to develop into a highly centralized authority for cultural affairs, for doctrine, jurisdiction, and administration. In the Western Roman Empire, the church of Rome was the only institution that was capable of providing an effective system of order and security.

In February 380, Emperor Theodosius the Great declared Christianity the only legitimate imperial religion, and, in 392, he banned all

forms of pagan worship. In this way, Emperor Theodosius the Great officially invited the Christian church to participate in the secular authority system. As a result of the religious policy of Emperor Theodosius the
Great, Pope Damasus I, who was the Bishop of Rome from 366 to his
death in 384, hastened to take advantage of opportunities to exercise political power. Pope Damasus I restored the Petrine theory, and he added
that not only did Jesus Christ instituted Peter leader of the church, but
also he transferred authority to Peter. Hence, according to Pope Damasus I, the Apostle Peter was the indisputable and absolute heir to Jesus
Christ's authority, and, furthermore, the Bishop of Rome is the direct heir
to Saint Peter's authority.

Pope Damasus I realized that, in order to consolidate his hegemonic
political role, he had to abandon the Greek language and the Greek philosophical tradition and to organize the church on the basis of the Latin
language and the Roman legal tradition. Thus, Pope Damasus I changed
the official language of the liturgy from Greek to Latin, and he commis-
sioned Jerome, a scholar from Dalmatia, to translate the Bible into Latin.
Jerome's Latin translation of the Bible is known as the *Vulgate* (from the
Latin term 'Vulgata,' meaning the common speech of a people). Jerome's
Vulgate contains many expressions and concepts of Roman law, and,
thus, it played a decisive role in the development of the West's legalistic
theology throughout the Middle Ages.

In the fifth century, Pope Leo I, who was the Bishop of Rome from
440 to his death in 461, endorsed Pope Stephen's and Pope Damasus's
Petrine theory, and, additionally, he argued that Jesus Christ gave Pe-
ter absolute monarchical authority. Furthermore, invoking principles of
Roman law (and not any biblical or other theological source), Pope Leo
I argued that the absolute monarchical authority that was given to the
Apostle Peter does not belong to the *person* of Peter, but it belongs to
the *Chair* of Peter, and, therefore, it is fully and exclusively transferred to
each and every person who manages to occupy the Chair of Peter, or the
"Holy See." According to Pope Leo I, the Pope of Rome has the *plenitudo
potestatis* (fullness of power), and, therefore, he is the *principatus* (supreme authority) of the church without any other presupposition due to
the very fact that he occupies the Chair of Peter (since, according to the

ecclesiology of Pope Leo I, the supreme church authority belongs to the Chair of Peter and not to the person of the Pope).

Moreover, in the fifth century, Pope Gelasius I, who was the Bishop of Rome from 492 to his death in 496, argued that the Pope of Rome has *auctoritas* (authority), whereas the Emperor has only *regia potestas* (guiding imperial power). The terms *plenitudo potestatis*, *principatus*, *auctoritas*, and *regia potestas* have been taken from Roman law and have been used by the Papacy in order to impose the subordination of the secular authority to the church of Rome.

In the fifth century, the Western part of the Roman Empire was conquered by the German invaders. The West had gradually been sub-jugated to various German tribes: in Africa were the Vandals; in Spain and Southern Gaul, the Visigoths; in north-western Spain, the Suevi; in south-eastern Gaul, the Burgundians; in Britain, the Saxons and the Jutes; in Itali, the Heruli. The old Roman authority was preserved only in the northern part of Gaul by Syagrius (c.430–c.486/87), the last Ro-man official in Gaul (*magister militum per Gallias*), whose defeat by King Clovis I of the Franks is considered the end of the Western Roman rule outside Italy. However, in September 476, Flavius Odoacer (German: Odoaker), a Germanic soldier, deposed Romulus Augustus (the last Western Roman Emperor), and he became the King of Italy (476–93). Odoacer was given the title of patrician, and he ruled over Italy as the vicar of the Eastern Roman Emperor (Byzantium). The West was then deprived of the imperial title, and, thus, Odoacer's reign signals the end of the Western Roman Empire.

The Franks and the other Germanic peoples underwent gradual Christianization in the course of Late Antiquity and the Early Middle Ages, without, however, allowing the mystery of the Incarnate *Logos* to alter the essence of their ethos. The quality and the deficiencies of the Frankish Christianity were eloquently described by Boniface,[16] the first Archbishop of Mainz, in a letter that he wrote to Pope Zacharias *On His Accession to the Papacy* (472 A.D.). In that letter, Boniface wrote: "Franks have not held a council for more than eighty years; they have had no archbishop nor have they established or restored in any place the canon law of the Church." Moreover, in the same letter, Boniface described the ethos of the Frankish church authorities as follows: "The Episcopal sees

16. Boniface was an Anglo-Saxon missionary who propagated Christianity in the Frankish Empire during the eighth century. He is known as the "Apostle of the Ger-mans." He is venerated as a saint in both Eastern and Western Christianity.

... have been given, for the most part, into the possession of avaricious laymen or exploited by adulterous and unworthy clerics for worldly uses. ... Among them are bishops who ... are shiftless drunkards, ... who march armed into battle and shed with their own hands the blood of Christians and heathens alike."

For the Franks and the other Germanic peoples, Christianity was a means to achieve greater social homogeneity and consolidate their power in the West, and, therefore, they adopted and enhanced the Roman church's legacy of secularization and legalism. Moreover, the Franks did not hesitate to turn the Roman church's legacy of secularization and legalism against the Papacy itself, especially when Charlemagne (the King of the Franks from 768, the King of Italy from 774, and from 800 the first emperor of Western Europe since the collapse of the Western Roman Empire) challenged the authority of the *sacerdotium* (priesthood). Charlemagne claimed the status of direct appointment by God, without need of endorsement by the Pope, and he appointed bishops by his own, rather than Papal, authority.[17]

On the other hand, in the Eastern Roman Empire (Byzantium), the relations between church and state were based on the theory of Eusebius of Caesarea. The Byzantine world-conception was based on Platonism and Christianity, in the sense that it was based on the relation between the divine archetype and its image in the historical sphere. This world-conception was introduced in the Byzantine political thought by Eusebius of Caesarea. In his *Thirty-year Discourse* (pronounced in the thirtieth year of Emperor Constantine the Great's reign, 335 A.D.), Eusebius of Caesarea argued that an earthly kingdom (i.e., every form of secular authority) is a divine gift given from God to the prince and an image of the Heavenly Kingdom. Through the previous argument, Eusebius of Caesarea diplomatically proposed a new political theory, according to which: (i) the Roman conception of the god-king should be abolished and every form of pharaonic authority should be discarded, and instead it should be declared that the emperor exercises his authority "by the grace of God" and not self-sufficiently (i.e., the emperor is an image of God and not a god-king); (ii) the emperor is accountable to God and not an unaccountable absolute authority. Emperor Constantine the Great endorsed the political theory of Eusebius of Caesarea, and he founded the political system of the Roman Empire on the political theses of Eusebius of Caesarea. As

17. Sabine and Thorson, *Political Theory*.

a result of this political theory, the Byzantine emperors gradually created a system of a close symbiosis of state and church. In the context of the Byzantine symbiotic relationship between church and state, both church and state think that, even though they are administratively distinct institutions, they spring from the same fundamental source (namely, from God) and, for this reason, they must act in concert and assist each other.

SCHOLASTICISM

Scholasticism is a method and a system, and it is applied to both theology and philosophy. This term was applied in the era of Charlemagne to the philosophical and theological teachings at the schools he established. A *scholasticus* was a person learned in the trivium (grammar, dialectic, rhetoric) and the quadrivium (arithmetic, geometry, music, astronomy), or in theology. The application of the term *scholasticus* was gradually broadened in the course of time, until, finally, the title was given to all students and academics of universities in Western Europe from about 1100–1700.

The principal sources from which the early scholastics drew their inspiration were patristic literature, elements of Greek philosophy, and, later, Arabian and Jewish theories. However, until the middle of the twelfth century, the scholastics had very poor access to Greek philosophy, since the Greek philosophical material at their disposal consisted only of Latin translations of: parts of Plato's *Timaeus* (by Cicero and Chalcidius), Aristotle's *Categories* and *On Interpretation* (by Boethius), and Porphyry's *Introduction to the Categories* (by Boethius and Victorinus). Plato's *Meno* and *Phaedo* were translated in the twelfth century. Aristotle's *Analysis* and *Topics* became known to the West in translation after 1128, and his metaphysical and physical works in about 1200. On the other hand, in the Eastern Roman Empire (Byzantium), throughout the Middle Ages, the basic texts of classical philosophy were part of the Byzantine educational program, and they were available to Christian and non-Christian researchers without censorship or restraint by the church.[18]

Since the era of Augustine[19] (354–430), who was Bishop of Hippo Regius (located in the Roman province of Africa), the Western thought

18. Reynolds and Wilson, *Scribes and Scholars*. Tatakis, *Byzantine Philosophy*.

19. Augustine of Hippo is venerated as a saint by the Western churches. However, he has been regarded with some reserve in the East. The Eastern Orthodox churches praise him for his piety and relentless deference to the teaching authority of the church and refer to him as 'Blessed' or 'Holy.' The Orthodox Church's view of Augustine is a

has been oriented toward an element that, throughout the Middle Ages, continued to develop in contrast to the spirit of the first Apologists and the Greek church fathers (e.g., the Cappadocian Fathers, Maximus the Confessor, etc.), and it has exerted a great influence on the character and the history of modern European philosophy. This element, which is a diachronic characteristic of the Western spirit, is the thesis that the certitude of consciousness about itself forms the basis of truth.

Augustine is the intellectual father of individualistic subjectivism. From the distinction between the sensible and the intelligible worlds, Augustine infers that the soul knows bodies only through an inward experience and not through its relation to the body, and also he argues that the salvation of man consists in the soul's elevation into the intelligible world. Augustine's thought signals a philosophical shift from the natural world to the soul. But, even though the previous shift resembles Plotinus's thought, it is something different. Plotinus, *contra* Plato's *Phaedo* and Porphyry's *Introduction to the Categories*, maintains that the mind (*nous*) does not simply participate in the essence of cosmos, and it is not simply related to the essence of cosmos, but, since, according to Plotinus, the mind dynamically contains a multiplicity (the forms) and a duality (knower and known, or intellect and intelligible), it constitutes the essence of cosmos, which implies an active and creative consciousness. In Plotinus's own words, "no distinction exists between being and knowing" and "the truest life is such by virtue of an intellection and is identical with the truest intellection."[20] However, the previous Plotinian syllogism does not lead to Augustine's individualism, because Plotinus argues that the mind (i.e., the quintessence of the human being) is essentially divine, and, therefore, the subject cannot become autonomous; that is, it cannot be individualized. According to Plotinus's *Ennead III*, God (the absolute One) is pure spirit, and He creates the soul (the second level of the divine emanation); the soul is the effect and image of pure spirit (and, like every effect or image, less perfect than the original), it is supersensuous and intelligible, it is active and has ideas, and, by contemplating the ideas, it forms the cosmos in the ideas' image. The soul produces matter (the third and lowest level of emanation)—which is absolute impotence and privation—in order to act on it and thus form the world.

---

balanced appraisal of him with due credit given both to his orthodox positions and to his faults.

20. Plotinus, *Ennead III*, 8.

According to Plotinus, the world *per se* is neither good nor evil; it is good in the extent to which it participates in being, and it is evil in the extent to which it participates in matter. Before Plotinus, Plato, in his *Sophist*, had already argued that being and non-being are the extreme terms of an ontological series, whose intermediate terms are the non-being of being and the being of non-being. Hence, the vision of truth is achieved through the sensation of the world, and the ancient Greek notion of beauty signifies the triumph of spirit, i.e., the triumph of the ideas over the amorphy (formlessness) of non-being. By contrast, Augustine maintains that knowledge is in no way derived from the senses, but it is only derived from the ability of the soul to contemplate immaterial, moral, and aesthetic truths within itself.

In his treatise *De libero arbitrio*, Augustine defines *ratio* as the logical process according to which the intellect discerns and connects the objects of knowledge, and, furthermore, he discerns two functions of human reason: *ratio superior* and *ratio inferior*. According to Augustine's *De trinitate*, XII, *ratio superior* discerns ideal reality in and through the human soul and leads to the truth, whereas *ratio inferior* uses the senses to look outward on the world of sense objects and cannot lead to the truth. Augustine contrasts the inner truth and certainty of impression (intellectual perception) with the uncertainty of sense perception. In Augustine's philosophical and theological works, the soul is the epitome of personality, and *ratio superior*, as the exclusive way in which the soul knows the truth, is combined with a Manichean rejection of sense perception. As a consequence, from Augustine's perspective, truth is not a matter of spiritual freedom, since it is constrained by *ratio superior*, and, therefore, the human being is ontologically heteronomous and cannot be united with God in this life (i.e., salvation is impossible in this life).

From the perspective of the Greek church fathers, the knowledge of God consists in the participation of man in God's way of life, and, hence, in a metaphysically grounded experience of freedom from every (logical and natural) necessity. On the other hand, for the West, especially after Augustine's theology, the knowledge of God is analogous to the knowledge of man, in the sense of an inward experience that stems from the human will, which continually forms and reforms the contents of consciousness. Augustine substitutes sensation with will, and he argues that the awareness of an external stimulus is a result of the soul's intentionality, whereas Neoplatonism distinguishes the mind (*nous*) from the soul (the soul being second level of the divine emanation), and, therefore, it also distinguishes an external stimulus *per se* from the act of its conscious recognition. Furthermore, according to Neoplatonism, the task of the soul is to unite spirit with matter.

Before Neoplatonism, Aristotle, in his *On the Soul*, had pointed out that ancient Greek psychology is a theory of the acquisition of knowledge through the senses. Additionally, in Plato's *Timaeus*, the soul, like the body, is characterized by "that sensation which we now term 'seeing.'"[21] Thus, even though cognition is not founded on bodily sensations, it is not founded on representations created by a subjective mind, either. Plato argues that cognition is founded on a peculiar mental *sensation*, in the sense that the mind does not reproduce an external object through a process of visualization or conceptualization, nor does it create mental models of an external object, but it *participates* in the transcendent idea of an external object, and, therefore, it knows an external object due to the experience of the light of the corresponding idea. As a result of this relation between knowledge and the light of the idea, Plato's philosophy is opposite to every form of individualistic subjectivism. By contrast, Augustine's Manichean distinction between the soul and the body implies the following: rational truth is reflected in human spirit, but the personal will of God can be known only by analogy with man's personal will. For this reason, Augustine can be regarded as the father of individualistic subjectivism.

The radical distinction between the sensuous and the supersensuous worlds also played a dominant role in the work of the Roman statesman and philosopher Boethius (c.480–524/25). Boethius's work exerted a very important influence on the entirety of medieval Western thought, for until the thirteenth century Boethius's books constituted the only significant intellectual link between Greek philosophy and the Latin world. However, this link was conditioned by the mentalities of the Latin world and by the scope of the Latin education. The primary scope of the Latin education was rhetorical rigor and, hence, syllogistic perfection. In the medieval West, the pursuit of rhetorical power led to the substitution of metaphysical pursuits by rationality. Thus, in the medieval West, the Greek term *logos* was substituted by the Latin term *ratio*, and Boethius proposed a Platonic interpretation of Aristotle's logic. Both Boethius and Augustine interpreted Aristotle's general concepts (universals) like Platonic ideas (i.e., like entities totally distinct from the material world),

21. Plato, *Timaeus*, 45d.

and they interpreted Plato's ideas like logical essences, which was absurd. The cause of this confusion of the medieval Western thought is that the Latin scholars who were concerned with metaphysical problems ignored that, from the perspective of ancient Greek philosophy, the problem of essence was never an intellectual/rhetorical power game. Aristotle's logic itself is primarily concerned with the human *logos'* potential to comprehend and express an external spiritual reality (the *logos* of the cosmos), and not with the abstract systems of formal logic. In contrast to the Greek term *logos*, which refers to an experiential understanding of truth through participation/sharing (*mēthexis*), the Latin term *ratio* means the individual ability to syllogistically arrive at a comprehensive exhaustive understanding of truth.

The formative period of scholasticism, beginning with the ninth and ending with the twelfth century, was founded on the works of Augustine and Boethius. As a conclusion, from the aforementioned arguments, it follows that this period is marked by an attempt to arrive at a comprehensive exhaustive knowledge of God according to the methodology and the criteria of the human soul (mind and sentiment). This attempt put an indelible imprint on the entire medieval Western thought and determined the course of scholasticism. The dominant philosophical path that the West followed during this stage of scholasticism is known as philosophical realism, since Aristotle's general concepts (universals) were conceived of, in Platonic fashion, as the real essences of things and as prior to things (*universalia sunt realia ante rem*).

In the ninth century, the first Western scholar who methodically studied Greek church fathers was John Scottus Eriugena, who translated a collection of writings of Dionysios the Areopagite, Gregory of Nyssa's treatise *On the Making of Man*, and Maximus the Confessor's *Ambigua* into Latin. In Eriugena's studies about the relation between faith and reason, the former takes precedence over the latter, but Eriugena does not underestimate the significance of reason. Moreover, in Eriugena's thought, faith follows the path of philosophy, and, for Eriugena, philosophy offers a cataphatic form of knowledge which underpins apophatic (mystical) theology. Eriugena endorsed the Augustinian formula "crede, ut intelligas" [22] ("believe so that you may understand"), and, inspired by Neoplatonism, he created a system of philosophical realism in which general concepts (universals) are self-subsistent essences, and they create

22. Augustine, *Sermones*, 43, 9.

and determine every other entity. For Eriugena, the cosmos (universe) is God who has given form to Himself, a partial unfolding of the divine nature, and a pure *theophany*. From the perspective of Eriugena's logic, God is the superessential and indefinable absolute universal, but He is still part of nature; therefore, in the context of Eriugena's logic, initially the individual is deduced from the general, and finally, in Neoplatonic fashion, the individual is absorbed back into the general. Eriugena maintains that the real is the rational, and the rational is the real.[23]

The thesis of the ontological autonomy of universals (general concepts) and the tendency of medieval Western philosophers to identify reality with the intellect characterize the work of Anselm (1033–1109), Archbishop of Canterbury, who was the leading proponent of philosophical realism (more accurately, essentialism) during the formative stage of scholasticism.[24] Following the legacy of Augustine and Boethius, Anselm attempted to offer logical proofs for the existence of God. In his *Proslogium*, Anselm articulated his so-called ontological proof of God, which consists in deducing the existence of God from the concept of God, in showing that the very concept of God implies its existence. According to Anselm's syllogisms, the concept of God is the notion of something greater than which nothing can be thought; thus, if God did not exist, this concept would not be the concept of the greatest thing thinkable (since it would not have existence). However, the monk Gaunilo, in his anonymously published book *Against the Reasoning in Anselm's Proslogium*, exposed the fallacy in Anselm's argument: the human mind's capability of constructing the existence of God by logic, Gaunilo maintains, is the same as human mind's capability of constructing the existence of any other thing by logic, that is, so far as it is thought. For instance, according to Anselm's argument, one might prove the existence of a perfect island: the definition of a perfect island as the most perfect conceivable island is enough, by Anselm's way of thinking, in order to prove that a perfect island exists.

In the eleventh century, Anselm's logic became an important cause of intellectual uncertainty, because the French philosopher and theologian Roscellinus, a contemporary of Anselm, argued that the content of Anselm's logic consists of names, not of real entities.[25] Thus, Roscellinus

23. McGinn and Otten, *Eriugena*.

24. Colish, *Mirror of Language*.

25. Picavet, *Roscelin*.

founded nominalism. According to Roscellinus, ideas are simply words (*flatus vocis*) or names, not substances. Hence, for Roscellinus, the genus and species have no substantial unity, and the union of individuals in the genus or in the species is a mere fabrication of language or the work of thought; only individuals are real. Nominalism paved a way to positive science.

However, in the twelfth century, Peter Abelard, a French philosopher, theologian and preeminent logician, put forward a new theory, known as conceptualism, which is an intermediate position between philosophical realism/essentialism (e.g., Eriugena, Anselm, etc.) and nominalism (e.g., Roscellinus). According to Abelard, universals are neither substances nor mere words, but they are products of intellectual abstraction. Abelard maintains that, through abstraction, the mind can separate form from matter, but form does not subsist outside the mind, since it is predicated of a class of things. Abelard opposes essentialism by arguing that we cannot predicate a thing of a thing, but we can predicate a universal of many things, and, therefore, a universal cannot be ontologically autonomous (i.e., it is not a thing). For instance, the concept of a human being does not subsist in the world, but it exists only through and within particular beings. Hence, knowledge is derived from both conceptualization and sense perception. Additionally, Abelard opposes nominalism by arguing that the universal is a word only in relation to the objects of which it is predicated, and, therefore, universals are not mere words, but conceptual predicates.[26]

As a response to the rising spirit of positive science and to Abelard's conceptualism, which addresses the problem of knowledge independently of theology, Bernard of Clairvaux (1090–1153), a French abbot and the primary builder of the Cistercian Order, admitted the significance of dialectic and science, but he emphasized the depth of Christ's humility and love, thus becoming the founder of medieval Western mysticism. Bernard of Clairvaux's mysticism is deeply problematic, because it is founded on ecstasy (that is, on the exodus of the immortal soul from the mortal body), and, therefore, even though it can lead to the union between the will of God and the will of man, it precludes the divinization of the whole human being as a psycho-somatic unity. In his work *On Loving God*, Bernard of Clairvaux argues that his vision of a loving union with God presupposes freedom from the mortal body, and, therefore, it consists in a psychological phenomenon of 'divinization' (i.e., a type

---

26. Brower and Guilfoy, *Abelard*.

of 'divinization' that is due to an ecstatic mental state[27]), and not in the actual divinization of the human being (as a psycho-somatic whole) by the grace of God.[28] Bernard of Clairvaux's psychological approach to the issue of the divinization of humanity gradually gave rise to a shift from Western Christian mysticism to a form of Christianity that consists in a religious system of morality. On the other hand, as I shall argue in the next section of this chapter, the Byzantines' *neptic* theology (Hesychasm) understands Christianity as the mystery of the literal divinization of man's psychosomatic *hypostasis* by the uncreated grace of God.

In the twelfth and the thirteenth centuries, the West experienced a period of philosophical and theological flourishing (known also as the period of the culmination of scholasticism) as a result of the influence that Arab[29] and Jewish[30] philosophers exerted on the Latin West during that period and, also, because, during the same period, the Latin West came in touch with Aristotle's original writings. However, it should be pointed out that the Arabs' treatises on Aristotle, which exerted a very strong influence on medieval Western thought, were based on Neoplatonism.

During the twelfth and the thirteenth centuries, the West continued to have fragmented knowledge of Greek philosophy and of the Greek church fathers' writings, and it depended on incorrect translations of the Greek philosophical and theological vocabulary, but, in this way, the scholastics managed to create a peculiar Western philosophical and theological identity which paved a way to the Renaissance. During this period

27. By the term 'ecstasy,' we mean a state of consciousness in which the subject is totally involved with an object of his awareness, whereas, in an ordinary state of consciousness, the subject is aware of other objects, too. Hence, ecstasy is an altered state of consciousness characterized by diminished or minimal awareness of other objects. For instance, Bernard of Clairvaux's conception of the loving union with God involves the cessation of awareness of the physical body.

28. Evans, *Bernard of Clairvaux*, 173–205.

29. Under the Abbasid Caliphate, the works of Plato, Plotinus, and Aristotle were translated into Arabic and influenced philosophy throughout the Islamic world. Neoplatonism flourished especially among the Persian philosophers of the tenth century and in the Fatimid court of Egypt in the eleventh century. Moreover, "without the Byzantines," Gelzer argues, "the Arabs . . . would have remained barbarians. . . . But they found Greek books in Antioch, in Alexandria, and in Odessa"; Gelzer, *Byzantinische Kulturgeschichte*, 17.

30. Since the Hellenistic era, the influence of Neoplatonism on Judaism had been so strong that many ancient and medieval Jewish scholars articulated a synthesis between Neoplatonism and the Jewish religion. Barry, *Greek Qabalah*. Bickerman, *Jews in the Greek Age*. Goodman, *Neoplatonism and Jewish Thought*.

of the cultural history of the West, the leader of philosophical realism/essentialism was Thomas Aquinas (1224–74), an Italian Dominican priest, philosopher, and theologian (honored as a saint and "Doctor Angelicus," "Doctor Communis," and "Doctor Universalis" by the Roman Catholic Church); the leader of nominalism was William of Ockham (c.1280/85–c.1349), an English Franciscan priest,[31] philosopher and theologian, and the leader of conceptualism was John Duns Scotus (c.1265/66–1308), a British Franciscan priest, philosopher, and theologian.

In his *Scriptum super libros Sententiarum* and *Summa theologiae*, Thomas Aquinas argues that the truth is one and that the soul, as a separate species and as the entelechy of the body, unites the domains of the sensuous and the intelligible into a unified natural whole (knowledge originates in Augustine's *ratio inferior* and culminates in Augustine's *ratio superior*). According to Thomas Aquinas, the soul is the supreme, *ne plus ultra*, intelligible creature of God, but it is immortal, immaterial and capable of comprehending the intelligible realm. However, Thomas Aquinas maintains, the soul is bound to the body, and, therefore, the soul does not directly understand the intelligibles, but only indirectly, through reason (*ratio*), which leads to the conception of the universal within the individual.

For Thomas Aquinas, the soul comprehends the essences of things through the conception of the corresponding species, and, also, it comprehends the accidental properties of things through their sensible species, or sensuous representations. But, from Thomas Aquinas's viewpoint, sensible species are neither Platonic/Neoplatonic emanations nor Democritus's idols (i.e., projections of bodies themselves, guided by one's eyes toward his soul). Thomas Aquinas argues that immaterial entities (namely, essences distinct from the sensible species by which they are represented) exist within material bodies, so that the comprehension of objects by the human mind is not externally determined by their representations, but it is determined by the inner principle of comprehension, that is by reason. With Thomas Aquinas's epistemology, rational thought, as an exact organ of knowledge, repudiates the ancient Greek theory of ideas (as entities independent of consciousness), since the ancient Greek theory of ideas is neither a rationalist theory of knowledge nor a system of mysticism (at

31. In 1328, Ockham was officially excommunicated for leaving Avignon (for Pisa) without permission. Louis of Bavaria, the Holy Roman Emperor, offered Ockham's group protection, and, in 1330, Ockham travelled to the imperial court in Munich, where he spent the rest of his life writing about political and ecclesiological affairs.

least if one endorses Bernard of Clairvaux's approach to mysticism), but it is a method of spiritual cleansing. In contrast to the ancient Greek theory of ideas, Thomas Aquinas's epistemology paved a way to the modern tradition of individual truth (subjectivism), which was founded in the seventeenth century by Descartes (see chapter 3). The ancient Greek theory of truth *qua* spiritual cleansing and participation in the external realm of ideas leads to a holistic understanding of society, whereas rationalism maintains that truth can be found through analysis or calculus,[32] and, ultimately, it identifies truth with the self-certitude of the *ego*.

According to Thomas Aquinas, the universal does not exist as such (universal *qua* universal), but it exists only in an individualized manner within material bodies due to the quantitative differentiation of matter. From this perspective, human knowledge originates in the senses, and its integration is brought about by reason. In the context of Thomas Aquinas's philosophy, reason reigns over the soul, and its cognitive power, leading to the knowledge of God, is the most important asset of the human being. Thus, Thomas Aquinas maintains, the intellect, or the ability to reason, is superior to the will (since the will of a rational being is determined by the knowledge of the good), and the intellect is superior to freedom (since the freedom of a rational being is underpinned by the necessity of reason). Inherent in the previous arguments of Thomas Aquinas is a latent form of the humanism that became explicit in the West in the context of modernity (see chapter 3).

William of Ockham's nominalism and Thomas Aquinas's essentialism can be regarded as the two sides of the same coin (i.e., of the Western rationalist humanism). William of Ockham's nominalism begins with the skeptical arguments that sense perception is not a source of certain knowledge and that universals (intelligible species) have no existence outside the mind (i.e., they are not inherent in things). According to William of Ockham, to assume mind-independent universals, as essentialists/realists do, is to make entities of abstractions, and, hence, it is an unnecessary doubling of the universe. This principle is known as "Ockham's Razor," since it shaves off the unnecessary universals.[33]

In his *Summa totius logicae*, William of Ockham argues that only particulars exist, and they can be known independently of abstract concepts, through simple psychological activities, or through representation.

32. Von Neumann, "Mathematician," 180–96.
33. Moody, *William of Ockham*.

Science, therefore, is wholly concerned with self-evident truths (tautologies) and truths known by experience. If one believes in the ontological autonomy of general concepts, then universals (even though, for William of Ockham, they exist merely as thoughts in the mind) function as necessary constraints on the reality of the particular/individual and, also, on God's freedom. Thus, in order to save God's and man's freedom from universals, William of Ockham proposes the complete abandonment of general ideas, and he reduces them to psychological representations, meaning to expressions of one's own inner states (intellections, acts of will, joy, and sorrow). William of Ockham's nominalism is the first ontological legitimization of the individual *qua* 'subject' (i.e., a historical actor filled with reason and will and, more precisely, a historical being capable of acting on the basis of reason and will) and of the individual's autonomy from communal authority.

According to Thomas Aquinas, the essence of politics consists in the deliberate guiding by man's reason of his will in social actions. Moreover, Thomas Aquinas argues that the state has positive value in and of itself on the grounds that it is an expression of God's providence and will for mankind and it secures peace.[34] In Thomas Aquinas's system, universals (general concepts) constitute authentic reality, whereas individuals belong to the realm of imperfect phenomena; consequently, society, as a system of relations, must be structured according to the eternal law, which is the wisdom of God and serves as an exemplar of law directing the actions of the created universe. The Pope is the authority that can explain and impose the will of the supreme universal, or the divine wisdom. On the basis of the previous arguments, the Pope managed to impose his *plenitudo potestatis* on medieval Western European societies. Thomas Aquinas's philosophical realism implies that the Pope has the right to behave like his archetype, or God, and, furthermore, since the individual has significance and value only because and in the extent to which it serves the universal, authorities have the right and the moral responsibility to suppress the individual for the sake of the universal.

Gradually, the medieval Western subject realized that the most effective way to fight against Papal absolutism consists in the refutation of philosophical realism. In the Middle Ages, several kings and local lords fought against the Vatican's political system. For instance, during the tenth and the eleventh centuries, kings saw themselves as the heads of

34. D'Entrèves, *Aquinas.*

hierarchical systems of personal loyalty, and local lords assumed rights over the persons and property of their followers to judge, punish, levy taxes, and receive rents and services; additionally, they viewed the local churches and monasteries in their area as part of their own domains. In the eleventh and the twelfth centuries, the belief in the supernatural authority of the kings undermined the authority of the Pope, and German emperors, especially Frederick I (Barbarossa), encouraged a dynamic revival of Roman imperial law. However, it was the bourgeoisie who, from the eleventh century onward, decided to unleash an attack on the philosophical foundations of the Papacy, specifically on philosophical realism.

According to Georg W. F. Hegel, 'civil society' (*bürgerliche Gesellschaft*) is the sphere of universal egoism, and the first medieval Western cities were created as a reaction against the feudal lords' violence.[35] The bourgeois (merchants, craftsmen, bankers, ship-owners, notaries, physicians, etc.) created their own civilization. Henri Pirenne argues that, in the Middle Ages, merchants started gathering around castles or abbeys, especially near ports.[36] Thus, the first medieval Western cities were created, not in the *bourg*,[37] but in the *faubourg* (out of the walls), and their autonomy was based on the bourgeois' needs for social order and security, freedom of movement, and an efficient system of taxation capable of protecting freedom (from feudal and generally arbitrary authorities) and social order. In the eleventh century, the bourgeois started acquiring political authority and promoting a form of parliamentarianism. The bourgeois understand society not as an expression or image of a universal, but as an association of individuals. Therefore, they endorse nominalism. William of Ockham argues that sovereignty derives from the people, who have the natural power to legislate and institute rulers.[38]

The individualistic humanism that stems from William of Ockham's nominalism is a more radical type of humanism than the one that stems from Thomas Aquinas's essentialism/realism. William of Ockham's

35. Pelczynski, *State and Civil Society*.

36. Pirenne, *Medieval Cities*.

37. Originally, the German word 'Burg' means an unwalled settlement formed around an abbey or around a throughway leading outward from the gate of a walled city. The words 'burgensis' and 'bourgeois' are derived from the word 'Burg' and mean an inhabitant of a Burg. From the ninth century onward, merchants, impoverished members of the nobility, opportunists, and fugitive serfs started building new walls, which replaced the old city walls, and, thus, they became permanent inhabitants of a city (i.e., bourgeois).

38. McGrade, *William of Ockham*.

nominalism can potentially justify unrestrained egoism. John Duns Scotus's conceptualism occupies the middle ground between Thomas Aquinas's essentialism/realism and William of Ockham's nominalism.

John Duns Scotus argues that universals exist in things as their essence, or general nature, and after things as abstract concepts in our minds. Hence, conceptual knowledge has a real object. However, John Duns Scotus maintains, the correspondence between knowledge and objects is not necessarily one of identity. In his *Opus Oxoniense* and *Opus Parisiense*, John Duns Scotus accepts the logical distinction between the 'genus' and the 'species,' and he clarifies that the genus necessarily implies the species, and that a species, in turn, necessarily implies individuals. From his perspective, essence, or universal nature, or 'whatness' (*quidditas*) is supplemented by the individual nature, i.e., by 'thisness' (*haecceitas*). For instance, just as 'man' is logically derived from 'animal' by the addition of the specific difference (namely, 'humanity') to 'life,' so Socrates comes from 'man' by adding the individual character, i.e., *Socratitas* (being Socrates), to the universal and specific essence. According to John Duns Scotus, the principle of individuation lies within this individual difference, and not, as Thomas Aquinas had argued, within matter; otherwise, the members of the same species would all be the same. In other words, the particular thing is what it is, not because of its matter, but because of its individual nature. This individuating difference is a quality conjoined with the general characteristics and inherent in them. Thus, by descending from universals (general concepts), we finally reach individuals, and, inversely, by ascending from individuals, we reach universals, the highest of which is being (*ens*), since it can be predicated of everything else.

John Duns Scotus's argument that the individual is the species plus the 'individual' difference and that the species is the genus plus the 'specific' difference underpins a theory of philosophical psychology according to which the soul is primarily concerned with being *qua* being, whose essence is its own way of being, without any further characterization. However, according to John Duns Scotus, the preoccupation of the soul with being *qua* being leads to uncertainty and skepticism about the soul and its energy. In particular, the immortality of the soul is not susceptible of rational demonstration, and, on this matter, faith alone can give us certainty (without entirely excluding doubt). Moreover, since the immortality of the soul is a rationally indemonstrable thesis, the proofs of God's existence are uncertain. Both Thomas Aquinas and John Duns

Scotus hold that we can syllogistically infer the existence of God from His works (*a posteriori*), the proof being latent in every rational creature and requiring only to be made actual, but they do not repose the same amount of confidence in natural reason. Whereas, in his *Summa Contra Gentiles*, 1, 3, Thomas Aquinas argued that, "by the light of natural reason," philosophers can prove truths about God demonstratively, John Duns Scotus contends that such proofs of God's existence are uncertain.

According to John Duns Scotus, revealed truths are rationally indemonstrable, and rationally demonstrable truths about the creation are different from the revealed truths of religion. As a result of the previous thesis, there are two distinct truths: the truth of the material world, which is susceptible of rational demonstration and can be sought through philosophy, and the truth of the spiritual world, which is only a matter of faith and can be sought through theology. For John Duns Scotus, the sensuous world is the realm of the intellect (i.e., of the most abstract and simple function of the soul and the distinguishing mark of a rational being), and the supersensuous world is the realm of faith, thus leading to the autonomy of the natural sciences from theology. The previous distinction is a consequence of John Duns Scotus's epistemological theses that knowledge is a result of the intellect's encounter with external objects, and that this encounter creates a visible image which is, more or less, a confused (or potential) perception and can be clarified (i.e., it can become an actual perception) by the will. Hence, in John Duns Scotus's system, knowledge is an instrument of the will, but will and love, which is a function of the will, are ends in themselves.

Thomas Aquinas's natural theology leads to an all-pervading unrestricted causal determinism, to which, presumably, even God conforms, since, in Thomas Aquinas's thought, the pure divine intellect is confused with divine wills. On the other hand, John Duns Scotus's attempt to save man's and God's freedom of will leads to indeterminism, since he argues that perception depends on the will; the degree of our knowledge is analogous to the degree of our will. From this viewpoint, one could validly make the argument that John Duns Scotus's philosophy paved a way to Nietzsche's doctrine of the "will to power" and to Heidegger's distinction between the authentic and the inauthentic modes of *Dasein's* existence (see chapter 3).

HESYCHASM: FROM PLATO'S CAVE TO
THE TABORIAN LIGHT

Hesychasm, or *nepsis*, is the hallmark of sanctity according to Christian Orthodox theology. The term *nepsis* comes from the New Testament (1 Pet 5:8), and it means to be alert and of sober mind. *Nepsis* is a state of watchfulness and sobriety acquired after a period of cleansing. Moreover, the term Hesychasm (Greek: *ho hesychasmōs*) comes from the New Testament (Matt 6:6), and it is a process of retiring inward by quieting (cleansing) the body and the mind in order, ultimately, to achieve an experiential knowledge of God (*theoria*, which is the Greek word for 'theory' and literally means seeing God). In the light of the arguments that I put forward in chapters 1 and 2, the emphasis that the Hesychasts, or Neptic Fathers, place on cleansing as a presupposition of true theology and on *seeing* God is a clear Platonic influence, and the understanding of Hesychasm presupposes that one is aware of the particular manner in which the Greek East understands Plato and Aristotle (which I exposed in chapter 1) and of the philosophical differences between the Greek East and the Latin West (which I exposed in the previous sections of chapter 2). In the eighteenth century, the monk, theologian, and philosopher Nikodemos of the Holy Mountain and Makarios of Corinth (Bishop of Corinth and theologian), both of whom are venerated as saints by the Eastern Orthodox Church, compiled the works of the Hesychasts, or Neptic Fathers, written between the fourth and the fifteenth centuries, into a collection that is called *The Philokalia*[39] (in Greek, the word *philokalia* means love of the beautiful/good).

Evagrius Ponticus[40] (345–99), Maximus the Confessor, and Symeon the New Theologian[41] (949–1022), three of the most influential Neptic Fathers, understand Hesychasm as a practice of inner prayer whose aim

39. In the nineteenth century, the *Philokalia* was translated in Russian. In the period 1979–95, Kallistos Ware, G. E. H. Palmer, and Philip Sherrard completed the English translation of the first four of the five Greek volumes of the *Philokalia*, which have been published by Faber and Faber.

40. Evagrius Ponticus, known also as Evagrius the Solitary, was a Christian monk and ascetic, and he was a disciple of Basil the Great, Gregory of Nazianzus, and the hermit Macarius of Egypt.

41. Symeon the New Theologian was a Byzantine Christian monk and poet. The Eastern Orthodox Church venerates him as a saint and has given him the title of "Theologian," not in the modern academic sense of theological study, but to recognize someone who spoke from personal experience of the vision of God.

is union with God in a way that transcends images, concepts, and language.[42] However, Gregory of Sinai[43] (1260s–1346) has pointed out that, even though images and thoughts are to be excluded, Hesychasm does not reject all feelings, because, rightly practised, the Jesus Prayer leads to a sense of joyful sorrow and to a feeling of spiritual warmth, which, the Hesychasts maintain, make the aspirant capable of experiencing the divine illumination that three Apostles, namely Peter, James, son of Zebedee, and John, experienced at the Transfiguration of Jesus Christ on Mount Tabor (Matt 17:1–9; Mark 9:2–8; Luke 9:28–36; 2 Pet 1:16–18). The Hesychasts emphasize that the light that shined at the Transfiguration of Jesus Christ is the uncreated light of God's glory.[44]

Kallistos Katafygiotis,[45] a fourteenth-century Hesychast whose treatise *On Union with God and Life of Theoria* is included in volume V of the *Philokalia*, exposes the Hesychasts' approach to divinization (Greek: *theōsis*) and the functions of the mind (Greek: *nous*). In particular, in the previous treatise, Kallistos Katafygiotis argues that all beings, including the mind, have received their movement and their natural characteristics from the *Logos*, who has created them, and that the movement of the mind, in particular, has as its characteristic the 'for ever,' which is infinite and unlimited. Therefore, Kallistos Katafygiotis maintains, it would have been beneath the nature and the value of the mind if it moved in a finite and limited way (i.e., if it had its movement in finite and limited things). According to Kallistos Katafygiotis, due to the mind's *logos* and nature, the perpetual movement of the mind needs to move toward something eternal and unlimited, and nothing is really (i.e., by its nature) infinite and unlimited but God, who by nature is One. Hence, the mind must gaze at and move toward the infinite One, God.

In the aforementioned treatise, Kallistos Katafygiotis argues that there are only three ways in which the mind ascends to the *theoria* (vision) of God: the self-mobilized way (Greek: *autokinetos*), the other-mobilized way (Greek: *heterokinetos*), and the mixed way. The self-mobilized way is performed with the mind's own will accompanied by imagination, and its

---

42. *Philokalia*, I, II, and IV.

43. Gregory of Sinai wrote fifteen treatises *On Stillness* and 137 treatises *On Commandments and Doctrines*; he is renowned also as a hymnographer, and with Gregory Palamas he helped to establish Mount Athos as a center of Hesychasm.

44. Louth, "Holiness and Vision," 217*ff.*

45. 'Kallistos Katafygiotis' is the pen name of an anonymous Hesychast. Upon ordination, many Hesychasts were given the name 'Kallistos.'

conclusion is the *theoria* of things related to God (i.e., an indirect and imperfect knowledge of God). The other-mobilized way is performed only with the will and illumination of God (i.e., it is supernatural, and, in such a state, the entire mind is found under divine possession, and it is caught in divine revelations). The mixed way consists partly of both the self-mobilized way and the other-mobilized way: as long as one works with his own will and imagination, he is in agreement with the self-mobilized way, and he partakes of the other-mobilized way as long as he unites with oneself by means of the divine illumination, and he sees God ineffably, beyond the mental union with oneself. Moreover, in the same treatise, Kallistos Katafygiotis makes the following remarks about faith, divine illumination, and union with God: when the mind uses its imagination in order to contemplate the ineffable, it is guided by faith; when the mind receives the divine illumination of God's grace, it is assured with hope; and, when the divine light takes hold of it, the mind becomes a repository of love toward humanity and much more so toward God. Thus, the triple alignment and movement of the mind, with faith, hope, and love, becomes perfect and divinizing.

In Nikiphoros the Hesychast's treatise *On Watchfulness and the Guarding of the Heart* (which is included in volume IV of the *Philokalia*) and in Symeon the New Theologian's treatises *The Three Methods of Prayer* and *153 Practical and Theological Texts* (which are also included in volume IV of the *Philokalia*), the following physical Hesychastic techniques are exposed: the aspirant should sit with his head bowed, with his gaze fixed on the place of the heart or on his navel, he should slow down his breathing rhythm, and, at the same time, he should search inwardly for the place of the heart. Moreover, in the previous state, the aspirant should recite the "Jesus Prayer," whose standard form is: "Lord Jesus Christ, Son of God, have mercy on me, a sinner." The significance of the Jesus Prayer has been emphasized by Gregory of Sinai and Gregory Palamas (1296–1359), two of the most influential Hesychasts, whose treatises are included in volume IV of the *Philokalia*.

In the thirteenth and the fourteenth centuries, the theology and the philosophy of Thomas Aquinas and William of Ockham as well as the poetry of Dante Alighieri laid the foundations of the Renaissance and of modern Western humanism. On the other hand, during the same period, Byzantium experienced its own variety of spiritual renaissance, which was founded on Hesychasm. However, in the Byzantine Empire, during the fourteenth century, a theological controversy known as the Hesychast controversy broke out between supporters and opponents of Hesychasm.

The Hesychast controversy influenced and was influenced by the political forces in play during the Byzantine Civil War (1341–47). The Byzantine Civil War broke out after the death of the Byzantine Emperor Andronikos III Palaiologos over the guardianship of his nine-year-old son and heir, John V Palaiologos. On one side was John VI Kantakouzenos (Byzantine Emperor from 1347 to 1354), who, on the accession of Andronikos III in 1328, was entrusted with the supreme administration of affairs, and, on the Emperor's death, was the designated regent and guardian of the nine-year-old John V Palaiologos. On the other side were the Empress-Dowager Anna of Savoy (the second wife of Andronikos III Palaiologos), the Patriarch of Constantinople John XIV Kalekas, and the Byzantine statesman and high-ranking military officer (Grand Duke) Alexios Apokaukos. John VI Kantakouzenos was primarily backed by the Byzantine aristocracy, which was a traditionalist social group, and he was an advocate of Hesychasm and especially of Gregory Palamas's theology. Anna of Savoy, Patriarch John XIV Kalekas, and Alexios Apokaukos were primarily backed by members of the lower and middle classes, they were significantly influenced by the culture of the West, and they were opposing Hesychasm.

A council held in Constantinople in August 1341 vindicated Gregory Palamas and his teachings, but another council held in Constantinople in 1344 opposed Hesychasm and excommunicated Gregory Palamas for heresy. Empress Anna and Patriarch John XIV had Gregory Palamas imprisoned. In 1347, a new council organized by Emperor John VI Kantakouzenos, who had victoriously entered Constantinople, affirmed the resolutions of the council of 1341 and excommunicated Gregory Palamas's enemies. The new Patriarch of Constantinople, Isidore, celebrated the triumph of Hesychasm by replacing the ecclesiastical hierarchy with thirty-two monks who were loyal to Gregory Palamas's theology, and he ordained Gregory Palamas as Archbishop of Thessaloniki. In 1368, the Patriarch of Constantinople, Philotheos, convened a council on Hesychasm, which proclaimed Gregory Palamas as a saint.

During the Hesychast controversy, the most prominent theological and philosophical opponent of Gregory Palamas was the Calabrian monk Barlaam. Barlaam was highly educated, he was an adherent of Plato and Aristotle, and he arrived in Constantinople around 1330. Due to his impressive academic qualification, Barlaam was appointed as a professor at the University of Magnaura, in Constantinople, and as a representative of the Eastern Orthodox Church during theological dialogues between Eastern and Western Christianity. However, Barlaam was significantly influenced by the scholastics' rationalism and humanism.

The first conflict between Barlaam and Gregory Palamas occurred when Gregory Palamas criticized the theological methodology and epistemology that Barlaam followed during the years 1333–34, when Barlaam was negotiating the union of churches with the representatives of Pope John XXII. Following Orthodox Christian dogmatics, Barlaam condemned the decision of the church of Rome to insert the *Filioque*[46] into the Nicene Creed, but, from Gregory Palamas's perspective, the theological methodology and epistemology that Barlaam followed in order to defend the Orthodox doctrine of the Holy Spirit was not in agreement with Orthodox Christian theology. In particular, Barlaam argued as follows: since God is ultimately unknowable and undemonstrable to humans, the Roman church's doctrine of the *Filioque*, according to which

46. *Filioque* is a Latin word meaning 'and [from] the Son.' In 809, a local council of Charlemagne's bishops in Aachen introduced the term *Filioque* into the Nicene Creed. The *Filioque* and the *Libri Carolini* (four books composed on the command of Charlemagne, who was illiterate, but he wanted to refute the Second Council of Nicaea and to challenge Byzantine civilization) were part of Charlemagne's cultural antagonism against Byzantium and of his attempt to control the church. Protopresbyter John Meyendorff and Protopresbyter John Romanides argue that the Franks' efforts to get Pope Leo III to approve the addition of the *Filioque* to the Nicene Creed were a consequence of Charlemagne's intention to disparage Byzantine spirituality (Meyendorff, *Orthodox Church*; Romanides, *Franks, Romans, Feudalism, and Doctrine*). According to the original Nicene Creed (as adopted in 325 by the First Ecumenical Council, that of Nicaea), the Holy Spirit proceeds from the Father, and the term 'proceeds' signifies the particular personal relationship between the Holy Spirit and the Father (Divine *Nous*), and not an authoritarian hierarchy. But, with the introduction of the *Filioque*, the Holy Spirit becomes a subordinate member of the Holy Trinity, and the Holy Trinity becomes an authoritarian Neoplatonic hierarchical system. Orthodox Triadology emphasizes that, for any given trait, it must be common to all Persons of the Trinity or unique to one of them: Fatherhood is unique to the Father, begottedness is unique to the Son, procession is unique to the Spirit, and Godhood is common to all. The argument that a trait (e.g., being the source of the Spirit's procession) can be shared by only two Persons of the Trinity implies that those two Persons are superior to the third Person, and, therefore, the balance of unity and diversity is overturned. In 810, Pope Leo III refused to approve the inclusion of the *Filioque* in the Latin Creed used in the church of Rome. However, in 1014, at the request of the German King Henry II, who had come to Rome to be crowned Emperor, Pope Benedict VIII, who owed to Henry his restoration to the Papal throne after usurpation of Antipope Gregory VI, approved the inclusion of the *Filioque* in the Latin Creed used in the church of Rome. The *Filioque* was one of the primary causes of the East–West Schism of 1054.

the Holy Spirit proceeds from both the Father *and* the Son, is meaning-less. On the other hand, Gregory Palamas wrote two treatises on the procession of the Holy Spirit, in which he condemned Barlaam's agnostic trends, and he argued that, even though God cannot be syllogistically demonstrated, God can be known through faith and divine illumination. The argument that the incomprehensibility of God is a consequence of man's cognitive weaknesses, and not an ontological characteristic of God, and the argument that divine illumination is only a symbol, and not es-sential to man's ontological perfection, are derived from scholasticism. Moreover, Barlaam's variety of apophatic theology is alien to Orthodoxy, because it is founded on the thesis that the material world is separated from the spiritual world and that the first is approached and studied through philosophical enquiry into the realm of the senses, whereas the latter is approached and studied through apophatic contemplation of the intelligible realm; this thesis echoes the views of John Duns Scotus. Moreover, John Duns Scotus's philosophy, which inspired Barlaam's vari-ety of apophaticism, reappeared on the philosophical horizon during the modern era through Martin Heidegger, whose philosophy begins with a theory of concepts and logical categories similar to the philosophy of John Duns Scotus, and it proceeds with Heidegger's own variety of John Duns Scotus's philosophy, since Heidegger articulated an apophatic ap-proach to the being-present-at-hand (see chapter 3).

In contrast to both the scholastics' rationalism and the nominalists' skepticism, Hesychasm emphasizes the difference between God's essence and God's energy: God's energy is the life-force of God's essence, and the fullness of God is present in His energy according to His will. Moreover, the Hesychasts often use the plural form of 'energy' (i.e., 'energies') in order to refer to God's particular energies, such as wisdom, love, provi-dence, creativity, etc. The main argument of Hesychasm is the following: both God's essence and God's energies are uncreated, but, even though God's essence and *hypostases* (i.e., the three Persons of the Trinity) are transcendent and totally inaccessible to humanity, humanity can partici-pate in God's energies and, therefore, humanity can be divinized.

According to the scholastics and Barlaam, those divine energies to which humanity can participate are created (and, hence, ontologi-cally inferior to God's uncreated essence), namely, from their viewpoint, God's grace is a created gift to humanity, and, therefore, humanity can know God only indirectly (i.e., from His creations). The scholastics and Barlaam arrived at the previous conclusion because they argued that 'entelechy' (i.e., the condition of a thing whose essence is fully realized, or actuality) is something totally separate from 'essence.' On the other hand, for the medieval Greek thought, including Hesychasm, 'entelechy' is the active, dynamic perfection of 'essence.' Thus, for the Hesychasts, God's grace is an uncreated, divinizing gift to man, and, therefore, man can know God directly, i.e., by participating in God's uncreated energies (His way of being), without, however, mingling with God's essence. According to Plato, Aristotle, and the Hesychasts, a being/thing exists authentically only if it is united with its *telos*. For the Hesychasts, in particular, the *telos* of man is his divinization; therefore, man exists authentically only if he is authentically united with God, and being *authentically* united with God means that one is a partaker of God's uncreated energies.

Man's participation in God's energies is a free personal relationship between God and man, and it takes place according to the degree of man's psychological preparation for such a divinizing experience. In contrast to the scholastics' rationalism, Hesychasm emphasizes that we should not try to conceive of God as the most general concept (God is not a coercive universal) and that the relationship between God and man is based on free will and not on logical necessity. According to the Hesychasts, true theology is the experience of participation in God's uncreated energies. Moreover, in contrast to the nominalists' skepticism, Hesychasm emphasizes that, even though there is absolute discontinuity between God's essence, which is uncreated, and the world's essence, which is created, and, therefore, God is totally free and unconstrained by His nature, man can actually know God by participating in God's energies. Thus, Hesychast epistemology consists in two theses: (i) since God's essence is totally unknowable due to God's ontologically grounded freedom (i.e., because God's essence is not determined by any logical category), God and the world do not constitute a hierarchical universal unity (for, otherwise, God's and man's freedom would be limited by a coercive universal *ratio*), and, therefore, *contra* Thomas Aquinas's natural theology, God cannot be known syllogistically; (ii) God can be known through a metaphysical type of knowledge, which consists in psychic cleansing and was originally described by Plato in *Phaedrus*, where he writes about the soul journeying in "this region beyond the skies," which is "the abode of the reality with which true knowledge is concerned, a reality without color or shape, intangible."[47]

47. Plato, *Phaedrus*, 247c–e.

In his *Republic*, Plato writes that the just man has cured his soul by keeping the three elements (i.e., reason, the emotions, and the appetites) which make up his inward self "in tune, like the notes of a scale," by setting his house to rights, by attaining "self-mastery and order" and by living "on good terms with himself," thus bounding "these elements into a disciplined and harmonious whole."[48] Moreover, in his *Phaedo*, Plato argues that psychic cleansing is a necessary presupposition of our transformation into the Good, because "it cannot be that the impure attain the pure."[49] Hence, according to Plato, the knowledge of the absolute good presupposes not only the ability to give an account, but also a psychic cleansing or cure.

In his treatises entitled *Triads in Defense of the Holy Hesychasts* (included in volume IV of the *Philokalia*), Gregory Palamas understands psychic cleansing as a process that leads to mental transparency, and he emphasizes the difference between the 'mind,' being the repository of God's uncreated energies within the human being, and the 'intellect,' being the faculty of abstract thought (among its functions are attention, conception, judgment, reasoning, reflection, and self-consciousness). According to Gregory Palamas, psychic cleansing consists in the elimination of everything that may impede the descent of the uncreated energies of God into the human mind. In other words, psychic cleansing signifies perfect mental transparency. Therefore, according to Hesychasm, every attempt to equate the mind with the intellect leads to a state of mental non-transparency and restricts the human mind to created means of knowledge, rendering man incapable of divine illumination. The knowledge that is based on the intellect is derived from created sources, whereas the knowledge that is based on the mind, and, hence, on God's uncreated energies (or grace), is derived from an uncreated source.

The Greek church fathers in general and the Hesychasts in particular emphasize that God alone is uncreated, and everything else, including the human soul, is created. In chapters 5 and 6 of his *Dialogue with Trypho*, Justin Philosopher and Martyr puts forward the following arguments: "if the world is begotten, souls also are necessarily begotten," and, furthermore, if the soul were life, "it would cause something else, and not itself, to live, even as motion would move something else than itself"; even though the soul lives, "it lives not as being life, but as the

48. Plato, *Republic*, 443d–e.
49. Plato, *Phaedo*, 67b.

partaker of life . . . the soul partakes of life, since God wills it to live." According to Hesychasm, the human soul and the body are united into a psycho-somatic nexus, and the soul should be understood as the *hypostatic* bearer of the impersonal life-force; in other words, it is what makes a human being a *hypostasis*.

In the first triad of his treatises *In Defense of the Holy Hesychasts*, Gregory Palamas argues that the heart is the essence of the mind, and the mind is a power of the heart: "the heart is the secret chamber of the mind and the prime physical organ of mental power." Additionally, in the same triad, he attacks the idea that man must drive his mind out of his body in order to attain spiritual visions as an erroneous belief, and he argues as follows: "We who carry as in vessels of clay, that is in our bodies, the light of the Father, in the person of Jesus Christ, in which we know the glory of the Holy Spirit, how can it dishonor our mind to duel in the inner sanctuary of the body?" Furthermore, in the second triad of his treatises *In Defense of the Holy Hesychasts*, Gregory Palamas adds the following: "When spiritual joy comes to the body from the mind, it suffers no diminution by this communion with the body, but rather transfigures the body, spiritualizing it. For then, rejecting all evil desires of the flesh, it no longer weighs down the soul that rises up with it, the whole man becoming spirit."

Hesychasm does not fight against the body, but it aims at liberating the body from the law of sin (i.e., from impersonal, uncontrolled impulses and instincts and from selfishness) and at establishing there the mind as an overseer. The Hesychasts lay down laws for every power of the soul and for every member of the body: they dictate to the senses what they have to receive and in what measure, thus achieving self-mastery; they purify the desiring part of the soul through love; and they improve the intellectual part of the soul by eliminating everything that prevents the mind from soaring to God, thus achieving *nepsis*.

According to Hesychasm, through its participation in the uncreated energies of God, the human soul can be divinized, and, thus, it can be satisfied or filled with the uncreated light of God's glory. In the language of ancient mystics, a soul which is a partaker of God's uncreated energies is called a standing soul. Such a soul is truly immortal. On the other hand, a soul which is submerged in the lower and the animalistic cannot reach immortality, but it will instead perish with the animalistic part (Eccl 3:19); this is the meaning of 'spiritual death,' whose archetype is 'Satan' (Rom 6:23; Col 2:13; Eph 2:1–3, 5:8; 1 John 5:12; John 12:31; 16:11).

Gregory Palamas argues that, through the soul, God's grace is extended throughout the body and that God's gifts to man are actualized through the body. According to Barlaam, apathy consists in the deadening of the passionate part of the soul. On the other hand, Gregory Palamas argues that apathy consists in the re-orientation of the passionate part of the soul from evil to good. Instead of condemning and rejecting the passionate part of the soul, Gregory Palamas points out that we love through the passionate part of the soul, and, therefore, if we deaden the passionate part of the soul, we are unable to fulfill Christ's Law, which is to love God and one's fellow humans (Mark 12:28–31).

It is very important to clarify that, for the Hesychasts, the three aspects of the human soul, which are mentioned in the fourth book of Plato's *Republic* (namely, the appetitive aspect of the soul, which is responsible for the human being's base desires, the high-spirited, or hot-blooded, aspect of the soul, i.e., the part of us that loves to face and overcome great challenges, and that loves victory, winning, challenge, and honor, and the rational aspect of the soul) are not organic, or essential parts of the soul, but they are only consequences of the exercise of freedom of will by man. Thus, according to Hesychasm, man is responsible for his psychological contents and states, and the essence of 'psychological illness' consists in the dispersion of man's mental energy upon the sensible realm. Hesychasm emphasizes that the mind does not have any organs, but it is an image of God, and, therefore, it is not naturally determined to succumb to material passions, nor is it naturally attracted to the sensible realm. Whereas the intellect, desire, and passion are powers of the soul, and, therefore, they are natural channels of knowledge, the mind is the region of supra-natural wisdom.

According to the Hesychasts, the intellect is naturally oriented toward and concerned with the world of the senses, and it organizes sense-data into a rational whole, whereas the mind is naturally oriented toward and concerned with the *Logos*. Hence, the mind should not be mingled with the intellect. As a result of the Hesychasts' distinction between the mind and the intellect, it is the mind, and not the intellect, that must be detached from the world of the senses. The intellect cannot function without processing sense-data, and, therefore, if the intellect is detached from the world of the senses, it enters into a sleep state, such as the yogic sleep, which is totally irrelevant to the Hesychasts' notion of mental stillness.

The intellect, being concerned with sense-data and their rational organization, does not have free will. The mind alone has free will, since it loves and seeks the supra-rational Good (i.e., it aims at participating in the divinity). It is exactly due to the distinction between the mind and the intellect that Hesychasm leads to the conclusion that the human soul is something more than the nervous system. The mind can be united with the supra-rational Good only if it is cleansed from the passions of the senses, and this can be achieved through repentance, or through the return of the mind to the heart. By being detached from the world of the senses and by returning to the heart, where it remains exclusively oriented toward the *Logos*, the mind experiences God's freedom, because then it is capable of making passionless choices, ones that are independent from natural determinism.

3

MODERNITY AND POSTMODERNITY

FROM THE MIDDLE AGES TO MODERNITY

As I ARGUED IN the previous chapters, ancient Greek civilization understands truth as an ontological reality, and, therefore, it seeks to unite the
multitude into an ideal whole. As a result, according to the ancient Greeks'
ethos, humanity cannot be separated from the cosmic order, and the cosmic order cannot be separated from the supra-cosmic order. However, in
the context of ancient Greek civilization, the unification of the multitude
into an ideal whole is characterized by a tragic element. According to
ancient Greek philosophy, the human mind is in communion with the
divine spirit, which governs and preserves the universe, and, therefore,
the human mind is simultaneously a cosmic energy and an individual
force. As a consequence, the human mind operates analytically and syn-
thetically according to an absolute metaphysical principle (often called
the Good) which is knowable and in which man can participate, but
man can know and participate in this absolute metaphysical principle
only in a human way (according to the terms of human reason) and
not in the divine way, since the human mind is not a pure cosmic force,
but it exists *hypostatically.*

Ancient Greeks developed physical and metaphysical philosophy
in order to safeguard their *hypostatic* way of being, meaning in order to
set themselves free from disorder and doubt without eliminating their

existential otherness. Thus, in contrast to Asian societies, the classical Greek *polis* rejected absolutism and totalitarianism without lapsing into social disorder. In his play *Persians*, 181–96, Aeschylus describes the chasm between the Greek political ethos and the Asian political ethos by writing that King Xerxes's mother saw the following prophetic dream: two gorgeously vested women, one adorned in Persian robes and the other wearing the Doric garb, were fighting against each other. However, ancient Greeks realized that human reason is unable to comprehend God, and this is the essence of the Greek tragedy. As the Greek lyric poet Pindar wrote in his *Olympian Odes*, VII, during Diagoras's triumphant ovation on the shoulders of his sons, a spectator shouted: "Die, Diagoras; you will not ascend to Olympus besides." In other words, man's own efforts cannot bridge the chasm between God and man. Christianity solved the previous problem by declaring that the manner in which the chasm between God and man can be bridged was revealed through the incarnation of the divine Logos; this is the main reason why Greeks adopted Christianity. The Greek church fathers' eschatology is the completion and perfection of the classical Greek philosophers' teleology.

From the perspective of the doctrine of the incarnation of the *Logos*, the unification of the multitude into an ideal whole is achieved supernaturally, through love, in the image of the Holy Trinity. On the other hand, every natural/essential type of unification of the multitude into an ideal whole is based on reason, that is, it is a rational system. Whereas every natural type of unification of the multitude into an ideal whole presupposes that its members are of the same substance, and it is characterized by deterministic egalitarianism, Christianity's supernatural way of unifying the multitude into an ideal whole is based on *hypostases* that are neither necessarily of the same substance nor necessarily equal to each other. Therefore, the key of Christian unity is the freedom of love, whose archetype is the relation between the uncreated God and the created world, and not any kind of natural determinism.

The eschatology of Eastern Orthodox Christianity consists in the divinization of the human being. In other words, from the perspective of Eastern Orthodox Christianity, the *telos* of the human being transcends humanity. On the other hand, since the era of scholasticism, the West has abandoned the goal of the divinization of man, and its existential goals are based on the assumption that the human being is an end in itself, thus giving rise to humanism. The West's philosophy, regardless of the partial differences among the different 'schools' of medieval and modern

Western philosophy, is characterized by a persistent attempt to prove that truth is ontologically founded on the subject. Thus, the medieval and the modern West's views on the problem of truth are always different from the classical Greek philosophers' ontology of truth and from the Greek church fathers' Triadology. In this chapter, I shall review the works of the protagonists of modern Western philosophy, and I shall compare and contrast them with classical Greek philosophy and with the tradition of the Greek church fathers.

CARTESIANISM: DESCARTES, SPINOZA, AND LEIBNIZ

René Descartes (Latinized: Renatus Cartesius; 1596–1650) is the founder of modern philosophy. He was born at La Haye, Touraine, the son of a noble family. He was educated in scholastic philosophy and mathematics at the Jesuits of La Flèche. He pursued the diversions of a cosmopolitan traveler, and he entered the armies of Maurice of Nassau (1617) and General Tilly (1619). During his adventurous life, the problem that stirred him was to find one absolute certain truth in philosophy, and, because he encountered several uncertainties in the external world, he decided to seek that truth inside himself. In particular, influenced by Galileo's mathematical physics, Descartes decided to reach such certainty in philosophy as characterizes mathematics through a contemplative enquiry into syllogistic reasoning and its capabilities, specifically by devising a method of correct reasoning. Thus, he focused his attention on the mind itself and on the degree of certainty that characterizes its functions instead of being focused on external objects themselves and on the mind's judgments about them.

The scholastics identified truth with the reality of a hierarchical structure of being at the top of which was God. Descartes took mathematics as the model of his philosophical method, and he proposed a rational approach to reality in order to find a certain and self-evident truth, namely, one which everyone endowed with common sense and reasoning capabilities will accept. Thus, Descartes's philosophical system, known as Cartesianism, signals a shift from the scholastics' hierarchy of being to a truth founded on individual certainty.

According to Descartes's *Discourse on Method* and *Meditations on First Philosophy*, philosophers should proceed from absolutely certain first principles, namely, from certain and self-evident first principles, and pass on to new truths which are equally certain. Descartes argues that, even though there is no idea of which he can be entirely certain, one thing is certain, and that is that he doubts, or thinks. He does not appeal to an empirical physical fact, but he reasons logically that doubt implies a doubter, and thinking implies a thinker, a thinking thing (*res cogitans*). Thus, he arrives at the conclusion that to doubt means to think, and to think means to be, and, eventually, he declared: *"cogito ergo sum"* (I think therefore I am). From Descartes's perspective, the *cogito* principle is a certain, self-evident starting point for his ontology and a criterion of truth.

In Cartesianism, the *ego* becomes a substitute for the reality of God, the universe, and man (i.e., God and the universe reduce to individual concepts). Therefore, the argument *"cogito ergo sum"* is ultimately equivalent to the statement 'I imagine therefore I am,' since the inference of existence from thinking presupposes that one appeals to imagination. Therefore, *contra* Descartes, the *cogito* principle does not lead to any real certainty, since every expression of doubt about perception is *ipso facto* an expression of doubt about consciousness and, hence, about reasoning. As a result, Cartesianism leads to a civilization founded on a multitude of individual subjective opinions and on the principle of individual rights. Instead of really overcoming doubt and skepticism, Descartes attempts to substitute rational reasoning for perception in order to achieve certainty through the egocentric autarchy of rational reasoning. This is a self-defeating attempt. Descartes proposed the principle of individual truth, hoping that, in this way, he could liberate man from metaphysical mistakes and prejudices and lead him to certain knowledge, but he actually subordinated and confined man to a quantitative notion of universality founded on a mechanical universe.

Descartes combines Augustine's thought with Galileo's celestial mechanics. As I argued in chapter 2, Augustine contrasted the inner truth and certainty of impression with the uncertainty of sense perception, and he argued that truth lies in impression. Cartesianism is based on Augustine's thought, but it emphasizes reason, instead of Augustine's sentimentalism, and it combines Augustine's individualistic subjectivism with the quantitative universalism of Galileo's celestial mechanics. In his treatise *Passions of the Soul*, Descartes argues that the eye, the universe, and the human body are mechanical structures.[1] Furthermore, in his

---

1. Descartes, *Passions*.

Dioptrics, Descartes exposes his mechanical theory of sight.[2] Descartes's mechanistic theory of sight and of the universe in general precludes any attempt to explain physical phenomena in terms of an indeterministically acting spiritual principle (such as a hypostatically existing God). His ambition was to explain consequences through causes and causes through consequences; in other words, he wanted to create a causal, deterministic cosmo-conception in order to overcome the confusion which was caused by the scholastics' abstractions. But the actual outcome of his philosophy was simply the creation of a metaphysical chasm between God and the creation. Descartes attempted to reconsider and possibly bridge the previous metaphysical chasm through deism, i.e., by holding that the Creator does not intervene with the functioning of the natural world in any way, but He has left it to run according to the laws of nature. But, instead of bridging the metaphysical chasm between the Creator and the creation, deism simply implies that the Creator's creative activity is meaningless and that the creation can be completely comprehended through geometry and the laws of motion.

Among Descartes's successors, Baruch (Benedict) de Spinoza (1632–77) was the philosopher that remained most firmly committed to Descartes's geometric method. The only work that appeared under Spinoza's own name during his lifetime was the exposition of Descartes's system, *Cogitata metaphysica* (1663). Spinoza's posthumous works, including the *Ethics* and the *Tractatus politicus*, appeared in 1677.[3]

Spinoza rejects the Cartesian distinction between God and the natural world, but he endorses Descartes's rationalism, since he endorses an individualistic conception of truth. The previous two theses of Spinozism lead to the logical conclusion that God is not, as Descartes argued, an external transcendent cause acting on the world from without (deism), but He is *in* the world and the world in Him (pantheism). According to Spinoza, God is the immanent principle of the universe. In particular, Spinoza argues that everything that is emanates from God's substance just as in mathematical reasoning the conclusions are eternal consequences of a first principle. Spinoza equates cause (*causa*) with reason (*ratio*); in other words, in his philosophy, thinking and being are identical, and, therefore, the universe is a causal chain in which each link is necessarily connected with the previous link just as a proposition is the necessary consequence

2. Ribe, "Cartesian Optics."
3. McKeon, *Philosophy of Spinoza*; Scruton, *Spinoza*.

of some other proposition in a mathematical demonstration. Thus, according to Spinoza, the geometric method is a way of knowing God, and God's *logoi* are not, as Maximus the Confessor and many other Greek church fathers hold, divine wills, but they are natural necessities. As a consequence, from Spinoza's viewpoint, the existential perfection, or salvation, of man consists in conceiving of the truth of God in the world; that is, it consists in thinking.

Spinoza's relationship with God does not consist in a personal faith, since, instead of *believing* in God, he *speculates* about God in the context of a causal, deterministic conception of nature. Therefore, he argues that the purpose of philosophy is to organize everything into a logically coherent whole, which he calls God. In Descartes's philosophy, God is radically separated from the world, and the *ego*, or mind, is diametrically opposed to the body on the grounds that the essential attribute of body is extension, i.e., bodies are passive, whereas the essential attribute of mind is thinking (*res cogitans*), i.e., it is active. By contrast, in Spinoza's philosophy, God (cause) is essentially united with nature (being), and the *ego* is not self-conscious, but it is reflected in the logically connected wholeness of being (which Spinoza calls God), and, in this way, it knows itself. Thus, in Spinoza's philosophy, both the subjective character of experience and the subject are eliminated, thinking consists in reasoning without emotions, and every psychological activity is a consequence of a corporeal cause.

Spinoza equates freedom with the order of the natural world, and, therefore, he rejects man's freedom of will, and he argues that the only right that man has is to control his passions through reason. From the perspective of Spinoza's ethics, to be free means to think. In Spinoza's universe, all ideas and thoughts constitute a unified mental whole which corresponds to the natural world, and every particular mind is a piece of this infinite mind. As a conclusion, in Spinoza's suffocating universe, the only way in which man can exist *hypostatically* (i.e., as a free person) is by becoming a fool. In fact, a peculiar form of Orthodox Christian asceticism is known as 'Foolishness in Christ.' Sergey Ivanov has pointedly described a 'holy fool' (*salōs* in Greek, and *iurodivyi* in Russian) as a person who feigns insanity and provokes shock or outrage by his deliberately non-conformist behavior.[4] One of the most prominent holy fools is Basil Fool for Christ (c.1468/69–c.1552), who gives his name to Saint Basil's Cathedral in Moscow.

4. Ivanov, *Holy Fools*.

The Serbo-German philosopher and mathematician Gottfried Wilhelm Leibniz (1646–1716) believed that philosophy must be as certain as mathematics, but he was also aware that rationalism may lead to a suffocating, deterministic world-conception, to which he did not subscribe. Therefore, he decided to restore the transcendentality of the rational universe's purpose. According to Descartes, the essential attribute of body is extension. On the other hand, in his treatises *New System of Nature* (1695) and *The Monadology* (1714), Leibniz argues that, in nature, motion seems to be lost and gained, and, therefore, there must be something that persists when motion ceases: this is 'force,' or the *conatus* (i.e., the tendency of a body to move or to continue its motion). According to Leibniz, the essential attribute of body is force, not extension.[5]

In Leibniz's philosophy, the geometric or static conception of nature is replaced by the dynamic or energetic view. Leibniz argues that extension presupposes the existence of dynamic bodies or forces; force is the source of the mechanical world, and the mechanical world is the sensible appearance of forces. According to Leibniz, the world is not, as Descartes contends, an automaton (self-operating machine), but it is a force, i.e., it is in a state of becoming, which manifests the world's creative life. Every unit of force, Leibniz maintains, is an indivisible union of soul and matter; soul is the principle of activity, and matter is the principle of passivity.

According to Leibniz, the activity of the soul does not consist in thinking, but it corresponds to 'monads,' which are immaterial, unextended, self-determining, and purposive substances (forces). Leibniz's monads are metaphysical and eternal points (centers of force), without which there would be nothing real, because, without monads, there could be no manifoldness. Every monad is a process of evolution, it animates matter, it has 'perception' and 'appetition,' and it realizes its nature with an inner necessity. Without monads, the body would be unable to move, and the soul would be separated from and alien to the body, as is the case with Descartes's dualism. According to Leibniz's *The Monadology*, the soul and the body co-exist and interact with each other in the context of a harmony pre-established by God.

In his theological treatises, Leibniz argues that God created the monads, and only He can destroy them. According to Leibniz's theology, God transcends all monads, and man is a limited monad, but he can maximize the qualities which every monad possesses to a certain degree,

5. Di Bella, *Individual*. Jolley, *Leibniz*.

and, in this way, man can achieve a partial knowledge of God, since, Leibniz maintains, God is supra-rational but not contra-rational.[6]

Through his theory of monads, Leibniz attempted to overcome the problems of Descartes's mechanistic philosophy, since he argued that the monads animate beings and lead them to a transcendent *telos* (i.e., to a state of transcendent purity, which in the Bible is called holiness). But Leibniz argued that, even though monads are united with regard to their *telos*, they are mutually distinct, and, therefore, they are entities-in-themselves. As a consequence, the knowledge of the whole, or of God, underpins and concerns each monad individually as a conscious entity. Hence, Leibniz understands *praxis* as the activity of a subject, and, also, he understands sensation as a result of the interaction between the geometric space and the subjective mind. Therefore, ultimately, Descartes's *cogito* principle is restored in Leibniz's philosophy.

BRITISH EMPIRICISM: LOCKE, BERKELEY, AND HUME

British empiricism is a major philosophical opponent of European rationalism, since British empiricists, such as Locke, Berkeley, and Hume, attempted to refute the foundations of Continental philosophy, which are intimately related to those of the realist trends of scholasticism. In addition, the disputes between empiricism and rationalism are intimately related to the disputes between Anglicanism and Roman Catholicism and to the Anglicans' attempt to refute the dogmatic authoritarianism of the Papacy by questioning the certainty of intellectual knowledge and the church's hierarchy and tradition and by counter-proposing a Christian system of morality founded on the empirical individual.[7] The philosophical roots of British empiricism go back to Ockham's nominalism.

John Locke (1632–1704) was repelled by the scholastic methods of instruction which still prevailed at Oxford University, where he studied philosophy, natural science, and medicine. During the period 1666–83, he was in the service of Anthony Ashley Cooper, 1st Earl of Shaftesbury, who was a prominent English politician during the Interregnum and the reign of King Charles II and a founder of the Whig party. Locke followed the Earl of Shaftesbury to Holland into exile. Locke returned to England in 1689, after the deposal of James II (the last Roman Catholic monarch to

6. Martin, *Leibniz*.

7. Sabine and Thorson, *Political Theory*, chapter 19.

reign over the Kingdoms of England, Scotland, and Ireland), and, under the reign of William of Orange, he held several important public offices.

Locke's book *An Essay Concerning Human Understanding* is a philosophical revolt against scholastic dogmatism, against Spinoza's abstract ontology, and against Thomas Hobbes's biological materialism. Moreover, it is an empiricist variety of Cartesianism and a methodical and clear enquiry into the problem of knowledge. Locke argues that the necessary starting point of philosophy is the study of thinking. In the first part of his *Essay*, Locke is focused on the problem of discovering the source of knowledge, since, if it is true, as Descartes and many others hold, that we have an innate knowledge of principles, we would have no reason for questioning its validity. Thus, Locke proceeds to refute the doctrine of innate ideas. Whereas Descartes argues that ideas are innate and identifies them with inward perception and certainty, Locke argues that ideas are derived from sensation, which supplies the mind with sensible qualities, and from reflection, which supplies the mind with ideas of its own functions (perceiving, thinking, believing, doubting, reasoning, knowing, willing).

Locke hastily inferred the relativity of general concepts (ideas) from the observation that general concepts differ from language to language, and, ultimately, based on his thesis about the relativity of general concepts, he rejected the doctrine of inborn ideas, i.e., he rejected the thesis that the mind has the innate capability of conceptualizing independently of empirical reality. In other words, Locke rejected the thesis that the human mind can function in a creative way. From Locke's perspective, the mind, in its first state, is a *tabula rasa* ('white paper'), all our knowledge is founded on and, hence, derived from experience, and the primary capacity of the human mind is intellect's ability to receive the impressions made on it, either through sensation (by outward objects) or through reflection (when it reflects on its own functions). The ideas thus received do not constitute knowledge *per se*, but they are elements of knowledge ('simple ideas'), which the mind can repeat, compare, and combine in different ways, and, therefore, it can make at pleasure new 'complex ideas.' According to Locke, no understanding can invent or frame one new element of knowledge ('simple idea'). As a result, Locke's theory of knowledge replaced certainty with the uncertainty of sensation, and it replaced 'substantial truth' with 'conventional truth.'

Through the doctrine of innate truth, Cartesianism attempted to preserve the objectivity of truth's spirit, which had been defended by ancient and medieval philosophers in different ways, and, therefore, even though Descartes was repelled by scholasticism, he compromised with the realist trend of scholasticism on the objectivity of truth's spirit. Locke's intention was to popularize Descartes's philosophy, but, more than that, Locke rejected Descartes's theory of innate ideas, and he endorsed nominalism. However, Locke failed to bear in mind that, even if ideas are not innate with regard to their content/essence, ideas may be innate with regard to their structure. By the term 'structure,' we mean an inner reality which is being self-organized and self-reorganized, and which is pervaded by its own order, which is the core of structure (the term 'structure' was originally used in physics, biology, and linguistics, and, gradually, it was adopted by scholars in ethnology, sociology, and philosophy). Intellect transcends logical reflection, because it can unite everything into a whole, and, thus, it can overcome the fragmentation and the partiality to which the empirical subject's truth leads us.

In the fourth part of his *Essay*, Locke argues that, whenever we study the truth of the natural world, we must content ourselves with probability. According to Locke, the pursuit of a perfect science of natural bodies (not to mention spiritual beings) is "lost labor." According to Locke, nature furnishes the mind with the first matter of our knowledge, from which the mind makes complex ideas (i.e., conventional forms). From Locke's viewpoint, certainty is attainable only in the area of conventional knowledge, like in the fields of morality and theology. Hence, general knowledge can only be derived from the contemplation of our own abstractions and, more specifically, from the agreement and disagreement of our ideas.

Locke argues that, as a result of our ignorance of the inaccessible reality of the natural world, the purpose of life consists in our attempt to overcome uncertainty. In Locke's philosophy, values stem from the inaccessibility of authentic reality, and, therefore, happiness is defined as the avoidance of pain. In other words, values are means by which we tackle the absence (inaccessibility) of authentic reality. From the perspective of Locke's negative definition of happiness, happiness is intimately related to the negation of nature *qua* death, since, for Locke, the natural end of being is death, whereas the moral end of being is self-preservation. Thus, the task of human legislation is to endow natural law and natural rights with the precision, the clarity, and the impartial enforceability that were lacking in the state of nature.[8] Moreover, according to Locke's previous arguments, happiness is not a good-in-itself, since it consists in the avoidance of pain, and, therefore, 'goodness' is identified with 'utility' (i.e., with the attractiveness of some state of affairs to an individual). As a consequence, the struggle for life is oriented toward the acquisition of goods that are useful for the satisfaction of needs, instead of being guided by the goal of existential completeness.

According to Locke, the satisfaction of needs provides us with self-assurance and liberates us from natural constraints. In the context of empiricism, the self-assurance of the *ego* is identified with moral utilitarianism, and conventional moral law is identified with God's will. The goal of self-assurance is the prime principle and the end of Locke's moral philosophy; therefore, actually, his moral philosophy is not so much a way of liberating oneself from the constraints of inaccessible nature as it is a way of liberating oneself from social constraints through values, which presumably are substitutes for the mysterious natural order. Hence, Locke's moral philosophy has the following consequences: (i) society is not founded on personhood, i.e., on a *hypostatic* way of being, but it is subjected to the rule of an impersonal state mechanism, which controls and regiments the masses through law; (ii) education does not consist in a process of spiritual formation, but it becomes a process of training mechanically behaving people who pursue existential completeness through material and sensual self-gratification.

George Berkeley (1685–1753) studied at Trinity College, Dublin, became Bishop of Cloyne in 1734, and he used Locke's empiricism in order to refute materialism and atheism. Hence, Berkeley endowed the basal empiricism of Locke with some post-empiricist principles. In Locke's philosophy, given that sensation is the ultimate source of simple and complex ideas, and general knowledge cannot be attained independently of sensation, the human soul has a passive role, and empiricism tends to become pure subjectivism. Thus, the following question emerges: which is the most important force in the realm of the intellect, inward experience or outward experience? Berkeley dedicated his books *An Essay towards a New Theory of Vision* and *A Treatise concerning the Principles of Human Knowledge* to the study of the previous question.[9]

8. Locke, *Two Treatises*, and *Human Understanding*.

9. Berkeley, *Philosophical Works*.

According to Berkeley, the solution to the problems of Locke's philosophy can be found within one's consciousness (i.e., in inward experience), without, however, rejecting the reality of the external world; he simply argues that the external world *qua* substance is unknowable. In Berkeley's philosophy, existence (*esse*) is identical with perception (*percipi*) (i.e., to be means to be perceived), and perception is a faculty of the mind and more specifically of the conscious mind. Not even general concepts are independent of perception.

According to Locke, general concepts constitute a common element of things, and they are derived from intellectual abstraction. In his *Essay concerning Human Understanding*, Locke argues that "ideas become general by separating from them the circumstances of time and space, and any other ideas," and, "by this way of abstraction, they are made capable of representing more individuals than one."[10] On the other hand, according to Berkeley, all things are perceptions of an essentially unperceived external world. A body is a solid, extended, figured substance, and it has the power of motion, a certain color, weight, taste, smell, and sound. Certain of its qualities (color, taste, smell, sound) do not inhere in it, but they are the effects of the body produced in a perceiving subject, and, therefore, they are called secondary qualities. Extension, solidity, figure, motion, and rest are considered to be inherent in the substance, or body, *per se*, and, therefore, they are called primary qualities, but, according to Berkeley, these so-called primary qualities are sensations in one's mind, too, and, therefore, they are just as secondary as the other qualities. In other words, for Berkeley, the material substance of a body is a bundle of sense perceptions. Berkeley rejected Locke's theory of general concepts as a remnant of the scholastics' universals, and he attempted to create a totally empiricist philosophy. According to Berkeley, things exist in our minds as bundles of mutually distinct sense perceptions, and these bundles are called concepts.

Berkeley argues that we can never perceive a thing as a whole, but we can only perceive it in parts, or ideas, which arouse sensations in us. Ideas are merely results of direct perception, and our knowledge of each thing consists in the inward experience of the corresponding ideas, meaning in the whole bundle of the corresponding sensations. This inward experience is an indirect perception, and it leads to concepts, i.e., ideas that do not correspond to particular sensations, but they have some significance. We

10. Locke, *Human Understanding*, III, iii, 6.

can, indeed, imagine, or represent to ourselves, the ideas of the particular things which we have perceived, and we can variously modify them (i.e., we may abstract), but we cannot, for instance, frame an abstract idea of a triangle (i.e., we cannot think of an idea corresponding to the description of the general idea of a triangle). In the Introduction to his *Principles of Human Knowledge*, Berkeley defines the general idea of a triangle as follows: a triangle which is "neither oblique nor rectangle, equilateral, equicrural, nor scalenon, but all and none of these at once."[11] Thus, Berkeley rejects Locke's general concepts, and he arrives at the conclusion that, apart from the mind itself (which is considered to be a supra-experiential element), everything else exists within the mind, and he replaces Locke's general concepts with bundles of particular perceived qualities.

According to Berkeley, God excites in us the ideas of sense according to natural laws, which can be learned by experience. In other words, the supreme Mind arouses in us ideas according to uniform rules. The ideas imprinted on the senses by God are real things, but they are ideas and exist in the mind, together with those excited in the imagination, which, being less vivid, regular, and constant, are more properly called 'ideas' or 'images' of things which they represent. Furthermore, according to Berkeley, words signify bundles of sensible symbols through which we communicate, and they copy God's order.

Both Locke and Berkeley understand the term 'idea' as a sense perception, but Berkeley adds that reality is immanent in the conscious mind. However, in his *Essay towards a New Theory of Vision*, Berkeley argues that concepts presuppose space. For Berkeley, time is the succession of ideas in individual minds, and space is sensible extension. In contrast to Newton's theory of absolute space and time, Berkeley argues that any idea of pure space is relative and that we cannot conceive of the idea of space as separate from body. Furthermore, he argues against the infinite divisibility of extension; a notion which, according to Berkeley, is the source of a great many geometrical paradoxes. Thus, from Berkeley's perspective, it is misleading to attempt to explain a given phenomenon by arguing that it is 'caused' by attraction, force, or gravity. According to Berkeley, the only true efficient causes are 'spirits,' by which he means active, indivisible substances, as opposed to 'ideas,' which, for Berkeley, are inert, fleeting, dependent things which do not subsist by themselves, but they are supported by or immanent in minds or spiritual substances.

11. Berkeley, Introduction (paragraph 13) to his *Principles of Human Knowledge*, included in his *Philosophical Works*.

Thus, in Berkeley's philosophy, man's active spirit and God's spirit cannot be known as ideas, but they can only be known as concepts. Berkeley's philosophy conforms to modern philosophy's general orientation toward the principles of individual certainty and individual truth.

The Scottish empiricist philosopher David Hume (1711–76), in section 12 of his treatise entitled *An Enquiry concerning Human Understanding*, argued that Berkeley's arguments about the uncertainty of sensible knowledge are not refutable, but they do not produce any conviction either.[12] Hume endorsed Berkeley's argument that concepts are not substances, and he replaced the distinction between inward and outward perceptions with the distinction between impression and representation, thus proposing a skeptical approach to the problem of knowledge. According to Hume, if all we can know are our own impressions, we cannot assert the reality either of spiritual or of material substances, and, furthermore, we find no impressions that justify our notion of necessary connection, or causation. By 'impressions,' Hume means our more lively perceptions when we see, or hear, or feel, or love, or hate, or desire, etc. (i.e., all our sensations, passions, and emotions as they originally appear in the soul), and, by 'ideas,' or 'thoughts,' he means representations, or copies, of such impressions (i.e., the faint perceptions of which we are conscious when we recall or reflect on an impression). Hume's theory of impressions is derived from Locke's and Ockham's philosophies.

Hume's philosophy is pure empiricism, because he argues that all our knowledge is derived from outward and inward impressions. Outward perceptions, or sensations, arise in the soul from unknown causes, and inward perceptions are occasioned by our ideas, or representations, which are due to the memory and the imagination. Through impressions, one can answer the question 'what,' but he cannot answer the question 'why.' In other words, he can discover nothing in his experience that explains the cause of impressions. In Hume's philosophy, knowledge consists merely in impressions, because, for Hume, impressions alone are characterized by cognitive significance, whereas sensations and one's judgments about them are uncertain. In particular, Hume agrees with Descartes and Locke in requiring that certain knowledge must be self-evident, but he argues that such knowledge can be found only in mathematics, which merely analyzes its own concepts. From Hume's perspective, 'reality' is the unknown substratum of our impressions.

12. Hume, *Enquiry*, 155.

Empiricism leads Hume to the argument that our knowledge of cause and effect is derived from experience. More specifically, Hume argues that custom leads us to infer that objects which we know by observation and experience that they are frequently conjoined, will always be so. However, Hume points out, custom is an instinct, and, hence, it may mislead us. In Hume's philosophy, there is no connecting principle, and, therefore, Hume is forced to appeal to custom as a psychic power which produces a belief in the connection of objects which we observe that they succeed one another. Moreover, in Hume's philosophy, custom structures the *ego* as a unity of impressions.

Based on the notion of custom, Hume proposes a natural type of religion and a practical system of morality, whose essence is the principle of utility. Hume argues that religion owes its origin in man's emotional and impulsive nature, and it is not the result of speculative reasoning. Additionally, Hume endorses a pragmatic attitude toward religion by arguing that the natural type of religion which he proposes is the only type of religion capable of harmonizing moral life with utilitarianism. Thus, Hume's approach to religion and morality does not aim at changing man himself and elevating him to a higher level of being, but it merely aims at achieving a socially functional compromise through custom. This attitude is a logical consequence of the empiricists' spiritual passivity. The essence of empiricism's spiritual passivity consists in the replacement of the pursuit of a metaphysical synthesis with an empirical enquiry into the functions of the mind.

ROUSSEAU'S PRIMITIVISM AND SOCIAL CONTRACT THEORY

The French moral and political philosopher Jean-Jacques Rousseau (1712–78) reacted against rationalism and against the arguments of leading figures of the French Enlightenment (the group known as the *philosophes*). Rousseau's contribution to moral philosophy is principally based on his two *Discourses*: in the first, i.e., in the *Discourse on the Sciences and Arts*, Rousseau argued that the spread of scientific and literary activity was morally corrupting for society at large, and, in the second, i.e., in the *Discourse on the Origin of Inequality*, he explained the foundations of his critique of the Enlightenment.

Whereas the English philosopher Thomas Hobbes[13] (1588–1679) argues that natural man is a wolf to his fellow man, Rousseau, in his two *Discourses*, asserts that natural man is a social being. However, according to Rousseau, the goodness and innocence of the 'primitive' (or 'savage') man are derived from a natural impulse to preserve himself, to develop his capacities, and to live together with other men. Moreover, Rousseau maintains, man is by nature prompted by sympathy for others and inspired by religious feeling and gratitude. Thus, in Rousseau's moral philosophy, man's sense of duty is not a product of reasoned thinking, but it is a matter of natural feeling. From Rousseau's viewpoint, a harmonious society cannot be created by egocentric rationalist beings, but it can only be created by the "noble savage," who is governed by social sentiments.

Rousseau argues that reasoned thinking and the way of life which underpins science and technology constitute a significant deviation from the way of life prescribed to man by nature. According to Rousseau, man is different from animals not because he is capable of reasoned thinking, but because he is capable of making choices. However, Rousseau maintains that natural man makes choices in conformity with the program of man's natural integration and perfection, and not according to the principle of spiritual freedom. In Rousseau's philosophy, reason is always intimately related to the satisfaction of the needs of the body. Therefore, external conditions (i.e., the events that take place in man's life and his needs) form man's natural spirit in the image of universal necessity. Making syllogisms similar to those of Hume, Rousseau argues that custom (i.e., the accumulation of experiences) gradually makes human reason capable of determining man's destiny.

In his books *Émile* and *The Social Contract*, Rousseau argues that, at the beginning of history, humans were innocent and were living as free individuals organically integrated into nature, and that moral corruption and injustice arose from social inequality and the resulting dependence of one individual on another. The primitive social harmony was destroyed by the first man who fenced a piece of land and declared it his private property.[14] The feeling of ownership destroyed social equilibrium. According to Rousseau, crime, war, misery, and generally wretchedness came with the development of private property, but bourgeois society is based on private property, and it has high hopes for science and tech-

13. Hobbes, *Leviathan*.
14. Rousseau, *First and Second Discourses*.

nology. Rousseau argues that the progress of science and technology corrupts morals (our natural inclinations), because it has its origin in indolence, and it produces and intensifies the slavish and the lordly vices.

Rousseau admits that the primitive natural way of life has been lost and humanity cannot return to that way of life, but he argues that we can retrieve some of the goods of the natural way of life even within a society based on scientific and technological progress, under the condition that such a society will not depend on a coercive rational authority, but it will depend on the principle of the general will (*volonté générale*), precisely on an agreement among the particular wills of individuals and groups.

Rejecting rationalism and statism, which were constituent parts of the dominant grand narrative of his time, Rousseau counter-proposes the merits of the primitive natural way of life and also the idea of virtue as it was cultivated in ancient city-states. According to Rousseau, the established type of modern state cannot cultivate virtue, because it is an artificial and mechanistic association in which the logic of money and power prevails. However, Rousseau argues that, if we understand the structure of the social body in a different way, modern state can promote virtue.

From Rousseau's viewpoint, the purpose of politics is to restore freedom to us, therefore reconciling us as essentially free beings to our modern life (i.e., to the 'progress' of civilization, which has substituted subservience to others and inequality for the freedom that characterizes the state of nature). Rousseau proposed his social contract theory in order to show how we can live together without succumbing to the force and coercion of others: we submit our individual, particular wills to the general will, created through agreement with other free and equal individuals. Thus, the individual surrenders its natural freedom for the liberty of citizenship. In his book *The Social Contract*, Rousseau argues that the most basic agreement, the social pact, is that on the basis of which we come together and form a 'people,' which by definition is more than and different from a mere aggregation of the wills and interests of its individual members. In addition to each individual's private will, the citizen has a collective interest in the well-being of the society, which, in turn, ensures his liberty as a citizen. Thus, in Rousseau's political philosophy, the citizen body is the only legitimate 'sovereign' of a body politic, and the 'government' is an agent of the popular will.

Through his revolt against reason, Rousseau expressed his opposition to the path through which rationalists seek truth, but he did not reject the ultimate goal of rationalism and generally of the Enlightenment, precisely the rationalists' and the Enlighteners' attempt to found truth on the human individual. As George H. Sabine and Thomas L. Thorson have pointedly argued, the true hero of Rousseau's primitivism was "the irritated and bewildered bourgeois."[15] Trying to manage his sensitivity and seeking an anodyne for his painful life experiences, Rousseau follows a philosophical path which is totally different from rationalism, since he gives primacy to passion and instinct over reason, and he argues that the value of life stems from common emotions. From this viewpoint, Rousseau's philosophy enhances the West's faith in the human individual, regardless of whether this human individual is an intellectual or a "noble savage." For instance, in the nineteenth century, Friedrich Nietzsche walked the same path as Rousseau in order to unleash his attack against Western civilization.

Rousseau argues that his ideal of a society formed by social contract is based on the ethos of the ancient Greek city-state. But, even though he was influenced by ancient Greek scholars, and he was looking back with admiration to the city-states of ancient Greece, Rousseau's political thought is conditioned by the way in which society and the individual are understood in the context of modern Western civilization. From the perspective of ancient Greek philosophy, man as a rational being is neither essentially nor primarily an 'individual', but he is understood as a composite of inclinations and forces, such as those that characterize the soul in Plato's dialogues *Phaedo*, *Republic*, and *Symposium*, and as a "political animal" in the service of society according to the terminology used by Aristotle in his *Politics*.

In ancient Greek civilization, social justice does not refer to the idea of protecting individual rights, but it refers to the idea that each citizen contributes to the prosperity of the community in proportion to his respective abilities (and, therefore, the modern notion of 'social equality,' which is founded on the notion of individual rights, is irrelevant in the ancient Greek city-state). According to Pericles's famous "Funeral Oration," quoted in Thucydides's *History of the Peloponnesian War*, II, 34–46, ancient Athenian citizens regarded a man who was not interested in public affairs as "a useless character." According to the culture of ancient Greek city-states, indifference toward public affairs is a shameful and disgraceful attitude. Hence, from the perspective of ancient Greek civilization, 'society' or 'republic' is primarily and essentially a type of

15. Sabine and Thorson, *Political Theory*, 531.

consciousness; it signifies existence through participation in the same spiritual horizon and through sharing thoughts, feelings, material goods, etc. On the contrary, in the context of modern Western civilization, the individual (regardless of whether the 'individual' is understood as a thinking subject or as a natural being) has primacy over society. Moreover, in the context of modern Western civilization, society is understood as a mechanical event, and not as an ontological reality.

There is a sharp anthropological and ontological difference between ancient Greek sociocentric way of thinking and modern European collectivist theories. Through the ambiguous ideology of social equality and through totalitarian structures, modern collectivist political theorists, such as Rousseau (who ushered the age of totalitarian democracy by equating the will of the collectivity, or 'the people,' with the will of God) and Karl Marx, interpret man as a being determined by historical and natural necessities, and, ultimately, they degrade him into a bio-economic unit. Such a degradation of the human being could not happen in ancient Greek and Byzantine sociocentric systems, because, in ancient Greek and Byzantine sociocentric systems, the system of collective ownership was not a form of co-operation among individual owners for the simple reason that, in those societies, there were no 'individuals' in the modern sense of the term.

KANT, THE ENLIGHTENMENT, AND COSMOPOLITANISM

The Enlightenment was an eighteenth-century intellectual movement that argued for the autonomy of reason from tradition and religion, and it is part of the broader phenomenon of modernity, whose essence consists in the assertion that the subject is an ontologically sufficient foundation of truth. One of the most important paradigmatic representatives of the Enlightenment was the German philosopher Immanuel Kant, whose philosophy has put an indelible imprint on the history of Western philosophy and political thought.[16]

Immanuel Kant (1724–1804) was born and died at Königsberg, East Prussia, and his philosophical reputation rests on his three *Critiques*: *Pure Reason* (1781), *Practical Reason* (1788), and *Judgment* (1790). During his earlier years, Kant followed Leibniz's philosophy, and, from 1760 to 1770, he came under the influence of British empiricism. Moreover, Newtonian

16. Hampson, *Enlightenment*.

physics and mathematical analysis made a great impression on him. By the year 1770, he had formed the basic principles of his own philosophy, which he presented in a Latin dissertation entitled *De mundi sensibilis atque intelligibilis forma et principiis.*

Influenced by Newton's physics and by the achievements of calculus, Kant subscribes to the mechanical explicability of the natural world (where the mechanism of nature, as he argues in the *Critique of Judgment*, V, 360, is the determination of nature "according to the laws of causality"), and he contrasts the realm of knowledge, which he methodically studies in the *Critique of Pure Reason*, with the realm of will and freedom, which he methodically studies in the *Critique of Practical Reason*, whereas, in his *Critique of Judgment*, under the influence of Rousseau, he attempts to bridge the gap between the realm of knowledge and the realm of will and freedom by arguing that nature, which we seek to know, has a purpose, which implies freedom, but this freedom is manifested as free motion and co-exists with constraint; that is, freedom conforms to a mechanical universal rhythm. In this way, Kant resolves the antinomy of free motion and constraint under the idea of mutual limitation, which, in the social sphere, corresponds to the sentimental factor.[17]

According to Kant, reason is an *a priori* structure in which categories are combined, and, after adequate processing, they can establish connections among empirical data, thus leading to the articulation of synthetic judgments. In this way, Kant manages to transcend the level of experience. In agreement with modernity, the ultimate goal of Kant's philosophy is to found truth and morality on the subject. Thus, Kant's pure reason precludes the knowability of *noumena* (i.e., things-in-themselves), and is limited to intellectually knowable *phenomena*. Furthermore, Kant's practical reason is founded on the subject's will, and not on an objective good. In both cases, the protagonist is the subject. The relation between Kant's *Critique of Pure Reason* and Kant's *Critique of Practical Reason* corresponds to the relation between a thinking subject and an acting subject.

The key difference between Kant's philosophy and Descartes's philosophy is the following: Kantianism is focused on phenomena (*Critique of Pure Reason*) and aims at achieving a moral goal (*Critique of Practical Reason*), whereas Descartes's philosophy is oriented toward a knowable object. But there is an underlying agreement between Kant and Descartes: they both recognize the subject as an ontological foundation of

---

17. Kant, *Three Critiques.*

truth. Descartes searches for the foundations of certainty in thinking. Kant seeks to know the foundations of sensation in the faculty of understanding, which has different forms of conceiving and connecting percepts, and it expresses itself in judgment. In Kant's philosophy, there is no knowable transcendent world, and, therefore, Kantianism signals the complete abandonment of the metaphysical tradition that originated from Plato's philosophy.

British empiricism and especially Hume's skepticism urge Kant to study the rational structure of the world in order to exorcize irrationality and chaos. During his studies, Kant realizes that he seeks universal and necessary knowledge of the things of the external world, but he cannot find such knowledge: philosophy analyzes concepts, and, therefore, philosophical judgments are lacking in experience, whereas mathematics is concerned with quantities and creates quantities, and, therefore, it does not need to appeal to experience. In other words, philosophy is founded on reason, and mathematics is founded on pure sensation.

According to Kant, perception can be analyzed into sensations, which constitute the content of experience, and into space and time, which constitute the form of experience. Sensations furnish the raw material which is arranged within the framework of space and time. Sensations, space, and time together constitute percepts. The mind receives sensations, and, additionally, it perceives them by virtue of its faculty of intuition;[18] for example, the mind sees the color, hears the sound outside itself, etc., in a spatio-temporal order. Furthermore, Kant maintains, the mind perceives space and time *a priori* (i.e., it intuits pure space and time).

In Kant's philosophy, the forms of arranging sensations in space and time are not themselves sensations, but they are *a priori* (i.e., they are inherent in the nature of the mind). Space and time are forms of sense perception and, hence, ways in which our sensibility apprehends objects. Since space and time are conditions of sensibility, it logically follows that they have validity only when they are applied to perceived things (i.e., to phenomena) and not when they are applied to things-in-themselves, meaning to things independent of our perception of them. Thus, in his *Critique of Pure Reason*, Kant argues that we know only our peculiar way of perceiving things, but we cannot know what things-in-themselves are apart from our sensibility. From this perspective, space and time are subjective, in the sense that we know only our peculiar way of perceiving

18. The term 'intuition' is derived from the Latin term *intueri*, which means to look at, envisage.

things, but they are also objective, in the sense that all phenomena are arranged in a spatio-temporal order.

The knowledge of phenomenal objects is based on the faculty of understanding (i.e., on a synthetic, thinking mind): the forms of sensibility are intuitional, but the faculty of understanding is conceptual (i.e., it thinks in concepts). The understanding has different forms of conceiving and relating percepts, and these forms are called categories of the understanding, or pure concepts. Thus, the understanding connects percepts by virtue of synthetic *a priori* judgments.

In an analytic judgment, the predicate merely elucidates what is already contained in the subject; for example, the judgment 'body is an extended thing.' Therefore, such judgments are by definition true and cannot qualify as genuine knowledge. Only synthetic judgments qualify as genuine knowledge, because they add something to the predicate, like the judgment 'every body has specific gravity.' But not all synthetic judgments give us genuine knowledge. Some synthetic judgments are derived from experience (i.e., they are *a posteriori*), and, therefore, they are lacking in necessity and in universality, like the judgment 'the horse is white.' To be genuine knowledge, a synthetic judgment must be necessary and universal, or *a priori*. Universality and necessity have their source in reason (i.e., in the understanding itself). According to Kant, we find synthetic *a priori* judgments in the foundations of physics and mathematics. Without such judgments, humanity would be logically compelled to endorse Hume's radical skepticism.

In Kant's philosophy, the synthesizing activity of the mind (manifested in the rule-based structuring of perceptions into a world of objects) is derived from "transcendental imagination," a term used by Kant in the first edition of his *Critique of Pure Reason*. According to Martin Heidegger, transcendental imagination is what Kant refers to as the unknown common source uniting sense and understanding.[19] In Kant's philosophy, transcendental imagination underpins consciousness and secures it against the changeability and volatility of phenomenal objects. Hence, by virtue of transcendental imagination, which ultimately is a variation of Descartes's *cogito* principle, consciousness becomes a pure and solid *ego*, which connects percepts according to its own forms (i.e., in its own way). To sum up: in Kant's philosophy, imagination forms space and time, safeguards the unity of the *ego* vis-à-vis the multiplicity

19. Makkreel, *Imagination and Interpretation*.

of the phenomenal world, and, thus, the subject imposes its categories of understanding on phenomena. As a result, thinking is derived from imagination, and, therefore, ultimately, we are logically urged to accept arbitrariness (i.e., choices based on an individual's own opinion or discretion) as the foundation of the *ego*! Kant was so horrified to find out the philosophically dangerous consequences of his theory of transcendental imagination that he omitted this term from the second edition of his *Critique of Pure Reason* in 1787, without, however, ceasing to glorify the *ego*.

Kant identified genuine knowledge with synthetic *a priori* judgments, on which he founded the distinction between the noumenon and the phenomenon. Thus, according to Kant, we can know only products of our minds, and the world is structurally united with the thinking *ego*. Furthermore, science can only convey knowledge of phenomena, and, therefore, reality and truth are mutually separated. Apart from abstract categories of the understanding, the only solid content of Kant's pure reason is the subject.

In Leibniz's philosophy, the subject derives its ontological autonomy from its inner self. In Kant's philosophy, the subject derives its ontological autonomy from pure reason through the moral law, which is a categorical imperative (i.e., it commands unconditionally). A categorical imperative is a universal axiom, and, therefore, it can simultaneously be a universal law and an individual duty. Hence, the subject whose individual morality is such that it has the authority and the value of a universal law can set aside the problem of the ontology of the universal good, and he can substitute pure reason, interpreted as the consciousness of duty, for the universal good, thus abandoning the morality of love, which is derived from and founded on one's relationship with the universal good. In his *Critique of Practical Reason*, Kant argues that the relation between the will and the law corresponds to the relation between practical reason and pure reason. Thus, in his *Groundwork of the Metaphysics of Morals*, Kant formulates his fundamental moral maxim as follows: "I ought never to act except in such a way that I can also will that my maxim should become a universal law."[20]

According to Kant, the will legislates, and reason determines the subject's way of life, so that a will is good when it is determined by respect for the moral law, which is a manifestation of reason. The will is subject to reason and, hence, to the moral law, so that, ultimately, the will

20. Paton, *The Moral Law*, 67.

legislates its own laws. In other words, Kant's moral philosophy extols duty for duty's sake, and it identifies free will with irrationality. Thus, with his moral philosophy, Kant seeks to accommodate transcendental imagination to the moral law. If it is to be stable and universal, 'good will' cannot be a subjective goal. Thus, in order to free 'good will' from the subjectivity of practical reason, Kant asserts that man is an end-in-itself. In particular, in his *Groundwork of the Metaphysics of Morals*, Kant argues as follows: "Act in such a way that you always treat humanity, whether in your own person or in the person of any other, never simply as a means, but always at the same time as an end."[21] The principle of humanity as an end-in-itself and the corresponding political order as a union of particular ends express a belief in the ontological autarchy of humanity, which, in the absence of a transcendent *Logos*, is secularized in conformity with the commands of pure reason. The sovereignty of pure reason implies that the *telos* of history is a historical goal (and not a transcendent one), and, therefore, it provides 'good will' with an objective end which is the source of the categorical imperative, and it determines what politics can legitimately do. Furthermore, the sovereignty of pure reason legitimates and underpins the creation of a system of world governance as a historical objectification and as an institutional guarantor of the universality of pure reason and the categorical imperative. In his *Metaphysical Elements of Justice*, Kant argues that the "task of establishing a universal and lasting peace is not just a part of the theory of right within the limits of pure reason, but its entire ultimate purpose."[22] Kant outlined his cosmopolitan political ideals in his essay entitled *Perpetual Peace: A Philosophical Sketch* (1795), in which he proposes the following Definitive Articles of a Perpetual Peace between States[23]:

I. "The Civil Constitution of Every State shall be Republican."

II. "The Right of Nations shall be based on a Federation of Free States."

III. "Cosmopolitan Right shall be limited to Conditions of Universal Hospitality," by which he refers to "the right of a stranger not to be treated with hostility when he arrives on someone else's territory."

The set of principles that Kant's *Perpetual Peace* enjoins constitute the settled norms of the modern international system, using the latter

21. Ibid., 91.
22. Reiss, *Kant*, 174.
23. Ibid., 93*ff.*

term in Frost's sense of a norm as settled "where it is generally recognized that any argument denying the norm (or which appears to override the norm) requires social justification."[24]

The sovereignty of reason, which Kant endorses, is overthrown when the *telos* of existence is the transcendent Good, namely, the bliss of union between man and God, in the sense of one's union with his lover (as it has been described by Plato and the Hesychasts). When the *telos* of existence is the transcendent Good, the path that leads to man's ontological perfection is freedom. On the other hand, Kant depends on the objectivity of moral law because he intends to found his pietist ethics on the categorical imperative. In order to settle the quarrel between the subjectivity of practical reason and the objectivity of the categorical imperative, Kant's moral rationalism gives rise to a subject whose inner world is extremely poor, since the Kantian subject is filled with a sense of duty which has replaced free will. As long as one subscribes to subjectivism, he cannot act freely. Subjectivism implies that the individual himself (and not a knowable transcendent Good) is the source of the goals and the principles that are dictated by his will. Kant argues that a moral act cannot depend on the principle of absolute Good (since, according to Kant, the Good as a thing-in-itself, i.e., as a noumenon, is unknowable), and, therefore, he has no other choice but to assert that the moral value of our acts is derived from 'good will,' in the sense that it is determined by the categorical imperative. Thus, from Kant's viewpoint, the moral status of an act is determined by the goodness of its end, and not by the good *itself*, which is a noumenon and, hence, according to Kant, unknowable. As a consequence of Kant's moral rationalism, man loses his spiritual freedom, and he is subjected to the formalism of pure reason.

When one is truly and, hence, unselfishly, in love, his good will toward his lover is not derived from the categorical imperative, but it is a manifestation of his free will, and, also, it is a way of life. Thus, Plato proposes *eros* (love) toward the absolute Good (which, in Plato's philosophy, is a knowable noumenon) as an epistemology and as a moral philosophy, and, similarly, the Hesychasts' epistemology and morality are based on *eros* toward Christ, the Incarnate Good. The Greek church fathers and especially the Hesychasts teach that Christian morality consists in an inward spiritual transformation (i.e., in the orientation of the mind toward

24. Frost, *Normative Theory*, 121.

the absolute Good and in one's unification with it) and not in the enforcement of outward moral rules.

The enforcement of outward moral rules can possibly correct one's behavior, but it cannot offer existential salvation. The suppression of passions does not save the soul, since a suppressed passion, most probably, will mutate and re-emerge as a new passion. The suppression of passions through the moral law resembles witch hunts, since it is a Sisyphean process. The soul can be saved only if one is aware of the ultimate goal that underpins and guides his passions; that is, only if he can look at the depths of his soul. Thus, the Hesychasts emphasize the purification of passion.

From the perspective of Western intellectual tradition, the ultimate psychological goal of passion is self-vindication. Thus, modern West emphasizes and promotes the ideal of the self-made man, the 'American dream,' the 'success stories' of several 'heroes' of capitalism, and self-affirmation through sexual promiscuity.[25] Moreover, in a society which is founded on the assumption that passion is necessarily underpinned and guided by the goal of self-vindication, failure to attain self-vindication through legitimate means often leads to an outburst of passion which causes criminal behavior. On the other hand, as I mentioned in chapter 2, the Hesychasts argue that there is another kind of passion, a purified, unselfish passion: this is the passion that makes man capable of fulfilling the New Law of Christ, which is love (Mark 12:28–31).

HEGEL'S OBJECTIVE IDEALISM AND COMMUNITARIANISM

Georg Wilhelm Friedrich Hegel (1770–1831) was born in Stuttgart and studied theology and philosophy at the University of Tübingen. He taught philosophy at the universities of Jena, Heidelberg, and Berlin. Hegel revolted against the Kantian distinction between the noumenon and the phenomenon, and he undertook to restore the unity between the subject and the object in a way that would be different from both ancient philosophy (in the context of which self-consciousness is based on and derived from the cosmic order) and medieval philosophy, which is focused on the will of an omnipresent and omnipotent God.[26]

Hegel argued that the Judeo-Christian approach to the 'transcendent' was the cause of modern philosophy's subjectivism and, furthermore, of

25. Brzezinski, *Out of Control*; Weber, *Protestant Ethic and Spirit of Capitalism*.
26. Harris, *Hegel's Development*; Taylor, *Hegel*.

the spiritual crisis of Europe. Thus, he attempted to refute the idealist philosophy of Johann Gottlieb Fichte (1762–1814), and, through the refutation of Fichte's idealism, he attempted to refute Kant's and Descartes's philosophies, too. In his book *The Science of Knowledge*, Fichte argued that the correspondence between the *ego* and the world (i.e., the thesis that there is a structural unity between the *ego* and the world) should be substituted with the correspondence between the *ego* and itself (i.e., the world is so much mind-projected raw material to be subdued to man's goal-pursuing activity); according to Fichte's subjective idealism, men's projects create the world.[27] Revolting against Fichte's philosophy, Hegel argues that subjective idealism causes a discontinuity and a chasm between the Absolute and its historical manifestation, and he undertakes to bridge this chasm by identifying the Absolute with reason. According to the viewpoints of Kant and Fichte, the Absolute is constituted by the unity between the subject and the object, and this unity is actualized within the subject. On the other hand, for Hegel, the unity between the subject and the object is dialectically actualized both within the subject and within the object. Thus, in Hegel's philosophy, history is an absolute value, and not a mere consequence of man's goal-pursuing activity.[28] In addition, the historical objectification of spirit is an object of the intellect, and the subject and the object are concepts.[29]

According to Hegel, the universe is a dialectical process, in which ends of universal reason are realized. This is a secularized teleological conception of the world. The intellect can only distinguish, oppose, and relate, but it is unable to conceive of the unity of opposites, which is the life and inner purposiveness of things. Furthermore, Hegel employs Fichte's and Kant's dialectical method, according to which one begins with an abstract concept (thesis), this concept gives rise to a contradiction (antithesis), and the contradictory concepts are reconciled in a third concept which, therefore, is the union of the other two (synthesis). Therefore, in Hegel's philosophy, truth, like rational reality, is a dynamic logical process. In other words, for Hegel, there is an inner necessity in thoughts, or notions, as if they were thinking themselves, and all the thinker has

27. Breazeale and Rockmore, *Fichte, German Idealism, and Early Romanticism*; Fichte, *Science of Knowledge*.

28. Hegel, *Lectures*.

29. Ibid. and Hegel, *Phenomenology*.

to do is to let his thought follow its logical course in accordance with the dialectical method.[30]

By arguing that there is no distinction between the 'real' and the 'ideal,' Hegel endorsed the starting point of Spinoza's philosophy, which identifies God with nature. However, Hegel modified Spinoza's thesis about the identity of God and nature, by arguing that the Absolute is the Idea, or universal reason, which expresses itself, not only in nature and in individuals, but in history, in right/law (property, contract, punishment), in morality, and in custom (family, civil society, State); in history and in these institutions, the Idea becomes actual; it appears in external form.[31] From Hegel's viewpoint, the reason which gave birth to human institutions is the same as that which seeks to understand them in the philosophy of right, i.e., the reason which unconsciously evolved into law, custom, and the state realizes itself (becomes aware of this evolutionary process) in the philosophy of right.[32] The world is the Idea in spatialized and temporalized form, and historical becoming is the dynamic movement of spirit (i.e., the dialectical itinerary of the Idea). According to Hegel's *Phenomenology of Spirit*, nature is a stage of transition through which the Idea passes in its evolution toward spirit (*Geist*) (i.e., the Idea), which embodies itself and is externalized in nature, returns into itself and becomes spirit; in spirit, the Idea reveals itself to itself.[33]

As a result of the aforementioned arguments, in Hegel's philosophy, the subject and the object of history are the Idea, or universal reason (truth-in-itself), which consists in the self-consciousness of thought, and, furthermore, each historical form is a conception of the self-consciousness of thought. Through Hegel's idealism, Cartesian subjectivism becomes a historical entity, and, therefore, instead of signaling the end of Descartes's philosophical tradition, Hegelianism revitalizes and enriches Descartes's humanistic legacy by substituting individual reason with the Idea. If everything is identified with the Idea, regardless of whether the Idea is a historical entity (as Hegel maintains) or an innate principle (as Descartes maintains), then the supreme being is man. However, in Hegel's philosophy, man purchases his ontological superiority at an extremely high price: history mediates between the subject and the object,

30. Hegel, *Phenomenology*.
31. Ibid. and Hegel, *Lectures*.
32. Hegel, *Philosophy of Right*.
33. Hegel, *Phenomenology*.

and, ultimately, it unites them in accordance with the dialectical method. Historical truth unites people within the framework of institutions, whereas individual truth undermines institutional unity. For this reason, Hegel praises the power and the authority of the state, and he is indifferent toward the freedom and the inner life of the individual human being. In particular, in his *Philosophy of Right*, Hegel argues that the essence of duty is objectified in institutions.

Ancient philosophy was focused and founded on the cosmic order. Medieval philosophy and theology were focused and founded on the certainty of a world that was obeying to the will of the omnipresent and omnipotent God who reveals Himself to man according to the Bible. On the other hand, modernity rejected the previous holism, it separated the subject (man) from the object (world), and, ultimately, it separated the *Logos* from the soul. Empiricism and the experience of irrationality urged modern philosophy to reconsider its assertions, and, therefore, Hegel decided to separate the individual from its spiritual substance, then to isolate spirit, and, finally, to interpret spirit as an all-pervading, impersonal, and coercive dialectical process. In this way, Hegel attempted to restore the unity between the subject and the object without appealing to either ancient or medieval philosophy. Hegel's attempt was based on the logic of modern science and technology, and, thus, he articulated a philosophy of objective idealism, which he substituted for Fichte's subjective idealism. In Hegel's philosophy, Kant's unknowable thing-in-itself is disclosed as the logic of history.

According to Hegel, spirit is actualized in history, and the different historical forms are stages of a unified evolutionary process. The essence and the value of historical phenomena are determined by the significance that they hold for spirit's self-evolution. By the term 'spirit,' Hegel means the subject that has returned to itself, and, according to Hegel, this subject exists as a people, and its spirit is the national spirit. Man exists as a conscious being within the nation, and, in the extent to which man's spiritual freedom is self-abolished and absorbed by the collectivity, man is elevated to the universal spirit. From Hegel's viewpoint, universality means man's identification with one's nation and history, right/law (*Recht*), or objectified spirit, means one's social *milieu* (civilization), and morality consists in the subjection of subjective, individual thought to the commands of universal reason/consciousness.

Hegel's account of international politics is set out in sections 321–40 of the *Philosophy of Right*. According to Hegel, the state is absolutely

sovereign (i.e., there can be no higher authority than the state). In opposition to Kant's cosmopolitanism, Hegel, in section 330 of the *Philosophy of Right*, maintains that international law springs from the relations
among sovereign states, and, therefore, the notion of an international
law that controlled state behavior must always remain at the level of an
"ought-to-be," since its actuality depends on the particular wills of the
different sovereign states. The individuality of the citizen presupposes the
individuality of the state. In section 324 of the *Philosophy of Right*, Hegel
argues that one of the roles of the state in its external aspect in the civil
society is to promote and protect its people's economic interests, and,
therefore, a specific civil society will be driven by its inner dialectic to
"push beyond its own limits," thus causing conflict and war. In Hegel's
world, where the individualities of states are unlimited, war is a necessary
feature of the international system, and, according to Hegel, war contributes toward the maintenance of the ethical health of peoples. Hegel's so-
called 'communitarianism'[34] is another variety of individualism, because,
through his communitarianism, Hegel simply attempts to substitute the
human individual with a quantitatively higher and, hence, historically
safer and more dependable individual; namely, the nation-state. In other
words, Hegel expanded the limits of the individual, but he did not transcend Western individualism.

Hegel remains intellectually anchored on the modern subject, and
he seeks a universal subject whose spirit will encompass everything. For
Hegel, the universal subject is history, and this subject's spirit is the logic
of historical becoming. In this way, Hegel recognizes only the reality of
the human being and completely rejects the reality of the transcendent
world. Furthermore, he identifies being with becoming, the historical
time. Thus, in Hegel's philosophy, history takes the place of God. Since
being is identified with historical *becoming*, it can never be a truth
independent of phenomena.

According to Hegel, man is Alpha and Omega, the beginning and
the end of history, and history *qua* the awareness of historical necessity safeguards order and happiness within and through the state. From
Hegel's perspective, man's existential fulfillment is determined by the
logic of historical becoming, and, therefore, it is necessarily a rational
goal, which is called the end of history. Hegel fails to realize that man's

---

34. Chris Brown has argued that Hegel's theory of international politics is "com-
munitarian," thus contrasting it with Kant's cosmopolitanism; Brown, *International
Relations Theory*, 60 *ff*.

existential fulfillment transcends the logic of historical becoming. On the other hand, classical Greek philosophers had realized that man's existential fulfillment is not achieved rationally, and, therefore, Plato argues that sight is possible only in the context and due to a third light (i.e., when each person pursues his ontological perfection without losing sight of the cosmos). Thus, even though ancient Greek scholars, such as Herodotus and Thucydides, founded history as a scientific discipline, classical Greek civilization was not founded on faith in history, because classical Greek philosophers never imagined a universal and, hence, logically necessary, form of happiness. From the perspective of classical Greek philosophy, happiness presupposes that one has a sense of reality, but happiness is structurally united with wisdom and virtue, which are *personal* achievements. For this reason, the highest ideal of the ancient Greek city-state was not the historical vindication of its regime, but the formation of virtuous and prudent citizens. In other words, in ancient Greek civilization, the city-state is treated as a means, whereas man as a moral and social being is treated as an end. As I argued in chapter 1, for classical Greek philosophers, true being is identified with a transcendent *logos*, or eternal order, in the framework of which history and historical becoming have only limited power, since the end of history is transcendent and not a historical goal itself. Therefore, from the perspective of classical Greek metaphysics, the Absolute can never be identified with a general concept, since, as I argued in chapter 1, it is transcendent. Only if one assumes that the faculty of thought is an ontologically sufficient foundation of truth, can he declare a program of general happiness ignoring or negating external reality, which transcends the subject.

Hegel's historical and, hence, secular teleology implies that the universality of a civilization is equivalent to and stems from the total dominance of the state over society (in the same way that a more general concept 'dominates' over a less general one). On the other hand, classical Greek metaphysics implies that the universality of a civilization is equivalent to and stems from the universality of the educated citizen, who has been 'molded' to the ideal of 'beautiful and good' (Greek: *kalōs kagathōs*). Thus, as Werner Jaeger has pointed out, Greek *paideia* (education) is the idea of perfection, or excellence.[35] Hegel's political thought is concerned with the improvement of humanity, but, in contrast to classical Greek political thought, it ignores the improvement of man as a person, and,

35. Jaeger, *Paideia*.

therefore, it legitimates absolutism and totalitarianism. Hegel's decision to completely negate 'eternity' and assert the absolute dominance of historical time has two important consequences: (i) the present is ontologically insignificant, because it is considered to be merely a stage of an all-pervading, impersonal, and coercive dialectical process, instead of acquiring significance by referring to a transcendent Absolute; (ii) the value of man stems from political authority, and political authority is the source of all values, thus paving a way to modern West's nihilism, with whose study Nietzsche is deeply concerned.[36]

THE CONTESTATION OF MODERNITY:
FROM NIETZSCHE TO FOUCAULT

From Nietzsche ...

The German philosopher Friedrich Wilhelm Nietzsche (1844–1900) first came to the public eye when he became professor of classical philology at the University of Basle in 1869. Three years later, he published his first major work, *The Birth of Tragedy from the Spirit of Music* (1872), in which he called into question the nineteenth-century mainstream theories about ancient Greek culture and especially about the origins and purposes of tragedy. Thus, his work was subject to a withering critique by his academic rivals. In 1789, Nietzsche resigned from the university, and he spent the next ten years of his life in southern Switzerland and northern Italy. The writings of this period, especially *Thus Spoke Zarathustra* (1833–34), *Beyond Good and Evil* (1886), and *On the Genealogy of Morals* (1887), are the core of his philosophy.

In his book *The Birth of Tragedy from the Spirit of Music*, Nietzsche proposes a new way of interpreting ancient Greek culture and modernity. In particular, he argues that, in order to understand classical Greece, we must contrast the Dionysian spirit with the Apollonian spirit, whose paradigmatic representatives were Socrates and Euripides. Furthermore, according to Nietzsche, Christianity is an extension of Socrates's spirit and the source of the European world's spiritual crisis.

Nietzsche argues that Greek tragic poetry is a fruit of the spirit of music, which influences us without the mediation of thought, and he urges us to restore our lost universal unity with nature through ecstatic

36. Cunningham, *Nihilism*.

experiences of joy and pain. Hence, from Nietzsche's perspective, the goal of universal natural unity expresses the Dionysian spirit, an irrational spirit which arrived in Greece from the Orient.

What Nietzsche finds attractive in tragedy is not the manner in which the mind controls passions, but the atmosphere of threat and mystery, and especially the horrifying uncertainty of human life. He identifies the Apollonian spirit with harmony, rhythm, and musical measure (i.e., with the *logos* of ancient tragedy). More specifically, Nietzsche identifies the Apollonian spirit with the tragic heroes' attempts to ponder over chaos, to create order from chaos, and, ultimately, to save us (the audience) from our passions through their passions. Pain without form (i.e., without the Apollonian spirit) becomes unbearable and can destroy us.

According to Nietzsche, tragedy is the product of the reconciliation between the Dionysian spirit and the Apollonian spirit in the context of musical passion, and the purpose of tragedy is to urge us to affirm life without any self-deceptions about salvation in a suffering-free world beyond and to offer us spiritual stillness, not through the oppressive Judeo-Christian urge for self-reproach, but through the negation of self-reproach. Thus, inherent in Nietzsche's philosophy is an ontological pessimism, in the sense that he argues that the only purpose of life is life itself; he affirms life even though he is aware that there is no other form of salvation apart from joy. Nietzsche believes that desire, passion, and will endow us with a deeper understanding of the truth of life than Socrates's philosophy does. Hence, Nietzsche maintains, the decline of tragedy was triggered by Euripides's decision to merge drama with philosophical thought, thus causing the displacement of the Dionysian spirit by the Apollonian spirit. From Nietzsche's perspective, the domination of the Apollonian spirit over human life is the cause of several centuries of human misery.

Nietzsche's book *The Birth of Tragedy from the Spirit of Music* is an attempt to refute Hegel's rationalism, which represents the Apollonian spirit, by appealing to Schopenhauer's voluntarism, which represents the Dionysian spirit. In 1819, the German philosopher Arthur Schopenhauer (1788–1860) published his book *The World as Will and Idea*, in which he accepts Kant's argument that the world of experience is a world of phenomena conditioned by the human understanding, but he departs from Kant's thesis that the thing-in-itself is unknowable. According to Schopenhauer, if man were merely an intellectual being (i.e., an outward-looking subject) he could only perceive phenomena arranged in space, time, and in causal relation. But, Schopenhauer argues, in his innermost consciousness, man comes face to face with his real, basal self, and, in the consciousness of activity, he becomes aware of the thing-in-itself, which is will (i.e., an impulse striving, craving, yearning). Moreover, man knows himself as a part of nature (i.e., as an extended organic body) too, but, according to Schopenhauer, it is the one will which, in self-consciousness, appears as the consciousness of activity, and, in perception, as one's extended organic body. Thus, the will is man's real self, and the body is an expression of the will.

Through his book *The Birth of Tragedy from the Spirit of Music* and through his appeal to Schopenhauer's voluntarism, Nietzsche expresses a thirst for authenticity and freedom, and he asserts that, through art, man can transcend the historicity of spirit. For Nietzsche, the creative power of the human being is superior to every kind of determinism and knowledge. Art and, more generally, sensible experience save us from blind impulses and also from the categorical imperative, since they prohibit truth from extinguishing the fire of life.

Nietzsche is concerned with the contest between the values of civilization, which is the realm of knowledge, and the yearning for the authenticity of passion, which is the realm of the will to power. Thus, for Nietzsche, art is not enough; sensible joy is not enough either, because the human mind exists and is active. Nietzsche realizes that sensible experience must be combined with theorizing about life, and, therefore, he introduces the three metamorphoses of the spirit in his book *Thus Spoke Zarathustra*: the camel spirit, the "weight-bearing spirit," which is a metaphor of a man who takes on the labor of philosophical thinking, and, thus, he is a collector of burdens, conquests, and scars; the lion spirit, which is a metaphor of a man who can say no to duty, who can create freedom, and who discovers that "God is dead"; the child-like spirit, which symbolizes innocence, forgetting, a new beginning, and a self-propelling wheel. Nietzsche's theoretical approach to life consists in striving to break boundaries and to overcome prejudice, and, therefore, the lion becomes a child when the individual who says "I will" rejects every value that is contrary to the law of his will: "the spirit now wills its own will . . . attains its own world".[37] According to Nietzsche, nihilism is the result of that "the highest values devaluate themselves,"[38] and the overcoming of nihilism

37. Nietzsche, *Thus Spoke Zarathustra*, 24.
38. Nietzsche, *Will to Power*, 9.

involves becoming a child, i.e., one who is creative and innocent as life is innocent (blameless) and creative: life is open for us to invent new values, "the sea, our sea, lies open again."[39]

The life of the Dionysian spirit, which breaks boundaries, has an innate boundary, because the mind is not the beginning of life, but it obeys the willpower instinct, on which Nietzsche's vision of a new world and a new man, the "superman" (*Übermensch*), is founded. Nietzsche identifies this innate boundary of the human mind with the will to power, and he argues that it is intimately related to what he calls nihilism. In Nietzsche's philosophy, nihilism signifies that action lacks any transcendent purpose, and, therefore, it signifies the liberation of the will to power from any restraint. Morality is a type of will to power, too, but it is characterized by logical/cultural restraints, because a moral being connects 'goodness' with 'true judgment.' On the other hand, from the perspective of the will to power, good is anything that is derived from power and increases one's power, whereas evil is identified with weakness, and, therefore, the will to power is beyond 'good' and 'evil.'[40] As a consequence, truth is identified with power and not with logical certainty, and, therefore, knowledge is intimately related to that impulse which leads to the devaluation of all values.

In Nietzsche's philosophy, the human being does not have a conscious center or origin, and, therefore, psychology reduces to mere symptomatology, in the sense that one phenomenon reduces to another one, and there is not an ultimate source, or first cause, of psychological phenomena. The previous symptomatology is called "genealogy" by Nietzsche, and, through his genealogical studies, Nietzsche attempts to prove that the world is not constituted by logic, but by our needs and desires, which determine our way of life.[41] Thus, Nietzsche does not interpret the will to power in a psychological manner, but he understands it as the resultant of several impulses which continually strive for power. Having substituted symptomatology for morality, Nietzsche interprets the crisis of modernity "in strictly physiological terms, as the mutual clash of instinctual systems."[42]

39. Nietzsche, *Gay Science*, 199.
40. Nietzsche, *Beyond Good and Evil*.
41. Conway, "Genealogy and Critical Method"; Nietzsche, *Genealogy of Morals*.
42. Conway, "Genealogy and Critical Method," 322.

Nietzsche's nihilism is summarized in his widely quoted statement "God is dead,"[43] which, by implying that we should negate the value of values, emphasizes that the will to power is necessarily connected with Nietzsche's "demolition project."[44] In the context of Nietzsche's physicalistic autonomy, the individual chooses truth, and, therefore he creates values instead of being subject to them. Thus, Nietzsche's objective is the devaluation of all values, and, furthermore, he espouses a radical utilitarian thesis according to which truth is whatever increases one's power.

Nietzsche's thought aims at overriding teleology, but Nietzsche's thought has a *telos* itself, namely, the autonomous post-moral individual, the "superman," who is the embodiment of the devaluation of values. Nietzsche argues that the "superman" is the *telos* of history, and, therefore, he subjects history to his own physicalistic norms, which supposedly determine and purify history. Actually, Nietzsche's philosophical Darwinism is a synthesis between the German idealists' ideal of personality (the subject that has dialectically returned to itself) and Herbert Spencer's[45] all-embracing conception of evolution.

Nietzsche's physicalistic theory of autonomy implies that the absolute *ego* of Nietzsche's "superman" exists only in natural time, since, in his thought, there is no teleological time. Teleological time presupposes values and contributes to the stability of value systems, whereas Nietzsche wants to demolish value systems and devaluate values. Values stem from and depend on a conception of time whose movement has a transcendent *telos* (i.e., an end other than natural death). If the *telos* of time is identified with natural death, then the will to power is meaningless, and the superman becomes a shadow of himself. For this reason, Nietzsche endorsed a cyclical conception of time, which can ignore values, since it does not refer to anything beyond itself. If time is a closed system, then 'good' and 'evil,' 'beauty' and 'ugliness,' 'usefulness' and 'uselessness' all have the

43. It first appeared in 1882 in Nietzsche's *The Gay Science* (in sections 108, 125, and 343), and it is also found in Nietzsche's *Thus Spoke Zarathustra*, which was composed in four parts between 1883 and 1885 and is most responsible for popularizing the phrase "God is dead."

44. Sachs, "Nietzsche's *Daybreak*."

45. The English philosopher and biologist Herbert Spencer (1820–1903) is best known for coining the expression "survival of the fittest," and, in common with other scholars of his era, including the members of Chapman's salon, he was persistently focused on an attempt to establish the universality of natural law, i.e., to show that everything in the universe (including culture, language, and morality) could be explained by natural laws of universal validity. Peel, *Herbert Spencer*.

same value, in the sense that there is no other value apart from affirming ourselves and existence through an endlessly repeated 'now experience.'[46] Thus, from Nietzsche's perspective, the essence of 'eternity' does not lie in values, but it lies in repetition, and it fills the superman with the cruel joy of maintaining one's existence without any eschatological hope of salvation and, hence, without any meaning.

Nietzsche's texts do not allow one to rest on a world of ideas, since they are characterized by a violent reactionary attitude and aim at exciting the reader. Nietzsche transforms man's action and thought into passions, and, thus, he urges us to subject the intellect to impulses. Even though Nietzsche envisages the superman as the embodiment of the will to power, the nature of his thought is essentially feminine, in the sense that the so-called 'feminine spirit' does not disclose beauty in an ideational way, but it is impulsive, fiery, exciting.[47] Nietzsche's philosophy is an intellectual shelter for those people who cannot endure a demanding world of values and principles, and instead they pursue an authentic relation to life through excitement; in other words, they conceive of authentic life as a kind of self-affirming sexual orgy.

... to Foucault

Nietzsche's attempt to articulate a way of liberating oneself from his misery through nihilism has inspired postmodernism. Postmodernism is an expression of the Western man's disillusionment with modernity and especially with the Enlightenment project, which is centered on the ability to think based on one's own will and one's own reason. In the second half of the twentieth century, after the tragic experiences of the two World Wars, of European totalitarianism, and of exploitative capitalist relationships, the scholars of the so-called 'Frankfurt School,' or critical theory, argued that the Enlightenment project, which was an attempt to create a rational, progressive, and cultivated society based on empirically discovered and/or logically deduced laws of the natural world and of the human being, became so detached from "lifeworld" as to lead to the commodification of man.[48] However, postmodernism's attitude is more radical than that of critical theory: it is in reality will-to-void. From the viewpoint of

46. Nietzsche, *Will to Power*.
47. Jung, *Feminine*.
48. Habermas, *Communicative Action*.

postmodernism, 'void' signals relief from the destructive activity of the modern subject. The French philosopher and historian Michel Foucault (1926–84), one of the most influential postmodern scholars, attempted to undermine the notion that there is such thing as a natural self, and he argued that "truth is a thing of the world. . . . And it induces the regular effects of power."[49]

Under the influence of Nietzsche's philosophy, Foucault's analyses are 'genealogical' in character, and they aim at unmasking operations of power that underlie the 'truths' and 'knowledge' of the modern world. Foucault, echoing Nietzsche, argues that there is neither constant human subject in history nor 'true' human condition or nature, and, therefore, there is no meaning or order to history.[50] Nietzsche's and Foucault's philosophies reduce truth and morality to relative judgments that reflect power relationships, and, eventually, they lead to an extremely dangerous relativization of the 'good' itself. Thus, Nietzsche's and Foucault's philosophies render humanity incapable of seeking the good-in-itself, and they can be used as philosophical underpinnings of totalitarianism, authoritarianism, and political crime.

The argument that any action, however disruptive or even murderous, is justified if it averts historical failure or defeat for one's principles and values implies that historical becoming has taken primacy over every principle and every value. Totalitarianism, authoritarianism, and political crime reveal a fundamental lack of conviction in absolute truths, and they suggest metaphysical insecurity. If a truth is absolute, then it does not need to be imposed through totalitarianism, authoritarianism, or political crime. Conviction in absolute truths suggests an aristocratic attitude toward history in general. It is a point uniquely captured in the words of Jesus Christ before the Roman governor of Palestine: "My kingdom is not of this world" (John 19:36).

According to Foucault, the human sciences have determined the categories within which we conceptualize our subjectivity and our criteria of normality and pathology. Thus, Foucault maintains, the modern state primarily governs through the use of the knowledge and practices of human sciences in order to construct its subject's subjectivity through what Foucault has called a "microphysics" of power.[51] Foucault sees power as

49. Foucault, *Power/Knowledge*, 131.
50. Foucault, *Language, Counter-Memory, Practice*, 153.
51. Foucault, *Discipline and Punish*.

a ceaselessly perpetuated, socialized, and embodied phenomenon. From Foucault's perspective, "power is everywhere" diffused and embodied in discourse, knowledge, and "regimes of truth."[52]

Nietzsche and Foucault fight against conviction in 'absolute truths', and they refuse to accept that there are truths over and above political power. Thus, from the perspective of Nietzsche and postmodernism, any discussion about truth is cognitively significant only if and in the extent to which it reduces to a discussion about power. However, their secular notion of power is inextricably linked to the pursuit of historically defined and historically determined goals, and, since, their philosophies preclude the pursuit of the good-in-itself, they lead to the conclusion that there is no significance at all in the witness of someone who criticizes and/or opposes the powers that prevail at any given time. This is an extremely dangerous and self-defeating way of understanding power. If one gives up his claims to truth, then all his principles and values are vulnerable to the contingencies of human history, and, therefore, far from becoming powerful, he becomes a victim of historical becoming.

KIERKEGAARD: THE REDISCOVERY OF THE SUBJECT

Søren Aabye Kierkegaard (1813–55) was one of the most influential philosophers and poets in the Danish "golden age" of intellectual and artistic activity. He is known as the "father of existentialism," and he has written important critiques of Hegel and German romanticism. Existentialism emphasizes the distinction between the essence of being and the presence of being. In his book *Existentialism and Human Emotions*, Jean-Paul Sartre defends the existentialist thesis that "existence precedes essence." The philosophers of existence, known also as the 'existentialists', argue that the only thing that is ontologically significant is that a being exists and is present, in one way or another, in front of me, or independently of me, or the manner in which it is identified with me. Hence, the only thing that is ontologically significant is that I am aware of my own existence. Thus, in his *Philosophical Fragments*, Kierkegaard argues as follows: "I always reason from existence, not toward existence. . . . I do not, for example, prove that a stone exists, but that some existing thing is a stone."[53]

---

52. Ibid.

53. Kierkegaard, *Philosophical Fragments*, 75.

In his work *Stages on Life's Way*, Kierkegaard argues that the first stage on life's way is the aesthetic stage, in which man chooses and experiences himself as the end of existence and indulges in material pleasures. The aesthetic stage is characterized by a quantitative way of understanding the absolute; this way of understanding the absolute consists in an "eat, drink and be merry" philosophy, a "wine, women, and song" lifestyle, and in making clever business deals. Additionally, the aesthetic stage is characterized by an infinitesimal division of existence into pleasant moments. Eventually, the sought-after pleasure ceases to satisfy. Moreover, man becomes painfully aware of the contradiction between the finitude of his lifetime and his infinite quest for the absolute. The sensational nature and the dead end of the aesthetic stage are described in Kierkegaard's *The Seducer's Diary*, where the seducer enjoys his self-assurance by manipulating the self-complacency of the sought-after person and, more specifically, by pretending that he is indifferent toward the sought-after person. According to Kierkegaard, Don Juan is the embodiment of the aesthetic stage, because, from Don Juan's perspective, the female beauty consists in the accumulation of beautiful women.

As long as the aesthete remains in the aesthetic stage, he constantly rotates the roles, the places, and the people in his life. By avoiding intense pleasures or pains associated with close intimacy and commitment (whether to a love, a friend, a cause, or a role), the aesthete is urged to continually distract himself with a variety of persons, experiences, or social roles. Thus, the aesthete's inner self is fragmented. Moreover, the aesthete is anxious that he may not have enough time to achieve his next material goal, and, therefore, feelings of despair take hold of him. The aesthete has the illusion that he is free of society's dictates merely because he is "morally neutral" (i.e., his choices are not in the ethical realm), but, in reality, he defines himself by a contradictory multiplicity of socially defined roles.

According to Kierkegaard's *Stages on Life's Way*, the second stage on life's way is the ethical stage, and the aesthete "leaps" into this stage through "irony," which echoes Socratic irony: the aesthete has now rejected the aesthetic stage, but he pretends that he is still in the aesthetic stage. The starting point of the ethical stage is the feeling of despair that is caused by the aesthetic stage. The ethical stage signals a dialectical transition from the negation of the aesthetic stage, in which one desires whatever attracts him, to the affirmation of the moral law. At this point, Hegel's influence on Kierkegaard's thought is clear: in his 1843 book *Repetition: A Venture in Experimenting Psychology* by *Constantin Constantius*, published the same day as *Fear and Trembling*, Kierkegaard argues that one's life becomes meaningful when he raises himself to the universal by bringing his immediate (natural) desires and inclinations under the moral law, which represents his *telos*, or what he *ought* to be. In the ethical stage, every decision that an individual makes is an ethical one. The ethical individual makes commitments to particular roles, and he considers the needs of others and community. In the ethical stage, there is no individual autonomy (since the law holds for all), but one's actions become meaningful, in the sense that they are governed by a norm, and, therefore, they are understandable.

The singularity of existence comes to light at the moment of conflict between the ethical stage and the religious stage, into which one "leaps" through humor, the tendency of particular cognitive experiences to provoke laughter. According to Kierkegaard's *Stages on Life's Way*, through humor, the ethical individual attempts to repulse the annoying and painful awareness that the 'important' and 'noble' ideals toward which one's moral consciousness is oriented represent base motives. Thus, Kierkegaard seeks a norm inherent in singularity itself, and, in his *Concluding Unscientific Postscript to the Philosophical Fragments*, Kierkegaard expresses such a norm in his assertion that "subjectivity is the truth," whereas "the crowd is untruth."

According to Kierkegaard's *Stages on Life's Way*, the third stage on life's way is the religious stage, in which commitment to others, to a 'cause', to a vocation, to one's 'role' in this life, whatever one has chosen that to be, gives way to the ultimate commitment; namely, to God. Kierkegaard argues that faith consists in man's unconditional surrender to God, and it can be understood as an act of self-sacrifice, which is painful, even though it endows man with unique spiritual wealth. Kierkegaard uses the story of Abraham and Isaac to illustrate his point: God commanded Abraham to sacrifice his son, Isaac (Gen 22:5-8); in other words, God required Abraham to override his commitment as a father and to act like a murderer; Abraham passed the test of faith by proving that his ultimate commitment was to God. In other words, faith is a painful passion, because it is intimately related to solitude, in the sense that a faithful individual sets himself apart from the sensible world. Through faith, man leaves the realm of physical self-assurance, and he attempts to exist in a deeper relationship with himself as a free agent.

In Kierkegaard's philosophy, the transition from one existential stage to another is a repetition of Hegel's dialectical method (thesis, antithesis, and synthesis) by means of the religious notions of 'fall' (thesis), 'repentance' (antithesis), and 'salvation' (synthesis). Therefore, even though, *contra* Hegel, Kierkegaard argues that the transition from one existential stage to another presupposes a movement that expresses the personal energy of spirit (as opposed to an impersonal logical process), Kierkegaard's dialectical perspective on existence implies that, with regard to morphology and direction, the paths and the solutions that the soul can pursue are determined *a priori*. In other words, from Kierkegaard's perspective, man's inner life is characterized by a subtle determinism, through which and due to which nature is merged with law, and, also, sensation is merged with knowledge within the framework of faith. Kierkegaard attempts to refute Hegel's philosophy by substituting Hegel's conception of reason *qua* history with man's inner life, and, from this perspective, Kierkegaard's philosophy does not override Hegel's philosophy.

Kierkegaard's rediscovery of the subject consists in disclosing a new type of dialectical relationship in the realm of man's inner life by relating man's freedom to the three stages of existence, which are also the three stages of man's spiritual life. Thus, the individual's inner life is determined by *a priori* spiritual forms, instead of creating spiritual forms. From this perspective, the individual is not spiritually free, because spiritual freedom presupposes spiritual indeterminacy. In Kierkegaard's philosophy, "repetition" (by which Kierkegaard means meditation), as a transition from being potentially to being actually, gives rise to an absolute individual. Kierkegaard's objective is to harmonize the individual with a given rhythm (i.e., the movement that is determined by the regulated succession of the three stages of existence) that allows the individual to achieve self-assurance by means of the individual's spiritual forms. Thus, Kierkegaard's philosophy is a system of religious romanticism, in the context of which even sacrifice is a way of self-assurance.

Kierkegaard appeals to the relationship between man and God in order to refute Hegel's objective idealism. However, Kierkegaard understands the relationship between man and God as a relationship between two individuals, and, therefore, he articulates a theology founded on the *ego*, which leads to subjectivism. The relationship between the 'I' of man and the 'You' of God is a totally private matter, and, therefore, even though it does not lead to moralism, it traps man in a realm of fruitless religious sentimentalism. Under Lutheranism's influence, Kierkegaard treated faith as an individual bond, and, thus, he transformed faith into a psychological category and, more specifically, into a human passion. Faith *qua* human passion gives rise to a solitary man, who is accountable only to God, and, therefore, in the historical realm, he is committed to himself alone. Kierkegaard's romantic conception of faith (i.e., faith as a religious sentiment) ignores the spiritual unity of church life, and instead it urges man to live a passionate relationship with an unmanifested absolute principle and to call this passionate relationship 'religious faith.' In the context of Kierkegaard's faith, man abandons and sacrifices everything apart from his own self.

On the other hand, for the Greek church fathers, faith refers to man's relationship with a God who manifests Himself to man through God's uncreated grace. Whereas Kierkegaard conceives of the church as a social institution, the Greek church fathers understand the church as a mystery and, more specifically, as the mystery of man's participation in God's uncreated energies. In the context of the Greek church fathers' teachings about the mystery of the church, the subject is oriented toward an external, transcendent truth, and, therefore, faith is not individualized. In the context of the mystery of the church, men are united by participating in the same transcendent truth, which transcends each and every one of them, and, simultaneously, it is available to all of them. The experience of truth *qua* spiritual unity presupposes a self which is available to the fellow man and seeks to transcend the limits of the *ego*. This is the essence of the Hesychasts' teachings about the divinization of man through man's participation in the uncreated energies of God.

HUSSERL'S PHENOMENOLOGY

The German philosopher Edmund Gustav Albrecht Husserl (1859–1938) was the principal founder of phenomenology, whose most prominent forerunners were Franz Brentano and Alexius Meinong.[54] As a philosopher with mathematical background and impressed by the achievements of mathematics and physics in the late nineteenth century, Husserl set himself the task of developing a general theory of inferential systems, which he conceived of as an epistemology, since he argued that every science is a system of propositions that are interconnected by a set of inferential relations. In his *Logical Investigations*, Husserl maintains

54. Moran and Mooney, *Phenomenology Reader*.

that the study of such propositional systems should start with their linguistic manifestations.[55] In particular, Husserl's analysis of these sentences and the propositions they express consists in studying the units of consciousness to which the respective speaker gives voice by expressing the proposition in question. These units of consciousness Husserl calls "intentional acts" or "intentional experiences," since they represent something as something. Moreover, according to Husserl, there are also non-intentional units of consciousness, such as pain. The difference between intentional and non-intentional experiences is that the former have intentional content.

According to Husserl, even objectless intentional experiences (e.g., our thought of the mythical horse Pegasus) have intentional content, since the intentional act is "merely as of," but not really of, an object. For instance, the thought of the mythical horse Pegasus lacks a corresponding object, but it has intentional content. Husserl rejected "representationalist" accounts of intentionality, and he attempted to conceptualize phenomenology as the only philosophical method capable of providing genuine knowledge, even independently of the existence of the world.

The investigations of phenomenology are primarily directed, not toward the empirical disclosure of the things of the external world, but toward the world as it is constituted in and by consciousness. In other words, phenomenology is primarily concerned with the presence of beings through their significations and through their physical properties. In this way, consciousness ceases to depend on its psychological content, whose source is sensation. In contrast to Locke and Berkeley, Husserl argues for the autonomy of rational enquiry into the ideal relational factors in experience, and he opposes the "psychologism" prevalent among many of his contemporaries, such as Theodor Lipps and Carl Stumpf.

In his book *Ideas: A General Introduction to Pure Phenomenology*, Husserl argues that empirical reality is the cause of knowledge, but knowledge is derived from the relation between phenomena and the unified spatio-temporal psychic entity, and not from empirical reality itself. As a result, the psychological aspects of knowledge are precluded, and, thus, phenomena are substances. Moreover, the significations of phenomena are independent of the physical realm, unchangeable, and they do not comply with the law of causality. According to Husserl, the significations of phenomena cannot be objectively determined, and they are not

55. Ibid.

subject to pragmatological analysis, but we can feel them as experiences that transcend sensible representations.[56] For instance, during a lonely walk, you may suddenly encounter another man; before you identify him through logical discernment (e.g., through his height, his weight, his facial characteristics, etc.), you attain knowledge of him through the significance that his presence has to you.

An essential feature of phenomenology is the technique of "bracketing" or "elimination" of the factual aspects of one's experience in order to focus attention on the essential, ideal aspect, which is the object of phenomenology. In other words, the phenomenologist is not concerned with particular facts as such, but with the ideal essences which are disclosed through the particulars. Husserl frequently uses the term *Epoché* (suspension of judgment) to refer to the purification of experience of its factual aspects.[57] In this way, consciousness is liberated from the constraints of perception, and ambiguous percepts are transformed into significations, so that the phenomenologist is not dependent upon the necessarily uncertain conclusions of empirical analysis. The attitude of phenomenological bracketing, which involves an initial suspension of judgment regarding the existence of the presentations of consciousness, must be preserved throughout to ensure the essential constitution of experience. For instance, pure mathematics brackets the factual aspects of man's experience of space and quantity, and its investigations are exclusively directed toward ideal relations.[58]

External objects furnish phenomenological consciousness as intentional reference with significations, and, therefore, signification is distinct from thought. The external world is present in consciousness only in the extent to which and in the manner in which it exists as a set of significations.[59] Hence, the world is created by the intentional reference of consciousness, which transforms the sensible structure of the world into a set of significations. In phenomenology, the importance of consciousness is equal to the importance that pure thought has in Descartes's philosophy.

Intentional reference opens phenomenological consciousness to the signification of the world, but simultaneously it keeps phenomenological consciousness directed, in Cartesian fashion, toward the *ego* and its

56. Husserl, *Ideas.*

57. Ibid.

58. Ibid.

59. Ibid.

presentations. Thus, ultimately, phenomenology is subjectivistic, and Husserl offers no criterion of truth capable of ensuring the objectivity of phenomenological knowledge. In other words, in contrast to Husserl's declared intentions, phenomenology is an epistemology of the ideal, and not of the real.

Husserl attempted to show that only spirit exists in itself and for itself and that, through the technique of "bracketing," it can become self-sufficient. The content of phenomenology consists in the energy of spirit (i.e., of the mind), which attains complete self-knowledge instead of being dispersed in the external world, where it can be attacked by skeptics. Since phenomenology is the science of objects that are constituted by the conscious mind through significations, intentional reference, being the producer of significations, elevates the conscious mind to the criterion and the subject matter of scientific knowledge. Therefore, for the phenomenologist, the only truth is the individual subject.

For one more time, with Husserl's phenomenology, we realize that the spiritual core of Western civilization is the principle of individual truth. For this reason, within the framework of Western civilization, rationalism, mysticism, romanticism/German idealism, and neoclassicism co-exist as different aspects and manifestations of the same principle; namely, of the principle of individual truth. Thus, the ideal objects of phenomenological enquiry must not be confused with Platonic ideas. Plato's theory of ideas is concerned with the vision of the external reality, whereas phenomenology is concerned with the forms through which the things of the world are constituted in consciousness.

HEIDEGGER'S EXISTENTIAL PHENOMENOLOGY

The German philosopher Martin Heidegger (1899–1976) is the most important representative of existentialism. In 1919, Heidegger became Husserl's assistant at Freiburg. During the period 1923–28, Heidegger was teaching at the University of Marburg, but then he returned to Freiburg to assume the chair vacated by Husserl on his retirement. In 1933, Heidegger joined the Nazi Party, and he was elected Rector of Freiburg University. In 1934, he resigned from his position as the Rector of Freiburg University, and he became increasingly distanced from Nazi politics, even though he did not leave the Nazi party. After the end of World War II, a university denazification committee at Freiburg banned

Heidegger from teaching, a right which he did not get back until 1949. In 1950, he was made Professor Emeritus. During the decades of the 1960s, the 1970s, and the 1980s, Heidegger's philosophy exerted a significant influence on left-wing political scholars, including Herbert Marcuse, whose political thought is marked by "Heideggerian Marxism," Hannah Arendt, and Jean-Paul Sartre.

Though closely associated with Husserl, Heidegger sought to take phenomenology in a new direction in his long and complex book *Being and Time*, first published in 1927. In particular, Heidegger sought to move phenomenology away from a purportedly 'Cartesian' emphasis on consciousness, practiced through the technique of bracketing, and toward a new form of phenomenology, emphasizing one's "being-in-the-world," one's "being-with-others," and what Heidegger called "fundamental ontology." Thus, Heidegger's approach to phenomenology has been called "existential" as opposed to "transcendental."

Heidegger is not concerned with the problem of essence, but he sets himself the task of recovering the question of the meaning of Being. Many of Heidegger's translators capitalize the word Being (*Sein*) in order to highlight that, in his book *The Basic Problems of Phenomenology*, Heidegger draws a crucial distinction between Being and beings (entities): the question of the meaning of Being consists in the investigation of what makes beings intelligible as beings, and whatever that factor is, namely Being as such (authentic Being), it is not itself another being among beings. Furthermore, Heidegger draws a distinction between the term 'ontical' and the term 'ontological': the former is concerned with facts about entities, whereas the latter is concerned with the meaning of Being (i.e., with how entities are intelligible as entities).

Heidegger argues that the study of Being as such has been forgotten, since the history of Western thought is characterized by the 'onticization' of Being (i.e., by the practice of treating Being as a being). As it has been pointed out by Søren Overgaard, from Heidegger's viewpoint, "an ontic knowledge can never alone direct itself 'to' the objects, because without the ontological . . . it can have no possible Whereto."[60] Heidegger argues that his fundamental ontology "aims . . . at ascertaining the *a priori* conditions not only for the possibility of the sciences which examine beings as beings of such and such type . . . but also for the possibility of those

---

60. Overgaard, "Heidegger's Concept of Truth," 76.

ontologies themselves which are prior to the ontical sciences."[61] In addition, Heidegger argues that fundamental ontology should be carried out through the notion of *Dasein* (there-being). The term *Dasein* is Heidegger's label for the distinctive mode of Being realized by human beings.[62] In other words, *Dasein* is Heidegger's term for the distinctive kind of entity that human beings as such are. "*Dasein* is ontically distinguished by the fact that, in its very Being, that Being is an issue for it."[63] In Heidegger's thought, the human being is the epitome and the most prominent representative of beings (entities).

In the context of Husserl's phenomenology, the movement of spirit (mind) is determined by the unchangeability of essences and of the conscious mind that constitutes them, and therefore, from Husserl's viewpoint, time is understood through the connection between cause and effect. On the other hand, from Heidegger's viewpoint, essence is time. According to Heidegger, 'essence' should not be identified with the concept of Being, but it is time; that is, he identifies essence with historicity.[64] From this perspective, and given that the human being is the epitome and the most prominent representative of beings (entities), nature is part of historical reality, since it is the field of human activity. Since, in Heidegger's thought, Being and time coincide with each other, in the sense that temporality is *Dasein's* own distinctive mode of being, we are urged to interpret Being as the temporal mode of man's being, as man's self-actualization, instead of contemplating super-temporal essences. Thus, Heidegger's philosophy is concerned with the forms of temporal existence; it is a philosophy of man's historical Being. Heidegger conceives of historicity as a living being. In the context of Heidegger's philosophy, man is identified with his dexterities, and the meaning of his existence is derived from *Dasein*. Thus, ultimately, Heidegger's view of existence consists in the awareness of Being.

From Heidegger's perspective, 'being' does not mean 'in existence,' but Being concerns sense-making (intelligibility), and the different ways in which entities make sense to us depend on the fact that we are *Dasein* (i.e., entities with a particular mode of being).[65] In Heidegger's own

61. Heidegger, *Being and Time*, 31.
62. Brandom, *Tales of the Mighty Dead*.
63. Heidegger, *Being and Time*, 32.
64. Heidegger, *Being and Time*.
65. Sheehan, "Paradigm Shift in Heidegger Research."

words, "Being (not entities) is dependent upon the understanding of Being; that is to say, Reality (not the Real) is dependent upon care," and,
furthermore, "only as long as *Dasein* is (that is, only as long as an understanding of Being is ontically possible), 'is there' Being. When *Dasein*
does not exist, 'independence' 'is' not either, nor 'is' the 'in-itself.'"[66]

After Hegel, modern European philosophy shifted toward the investigation of the historical dimension of the reality of the human being.
Before Hegel, the starting point of the philosophical investigation of the
reality of the human being was a super-temporal 'absolute,' whereas, after
Hegel, the new starting point of the philosophical investigation of the reality of the human being was temporality as a historical experience. Thus,
before Hegel, freedom was being understood as the freedom of choosing
the absolute good, but, after Hegel, freedom started being understood as
the pursuit of a creative activity into which nature, society, biology, and
history are somehow integrated.

When modern philosophy recognized historicity as an ontological
foundation of human existence, philosophical research shifted toward
historical reality and ceased to be concerned with theoretical contemplation. This philosophical shift signals a deviation from Hegel's philosophy
itself, since the determinism of Hegelian philosophy was challenged by
the indeterminism of post-Hegelian philosophers of history. The post-
Hegelian philosophers of history, including Heidegger, do not care about
knowing the absolute truth, but they primarily aim at conceiving of the
spiritual existence of man in the context of an ontology of historicity
and at describing the experience of temporality as an objective cultural
reality. Thus, in the post-Hegelian era, a significant number of Western
scholars started despising 'grand narratives' and focusing on partial approaches to truth. Pre-modern communities were referring to a clearly
defined meaning of existence, either in the sense of cosmic harmony or
in the sense of God's goodness.[67] On the other hand, when, in the context
of modernity, man started focusing on his own historical achievements,
the meaning of existence became a puzzle and a private matter. Thus,
ultimately, modern philosophy has no other option but to perceive life
from the standpoint of a living man, and not from the standpoint of the
absolute or God, and to interpret life according to the manner in which

---

66. Heidegger, *Being and Time*, 255.
67. Eliade, *Myth of the Eternal Return*.

man understands his existence, especially from the phenomenologist's pre-reflective perspective.

In conformity with his contemporary civilization, Heidegger attempted to release philosophy from the metaphysics of the subject. Heidegger criticizes all his predecessors in the history of Western philosophy, he conceives of Being as difference (i.e., as a principle without ontological subsistence), and he argues that *Dasein* exists as a structure and not as a subjective consciousness; on the other hand, his philosophy serves the goal of secular transcendence, which has been motivating Western philosophy from the Renaissance onward. By the term 'secular transcendence,' I mean man's attempt to transcend his existential conditions by his own means. Heidegger's philosophy is an integral part of the Western tradition of 'secular transcendence.' In his *Being and Time*, Heidegger emphasizes that historicity is the fundamental determination of *Dasein*, and he vigorously rejects metaphysics, in the sense that he vigorously rejects the distinction between the subject and the object, since this distinction separates truth from immediate reality. The *ego* upsets Heidegger only in the extent to which it preserves elements of the consciousness of the external world and, therefore, of the transcendent.

Heidegger's goal is to purify the human being of every element of the consciousness of the external world by proposing us to understand Being as difference and the human being as the presence of Being. From this perspective, Heidegger rejects the modern aspiration to 'planetary domination' of the earth and technological mastery of nature, by arguing that it is the outcome of a dichotomous understanding of Being (i.e., of an understanding of man as a 'subject' imposing one's intentionality on a submissive object-world). According to Heidegger, this dichotomous understanding of Being was originally introduced in Plato's myth of the Cave, it became enshrined in Western metaphysics through the subject-predicate logic of Aristotle, and it culminated in rationalism, empiricism, and German idealism. However, from the perspective of the arguments that I put forward in chapters 1 and 2, Heidegger ignores the essential difference between Greek philosophy and Western philosophy, and, therefore, his interpretation of Platonism and Aristotelianism is deeply misguided, since it expresses a purely Western approach to Plato and Aristotle.

Far from treating the world as a submissive object, ancient Greeks 'see' the ideas of beauty and justice *in* the world, and, furthermore, the Greek church fathers emphasize that the *logoi* of beings and things in the world are divine wills, and, therefore, they are united within the *Logos* (or

Word) of God (John 1:3; Col 1:16). In addition, according to the Greek church fathers, man is the mediator between the visible and the invisible, between the created nature and the uncreated one, between earth and heaven, and between the male and the female through love. For the Greek church fathers, the distinction between the subject and the object implies that the universe reveals its vocation through man and, furthermore, that man accomplishes the aforementioned mediation *only in the extent to which* he is in harmony with the divine *Logos*.[68] The goal of the metaphysical thought of Plato, Aristotle, and the Greek church fathers is not to transform everything into a field of human activity, but to change everything so as to glorify God in the context of temporal becoming. The temporal life of God (i.e., the presence of God in history) endows time with a form of completeness that is not secular, and, from this perspective, the meaning and the value of life transcend the *ego*, like the suffering/crucified Jesus Christ, so that the meaning of man's life lies in being open to something/someone that is outside oneself. By recognizing that the meaning of your life lies in being open to something/someone that is outside yourself, the end of time ceases to be death, since then, in contrast to Heidegger's assertions, the meaning of the *ego* and of *Dasein* is transcendent.

---

68. Bahrim, "Anthropic Cosmology of St. Maximus the Confessor."

4

THE THREE BASIC POLITICAL
THEORIES OF MODERNITY

THE THREE MAJOR POLITICAL ideologies of modernity are the following: Liberalism (including right-wing/conservative liberalism and left-
wing/'progressive'/social liberalism), Communism (including Marxism,
socialist schools of thought, and social democracy), and Fascism (including Mussolini's fascist model, National-socialism, Franco's National
Syndicalism, Perón's ideology of Social Justice, Salazar's regime, etc.). The
previous three ideologies have vigorously fought against each other, and
they are the causes behind the most important and dramatic political
events of the twentieth century. In what follows, I shall study these three
political ideologies in chronological order.

FIRST POLITICAL THEORY: LIBERALISM

The intellectual origins of liberalism can be traced back to nominalism
(in the light of the arguments that I put forward in chapter 2) and to
the civic ethos of medieval Western townspeople and especially of the
commercial regimes of the Venetian and the Dutch republics. However,
the origins of modern liberalism can be seen most clearly in the thinking
and politics linked to the English Revolution of 1688, precisely in British
empiricism and constitutionalism. The principles of constitutionalism,
religious toleration, and commercial activity, which were promoted by
the English Revolution of 1688, became a standard for European and

American liberals in the eighteenth century.[1] The French political philosopher Charles-Louis de Secondat Montesquieu (1689–1755), strongly
influenced by Locke and Spinoza, created an idealized portrait of English
politics, and he argued that his political model was the best regime for the
modern man. The successful American revolutionaries of the last quarter
of the eighteenth century were attracted to Locke's political philosophy,
which was seen as the most important intellectual underpinning of the
English Revolution of 1688. The motives and the results of the French
Revolution of 1789 were more mixed, but, in rhetoric and institution, the
French Revolution of 1789 was a liberal revolution, in the sense that it
proclaimed the liberty of the individual, promoted respect for the right to
private property, and it praised the 'self-made' man. Moreover, during the
nineteenth century, liberal revolutions and reforms occurred throughout
the European continent, often in alliance with nationalist and democratic
movements. Liberal thinkers such as Alexis de Tocqueville (1805–59),
John Stuart Mill (1773–1836), Lord Acton (1834–1902), and John N.
Figgis (1866–1919) attempted to reconcile democracy with liberalism
(thus often criticizing Rousseau's notion of unlimited popular sovereignty), and particular national (ethnic) loyalties with cosmopolitan
theories of human rights; additionally, they pioneered the Western model
of pluralist society.

In continental Europe, many nineteenth-century liberals were pre-
occupied with national unification (especially in Germany, Italy, the Central Europe, and Greece), and, therefore, they were less opposed to the
unifying and centralizing power of the state than many of their British
and American liberal contemporaries, who were more attracted to anti-
statist *laissez-faire* economic doctrines and policies. However, in the late
nineteenth and early twentieth centuries, the liberal justification of state
intervention expanded in Britain in the context of the new social liberalism promoted by Thomas H. Green (1836–82) and Leonard T. Hob-
house (1864–1929) and the new political economy developed by John M.
Keynes (1833–1946); in fact, J. M. Keynes rejected both 'state socialism'
and 'economic anarchy,' and he argued that poverty and "the economic
struggle between classes and nations" (which could produce war) could
be overcome by social intervention. During the late nineteenth and early
twentieth centuries, in the United States, social liberalism was identified
with the so-called 'progressive' political thought, which was expressed by

1. Duverger, *Introduction à la Politique*; Manning, *Liberalism*; Ruggiero, *European
Liberalism*.

such writers as Herbert D. Croly (1869–1930) and John Dewey (1859–1952). In addition, during the same period, in continental Europe, social liberals and 'progressive' thinkers were tracing their origins back to Rhenish industrialists, such as Friedrich Harkort (1793–1880), known as the "Father of the Ruhr," and some of them seemed more akin to socialism than to original liberal individualist doctrines, thus opening the way to a synthesis between liberalism and socialism (e.g., the "Gotha Program," i.e., the party platform adopted by the nascent German Social Democratic Party at its initial party congress, held in the town of Gotha in 1875, Edward Bernstein's social democratic theory, Anthony Giddens's "Third Way" social democracy, etc.). In Britain and in continental Europe, the new liberalism, which was prone to a synthesis between liberal principles and social democratic pursuits, was not, at least at first, unreservedly accepted by the official liberal parties, but, on the other hand, social democratic parties rushed to harbor it. In the United States, since the "Great Depression" of the 1930s, the 'progressives' (i.e., left-wing liberals) have captured the label 'liberal,' whereas the older liberals (right-wing liberals) have been known as 'conservatives.' From the conservatives' viewpoint, the new liberals had conceded too much to socialism, whereas, from the new liberals' viewpoint, the conservatives were politically fixated on outdated liberal policies that no longer served the ends of liberalism.

During and after World War II, conservative liberalism was reinforced, and its popularity increased as a result of the Anglo-American elite's ideological war against the Nazis and the Soviets. In the 1950s, some liberal intellectuals, such as Friedrich A. von Hayek (1899–1992) and Karl R. Popper (1902–94), even argued that ideologies were insignificant, that liberalism was a universal truth (not merely one among the many ideologies), that liberalism was naturally superior to its rivals, and that normal liberal politics consisted merely in the antagonism among interest groups, not in ideological disputes.[2] However, this arrogant liberal rhetoric was shattered by the return of ideological polarization in the 1960s and the 1970s. The failure of social liberalism's management to extend the post-war economic boom into the last quarter of the twentieth century contributed to the political reinforcement of conservative liberalism, of which the British Prime Minister Margaret Thatcher and the U.S. President Ronald Reagan were characteristic representatives. The political debate between social liberalism (revitalized by such social

2. Barry, *Hayek's Social and Economic Philosophy*.

democrats as the French President François Mitterand and Jacques De-
lors, the eighth President of the European Commission) and conservative
liberalism continued until the end of the Cold War. After the end of the
Cold War, and as a result of the intensification of the process of globalization, especially in the fields of finance and communication, both social
liberalism and conservative liberalism pursue and underpin the same
globalist strategy, and they differ from each other only with regard to
tactics and methodological issues.

In summary, we can discern the following stages of the development
of liberalism:

- **Original or primitive liberalism:** it is an offshoot of nominalism
  and British empiricism, characterized by individualism, skepticism,
  and social-contract theory. The political economy of original or
  primitive liberalism is known as *laissez-faire* capitalism, and it is derived from physiocracy, which, philosophically, is an offshoot of the
  determinism of Newtonian mechanics and Spinozism. Physiocracy
  is founded on François Quesnay's depiction of the economy as a cir-
  cular flow, which implies that the different elements of the economy
  are as integrally interconnected as are the blood vessels of the body.[3]
  In the context of physiocracy, man is ontologically united with the
  world, and he is determined by natural laws. In 1776, the Scottish
  moral philosopher and political economist Adam Smith (1723–90)
  published his seminal book *An Inquiry into the Nature and Causes of
  the Wealth of Nations*, through which he attempted to place the economic rationale of the physiocrats within a scientifically rigorous
  analytical setting by arguing that the market mechanism is a self-
  regulating 'natural' order and that the price system organizes the
  behavior of people in an automatic way. Thus, Adam Smith is widely
  recognized as the founder of 'classical economics.' The physiocrats
  and the classical economists follow a positivist epistemology, which
  has been summarized by John Cairnes as follows: "Political Economy is a science in the same sense in which Astronomy, Dynamics,
  Chemistry, Physiology are sciences."[4]

- **Social liberalism:** it includes liberal nationalism, which is philosophically derived from Hegelianism; liberal humanism/cosmopol-
  itanism, which is philosophically derived from Kantianism; liberal

3. Samuelson and Nordhaus, *Economics*, 376.
4. Cairnes, *Political Economy*, 35.

social democracy, which is philosophically derived from a synthesis among Kantianism, Marxism, phenomenology, and existentialism. In the beginning of the twenty-first century, the phenomenological and existentialist aspects of social liberalism were emphasized by the internationally renowned financial speculator and political theorist George Soros,[5] and Jonathan Salem-Wiseman[6] investigated the significant yet elusive relation between Heidegger's *Dasein* and the liberal conception of the self.

- *Conservative liberalism:* it consists in a synthesis among Adam Smith's free-market economics, Hegel's ethnocentric communitarianism, religious and social traditions as spiritual underpinnings of the political *status quo*, and Heidegger's notion of *Dasein*. Two characteristic representatives of conservative liberalism are Leo Strauss[7] (1899–1973), who spent most of his academic career as a professor of political science at the University of Chicago, and Pal Oskar Kristeller[8] (1905–99), a highly influential professor of philosophy at Columbia University in New York; both Strauss and Kristeller have been characterized as "methodological Heideggerian"[9] scholars, in the sense that they espoused Heidegger's "exegetical" practices.

SECOND POLITICAL THEORY: COMMUNISM–SOCIALISM

After the decline of the feudal system and of the political authority of the Roman Catholic Church, and as liberalism was continually expanding throughout Western Europe, a new political movement emerged and disputed liberalism's ideological monopoly on modernity. This new political movement was based on socialist and communist ideas, and the most systematic and penetrating exposition of its ideology is due to the German social scientist, historian, and revolutionary Karl Marx (1818–83) and the German industrialist and philosopher Friedrich Engels (1820–95). The constitutional liberalism and rebellious literary nationalism of the

5. Beinhocker, "Reflexivity, Complexity, and the Nature of Social Science."

6. Salem-Wiseman, "Heidegger's Dasein and the Liberal Conception of the Self."

7. Pangle, *Classical Political Rationalism*; Strauss, *Natural Right and History*, and *Political Philosophy and Other Studies*.

8. Kristeller, *Classics and Renaissance Thought*.

9. Woessner, *Heidegger in America*.

1830s appealed to Engels, but, after meeting Marx on his way to England in 1842, he started collaborating with Marx. By 1844, a friendship was established that lasted until Marx's death in 1883, and Engels became Marx's literary executor.

Marx's political and economic theory is intellectually founded on a materialist variety of philosophical realism/essentialism (thus, in the light of the arguments that I put forward in chapter 2, there is a strong philosophical link between Marx's thought and the realist/essentialist trend of scholasticism), on an inversion of Hegel's dialectic, and on the deterministic world-conception of physiocracy. Thus, Marx's political and economic theory is a purely Western ideological phenomenon.

Marx was greatly influenced by Hegel's dialectical theory and especially by the so-called "Young Hegelians," such as Ludwig Feuerbach, the father of modern philosophies of the will and pre-conscious drives.[10] However, Marx criticized Hegel's mystification of the dialectic, and he argued that, with Hegel, the dialectic "is standing on its head. It must be inverted, in order to discover the rational kernel within the mystical shell."[11] Thus, Marx based his conception of communism on a contrast between the alienation (estrangement) of labor under capitalism and a communist society in which human beings could freely develop themselves through economic co-operation. By extracting the "rational kernel" of Hegel's dialectic (i.e., the conception of the self-creation of man as a process), Marx articulates a philosophy of history defined by economic contradiction, in the context of which labor is the essence of man, and man's alienation from his social world and the dialectic of negativity constitute the engine of social change.[12]

Marx criticizes Hegel for creating concepts that reside solely in consciousness and, therefore, in abstraction from nature and material man, but, on the other hand, Marx praises Hegel for realizing the importance of these concepts. The result of situating alienation (i.e., self-objectification) within consciousness is that alienation becomes that of thought (i.e., the alienation of consciousness). Thus, alienation fails to be grounded on the production and reproduction of material life.[13] If man can only alienate thought, all that he can reclaim is his thought. But Marx maintains that

10. Aris, *Political Thought in Germany*.

11. Marx, *Capital*, I, 103.

12. Marx, *Manuscripts*.

13. Ibid.

Hegel's confinement of alienation to consciousness renders man unable to reclaim power over the commodities that are alienated in the context of capitalist production. In other words, according to Marx, Hegel's phenomenology of spirit grasps steadily man's alienation, but it fails to escape the realm of consciousness and place man in the material world. Alienation, Marx argues, would be overcome in communism, which would involve a reunification of man with the products of his labor (i.e., with his work process) and with the natural world.

Marx explained the historical and material basis for the aforementioned arguments in his book *The German Ideology*, whose basic thesis is that "the nature of individuals depends on the material conditions determining their production."[14] From Marx's perspective, the economic structure of society, which is perpetually constituted by the sum total of the relations of production, is "the real foundation, on which rises a legal and political superstructure and to which correspond definite forms of social consciousness."[15] According to Marx, the action of groups and individuals is the engine of historical becoming, whose general form is class conflict.[16] Marx's materialist conception of history is focused on the application of Hegel's dialectic in order to explain political action and forms of government. In Marx's own words, "with the change of the economic foundation the entire immense superstructure [i.e., the realm of politics and law] is more or less rapidly transformed," and this transformation, according to Marx, "can be determined with the precision of natural science."[17]

In his book *Dialectics of Nature*, Friedrich Engels formulated the following three laws of dialectical materialism: (1) the law of the unity and conflict of opposites; (2) the law of the transition from quantitative changes into qualitative changes; (3) the law of the negation of the negation, which is a synonym of 'synthesis.' After reading Hegel's book *The Science of Logic* in 1914, Vladimir Lenin made the following brief notes outlining three "elements" of logic or dialectics: (1) "the determination of the concept out of itself" (i.e., the thing itself must be considered in its relations and in its development); (2) "the contradictory nature of the

---

14. Marx, *Selected Writings*, 161.

15. Marx, "1859 Preface to *A Contribution to the Critique of Political Economy*," 4.

16. Marx, *Selected Writings*.

17. Marx, "1859 Preface to *A Contribution to the Critique of Political Economy*," 5.

thing itself (the other of itself), the contradictory forces and tendencies in each phenomenon"; (3) "the union of analysis and synthesis."[18]

In his *Critique of Political Economy*, Marx asserted that the original formation of capital was due neither to land ownership, nor to medieval guilds, but to usurers' and merchants' wealth. However, usurers and merchants managed to accumulate their immense wealth, because, in the fifteenth century, the Papacy approved of the thesis that money has an intrinsic virtue due to which it can multiply itself. The previous thesis had been proposed by scholastic theologians, who, in this way, legitimated usury. As a result of the previous 'theologically' grounded legitimization of usury, the West started conceiving of material wealth as a value in itself and provided capitalism with its necessary cultural/spiritual underpinnings, which were glorified by Protestant Europe.[19]

Marx has correctly pointed out that the first owners of capital found and used freely traded labor (the most profitable commodity), they violently estranged peasants from the objective conditions of their life (i.e., from the land, their tools, etc.), and also they violently estranged craftsmen from small workshops in the context of a ruthless process of "primary accumulation" of capital. However, even though the primitive accumulation of capital, as it has been described by Marx, was an important underpinning of the industrialization of Western Europe, the primary cause of the industrial civilization is the great spiritual significance that financial wealth acquired in medieval Western Europe.

Money existed in ancient and medieval societies, but it could not be transformed into 'capital', because, in ancient and medieval societies, financial wealth had no spiritual significance, and, for this reason, ancient and medieval people were creating personal bonds with the land and with their crafts. Thus, in ancient and medieval societies, labor was not a freely traded commodity. Marx has argued that the previous system changed and society's transition to capitalism became possible because, at some point, feudal lords asserted the primacy of the exchange value of their financial income over the use-value of their income, and, therefore, they transformed their wealth into a means of individual power.[20]

In his *Critique of Political Economy*, Marx correctly recognized the historical significance of financial wealth, but, due to his materialist

18. Lenin, *Collected Works*, vol. 38, 220–22.

19. Weber, *Protestant Ethic and Spirit of Capitalism*.

20. Marx, "1859 Preface to *A Contribution to the Critique of Political Economy*."

philosophy, he did not investigate the anthropological and cultural aspects of the financial system, and he confined his research work to the consequences of the financial system. Thus, he failed to understand the spiritual presuppositions of the industrial civilization. The significance of the spiritual presuppositions of the industrial civilization becomes easily understood if one bears in mind and studies the resistance of non-Western civilizations to the capitalist model of political economy. The expansion of capitalism is united with and dependent upon cultural imperialism.[21]

Furthermore, it should be mentioned that, in Byzantium, there were usurers and merchants, but Byzantium did not give birth to capitalism, because Byzantine civilization never transformed material wealth into a means of individual power, and it never asserted that material wealth is linked to salvation. Thus, Byzantine civilization precludes capitalism. Capitalism is the historical form of societies culturally founded on financial wealth and individualism.

'Individual ownership' is not an exclusive characteristic of capitalism, since it existed in pre-capitalist societies, too. 'Ownership' is a type of legal relation, and it should not be identified with 'capital.' Capital may be owned by the state, by private individuals, and by partnerships between the public and the private sectors, but capital is not a consequence of any particular type of ownership; capital is a consequence of the employment of 'free' (i.e., commodified) labor by a profit-seeking economic entity, regardless of whether it is a state-owned, a private, or a mixed enterprise. Thus, for instance, in societies with strong pre-capitalist, or anti-capitalist traditions, such as Greece, low-class and middle-class people tend to use material wealth in order to buy land, houses, and apartments, which they understand as symbols of their hard work, instead of speculating through financial instruments. This attitude is not easily understood by countries founded on the capitalist ethos, and, thus, for instance, on February 5, 2014, the German newspaper *Bild* published a stunningly superficial article entitled "Griechen reicher als wir!" ("The Greeks Are Richer than Us!"), which contained a vitriolic criticism of the high *per capita* real estate ownership in Greece.

Marx's political and economic theory is part of Western civilization, and, more specifically, it is part of Western utopian thought, in the sense that it aims at giving a rational solution to social problems once and

21. Tomlinson, *Cultural Imperialism.*

for all. In other words, communism is a theory of the total salvation of humanity within the limits and according to the imperatives of historical reason. Thus, Marxism can co-exist with liberalism in the context of the same civilization (namely, in the context of Western civilization) in the same way that, for instance, philosophical realism/essentialism and nominalism co-exist in the context of scholasticism. Furthermore, in the nineteenth and the twentieth centuries, the West gave rise to several combinations of Marxism and nationalism in the context of dependency theories[22] as well as to several combinations of Marxism and liberalism in the context of social democracy[23].

On November 9, 1918, as Prince Maximilian of Baden, a liberal politician, was voluntarily handing over Germany's chancellorship to Friedrich Ebert, leader of the Social Democratic Party of Germany (SPD), he said to him: "Mr Ebert, I entrust you with the German Reich," and Ebert responded: "I have lost two sons for this Reich," since two of Ebert's four sons were killed in World War I.[24] The 'First Reich' was the 'Holy Roman Empire' of the German nation, and the 'Second Reich,' to which Ebert and Prince Maximilian of Baden were referring in their previous discussion, was the constitutional monarchy of the German nation-state, which was created in 1871.

Friedrich Ebert was elected leader of the SPD on the death of August Bebel (1840–1913), who was a German Marxist politician, writer, and orator. Before World War II, the SPD was the biggest political party in Germany and the biggest labor party in Europe. In October 1918, Ebert was a pivotal player in organizing a coalition government of socialists and liberals under Prince Maximilian of Baden, and he offered significant support to the short-lived government of Prince Maximilian of Baden, who was overseeing Germany's transformation into a parliamentary system during the "October reforms" at the end of World War I. Ebert's rise to power on November 9, 1918 signaled the beginning of a new era in which center-left parties control the masses and especially the working class in conformity with the fundamental institutions of the liberal political system, and, therefore, they do not threaten capitalism.

Gradually, the SPD abandoned the Marxist criticism of capitalism, and, with its conformist and centrist policy, it offered significant

22. Amin, *Imperialism and Unequal Development*; Emmanuel, *Unequal Exchange*.
23. Clarke, *Liberals and Social Democrats*; Giddens, *Third Way*.
24. Brockhaus Deutsche Geschichte, *Deutsche Geschichte*.

underpinnings to German militarism and fascism. For instance, from 1898 until 1912, the SPD was opposing increases in military spending, but, in 1913, it voted for an Army Bill which would increase the size of the German Army at a cost of billion marks. The most prominent opponent of the SPD's shift toward the center of the political spectrum was Karl Liebknecht (1871–1919), a German socialist and co-founder with Rosa Luxemburg of the Spartacist League and the Communist Party of Germany. Karl Liebknecht's father, Wilhelm Liebknecht, was a co-founder with August Bebel of the then Marxist SPD. Karl Liebknecht opposed World War I in the *Reichstag*, and he played an active role in the Spartacist uprising of 1919. The uprising was suppressed by Ebert's social-democratic government and *Freikorps* (paramilitary organizations).

In 1918, the elite of the German military-industrial complex believed that Germany could impose its will on Europe, but was concerned about the spread of radical ideas in German society and about the influence of the Soviet Union. Thus, the elite of the German military-industrial complex arrived at the conclusion that it needed the German Social Democratic Party in order to contain a new wave of working-class unrest and, in general, in order to control and manipulate German society through social democracy. The German industrialist Robert Bosch posed the issue as follows: "When the house is burning you may have to put out the fire with water from a cesspool, even if it stinks a bit afterward"; the stinky water mentioned by Bosch was social democracy. Moreover, General Erich Ludendorff, representing the German military-industrial complex, proposed the creation of a coalition government based on the majority parties of the *Reichstag*, i.e., on the SPD, the Center Party (a Roman Catholic political party formed in 1870), and the FVP (the German liberals), under Prince Maximilian of Baden. The SPD justified its participation in the liberal government of Prince Maximilian of Baden on the grounds that Germany was in a difficult position and the SPD should prove its patriotism.

In 1918, the sailors' revolt in Kiel gave an opportunity for the SPD to offer significant services to Germany's military-industrial complex. The sailors' revolt started during the night from 29 to 30 October 1918. On the evening of November 4, 1918, a meeting of revolted sailors and workers representatives in the union house led to the establishment of a soldiers' and workers' council. On the same evening, the SPD deputy Gustav Noske arrived in Kiel, and, due to his attractive social democratic political profile, he was enthusiastically welcomed by the protesters, who did not know that Noske had orders from the new government and the SPD leadership to bring the rebellion under control. Noske had himself elected chairman of the soldiers' and workers' council, and, therefore, having peacefully placed the revolted masses under his control, he managed to prevent radical social changes. Three decades later, Noske was writing about the sailors' revolt in Kiel that, if he had raised the red flag of revolution in Kiel, then a revolutionary wave would have overwhelmed Germany.[25]

Ebert's first action as Chancellor was to issue a proclamation asking Germans to remain calm, get off the streets and to restore peace and order. On November 10, 1918, the Social Democrat Friedrich Ebert, at the time the Chancellor of Germany, and Wilhelm Groener, Quartermaster General of the German Army, signed the Ebert–Groener pact, with which Groener assured Ebert of the loyalty of the armed forces, and, in return, Ebert promised that his social democratic government would take prompt action against leftist uprisings and that the military would retain its 'state within the state' status.[26]

THIRD POLITICAL THEORY: FASCISM

Fascism came into being together with the twentieth century. It is a synthesis of organic nationalism, anti-Marxist socialism, social Darwinism, Nietzsche, Heidegger, the psychology of Gustave Le Bon, and the sociology of Vilfredo Pareto.[27] Fascism opposes materialism, liberal democracy, and Marxism, and regards them as different aspects of the same materialist evil. This revolt against materialism underpins the political alliance between anti-liberal and anti-bourgeois nationalism and an anti-Marxist, revolutionary variety of socialism. The fascist ideological synthesis highlighted the defects of a political culture inherited from the eighteenth century and the French Revolution, and it rejected liberal individualism.

The fascist ideological synthesis was clearly expressed in the 1910s in such publications as *Les Cahiers du Cercle Proudhon*, published by the Cercle Proudhon, a political group founded in France in 1911 by George Valois and Édouard Berth and inspired by the French philosopher Georges Sorel (1847–1922), who founded revolutionary syndicalism. Sorel

25. Ruge, *Novemberrevolution*.
26. Ruge, *Weimar*.
27. Hamilton, *Fascism*; Laqueur, *Fascism*.

replaced the rationalistic foundations of Marxism with anti-materialist, voluntarist elements.[28] Sorel's form of socialism, known as revolutionary syndicalism, is a philosophy of action based on intuition, activism, and the cult of energy and *élan*. Thus, Sorel argues that the most effective way of activating the masses is not based on reasoning, but it is based on myths, by which he means systems of images which excite imagination and sustain the warrior outlook. The combination of Sorel's anti-Marxist socialism and the theories of organic, exclusive nationalism that were developed by the French nationalist politicians and writers Maurice Barrès (1862–1923) and Charles Maurras (1868–1952) and by the Italian nationalist politician and writer Enrico Corradini (1865–1931) gave rise to the fascist revolutionary movement.

Giovanni Gentile (1875–1944), the preeminent Italian fascist intellectual, articulated a neo-Hegelian fascist doctrine, in the context of which the human individual is not an atom, but, as long as man is outside the organization of society, he has no significant freedom.[29] According to Benito Mussolini (1883–1945), who ruled Italy from 1922 until 1943, outside the state, "no human or spiritual values can exist, much less have value."[30] Mussolini's conception of liberty consists in the liberty of the state and of man as a member of the state. Furthermore, according to Alfredo Rocco, Mussolini's minister of justice, individual rights were significant only in so far as they derived from the rights of the state. From this perspective, Italian fascism is clearly a neo-Hegelian mutation of liberalism, in the sense that it preserves the individualistic ethos of Western civilization, but its individualism refers, in Hegelian fashion, to the rights and the ontological autonomy of the state. For this reason, fascists aim at creating a totally coherent state. Mussolini argues as follows: "We are . . . a state which controls all forces acting in nature . . . everything in the state, nothing against the state, nothing outside the state."[31] In the same spirit, the French fascist Marcel Déat (1894–1955) articulated a vision of "the total man in the total society."[32]

Fascism's focus on the individuality and the ontological autonomy of the state is intimately related to fascists' concern with the will of the

28. Sorel, *Violence.*
29. Gregor, *Giovanni Gentile.*
30. Mussolini, *Fascism,* 11.
31. Ibid., 40.
32. Déat, *Parti Unique.*

state. Gentile and Mussolini argue that the state is a conscious entity and has a will of its own. From this perspective, fascists aim at applying Nietzsche's notion of will to power and Heidegger's notion of *Dasein* to the fascist theory of the state. From the viewpoint of fascism, the state is the real bearer of will to power, and, additionally, *Dasein* is the state.

The combination of fascist doctrines and a biologically (i.e., racially) expressed desire for the transcendental gave birth to the ideology of the National Socialist German Workers Party (NSDAP), better known as the Nazi party, which was formed in 1919 and, under Adolf Hitler, ruled Germany between 1933 and 1945.[33] A paradigmatic philosopher of Nazism was Alfred Rosenberg (1893–1946), whose book *The Myth of the Twentieth Century* (1930) contains racist and *volkish* ideas, and it is characterized by revolutionary utopianism focused on Nordic mythology and the Nazi vision of the triumph of the Aryan race.

Even though fascism is an anti-liberal revolutionary ideology, it was used by liberal Anglo-American elites and by the elite of the German military-industrial complex in order to inhibit the ideological expansion of Marxist communism in Western Europe and in order to curb the geopolitical power of the Soviet Union in the 1920s and the 1930s. Benito Mussolini himself started his fascist political career in 1917 with a help of £100 weekly wage from MI5, the well-known British intelligence agency.[34] In 1917, Sir Samuel Hoare, a Conservative MP and MI5's head in Rome, who ran a staff of 100 British intelligence officers in Italy at the time, recruited Mussolini, then a thirty-four-year-old journalist, for MI5. Hoare, later to become Lord Templewood, mentioned the recruitment in his 1954 memoirs, and Cambridge historian Peter Martland has methodically investigated the details of Mussolini's recruitment by MI5.[35] Moreover, on June 13, 1940, Adolf Hitler granted a revealing interview to Karl Henry von Wiegand, a veteran reporter from the *Hearst* Newspapers. In that interview, Hitler supported the Monroe Doctrine, and he emphasized that he had no intention of destroying the British Empire.[36] Regarding many senior Nazi leaders' attempt to conclude peace with the British Empire, John Toland writes that, after Rudolf Hess's May 10, 1940

33. Nolte, *Fascism.*
34. Kington, "Recruited by MI5."
35. Ibid.
36. Fischer, *Hitler and America.*

solo flight to Scotland, "irritate as he was, Hitler . . . realized that his deputy had made the hazardous flight for him."[37]

The end of World War II signaled the defeat of fascism by liberalism, but, throughout the Cold War, liberal Western elites never ceased to treat fascism as an ideological weapon that could be used against political movements and governments supported by the Soviet Union and generally against governments of developing nations that were not conforming to the U.S. model of development (i.e., to the U.S. conception of economic, social, and political 'progress'). Thus, Robert S. McNamara (1916–2009), during his service as Secretary of Defense under U.S. Presidents John F. Kennedy and Lyndon B. Johnson, developed and promoted the doctrine that the Army was the most effective modernizing force in developing nations, in the sense that, in developing nations, the Army was the most effective local institution for imposing and implementing the U.S. model of development.

Modern Western societies promote the acculturation of the so-called 'backward' societies by diffusing capital, technology, and institutions in the developing world. This diffusion process, i.e., the paternalistic policy of modern West, underpins the modernization process of the so-called 'backward' societies. Thus, modern West's plans for the modernization of the so-called 'backward' societies reflect not only the interests but also the values and the mentality of modern West. When the so-called 'backward' societies exhibit resistance to modern West's development and modernization plans, modern West often attempts to impose and implement its development and modernization policy in the developing world through fascist regimes and especially through the Army.

Lucian W. Pye (1921–2008), a political science professor at the Massachusetts Institute of Technology, focused his research work on the modernization of Third World nations, and he became regarded as one of the foremost practitioners and proponents of the concept of 'political culture' and of political psychology. Pye served as advisor to U.S. President John F. Kennedy, and he played a key role in the formation of the liberal imperialist policy of the Kennedy-McNamara administration. In his book *Aspects of Political Development*, Pye argues that the Army is the most modernized institution in transitioning societies. Moreover, in the same book, Pye argues that the acculturation process in the Army tends to focus on the acquisition of economically significant skills, and,

37. Toland, *Adolf Hitler*, 666.

in developing countries, the Armed Forces can provide the citizen with a sense of rights and duties and with an appreciation for political action.[38]

By 1962, the White House and the U.S. Pentagon had devised a new strategy of counter-insurgency to combat communist guerillas. McNamara's liberal imperialist policy led to the creation of American special forces like the Green Berets and secret paramilitary operations throughout Asia and Latin America. The policy of McNamara's liberal imperialism often led to the support of fascist regimes (military juntas), such as Franco's regime in Spain (1936–75) and the Greek military junta of 1967–74. Moreover, when in 1964 Brazil's generals overthrew the democratically elected President Joao Goulart and proclaimed that their junta saved the nation from communism, U.S. President Lyndon B. Johnson promptly recognized the new military regime. According to this strategy of liberal imperialism, in 1965, U.S. President Lyndon B. Johnson, without even bothering to consult U.S. Congress, dispatched 23,000 marines to the Dominican Republic in order to support and consolidate the fascist military *coup* that overthrew the legally elected President Juan Bosch and to suppress Bosch's constitutionalist forces. Johnson argued that the popular democratic movement in the Dominican Republic had fallen into the hands of communist conspirators.

The Nixon administration (1969–74) supported fascist military regimes in Greece and Cyprus,[39] sold jet aircraft to the fascist governments of South Africa and Portugal, then engaged in difficult counter-insurgency campaigns in Africa, and it violated United Nations sanctions against Rhodesia. In 1970, U.S. President Richard Nixon and his National Security Adviser, Henry A. Kissinger, authorized the Central Intelligence Agency (CIA) to encourage a military *coup* in Chile in order to prevent the inauguration of the democratically elected socialist presidential candidate Salvador Allende[40], but the plan was not successful. The CIA provided funding for the mass strikes against Allende's government in 1972 and 1973 and for extensive black propaganda in the newspaper *El Mercurio*.[41] CIA's first approach to stop Allende was called "Track I" approach, and CIA's second approach, the "Track II" approach, consisted

38. Pye, *Political Development.*

39. Papandreou, *Democracy at Gunpoint.*

40. Kornbluth, *The Pinochet File.*

41. Ibid.

in the encouragement of a military overthrow.[42] On September 11, 1973, Allende died during a military *coup d' état* that was launched by Army Commander-in-Chief Augusto Pinochet and actively supported by the CIA.[43] Augusto Pinochet's fascist regime, which lasted from 1973 to 1990, implemented a free-market oriented economic policy under the guidance of the neoliberal "Chicago Boys" (a group of Chilean economists, most of whom trained in the Department of Economics at the University of Chicago under Milton Friedman and Arnold Harberger), and many of Pinochet's officers were paid contacts of the CIA or the U.S. military.[44]

In 1976, Henry A. Kissinger, who was Secretary of State under U.S. President Gerald R. Ford, took a similar line as he had toward Chile when Jorge R. Videla, a senior commander in the Argentine Army, came to power in a *coup d' état* that overthrew the elected government of Isabel Martínez de Perón. Through a process called the National Reorganization Process, Videla's fascist military regime consolidated its power, launching brutal reprisals and "disappearances" against political opponents.[45] The National Reorganization Process regime lasted from 1976 until 1983. Previously secret State Department documents, including some published by the Argentine newspaper *Clarin*, show that U.S. officials had prior knowledge of Videla's intentions and supported him. More than a week before Videla's *coup d' état*, U.S. Ambassador Robert Hill sent to William Rogers, who was the U.S. Assistant Secretary of State for Latin America, a secret cable reporting that the commander of Argentine Navy, Admiral Emilio Massera, had requested that the U.S. embassy "indicate to him one or two reputable public relations firms in the U.S. which might handle the problem for a future military government."[46] While Rogers suggested delaying official recognition of Videla's dictatorial government, the U.S. Secretary of State Henry A. Kissinger ordered full U.S. support to Videla, and among those who implemented this policy in 1976 were Richard Cheney, then the White House Chief of Staff, and Donald Rumsfeld, who was Defense Secretary.[47] About twenty years later,

42. Ibid.
43. Kornbluth, "CIA Acknowledges Ties to Pinochet's Repression."
44. Ibid.
45. Osorio et al., "On 30th Anniversary of Argentine Coup."
46. Ibid.
47. Ibid.

Richard Cheney became the U.S. Secretary of Defense under President George H. W. Bush, and he became the 46th Vice President of the United States from 2001 to 2009, under President George W. Bush. Donald Rumsfeld served again as Secretary of Defense from 2001 to 2006, under President George W. Bush.

The moral and philosophical legitimization of fascist regimes by liberal elites continued and was rigorously formulated in Jeane Kirkpatrick's celebrated 1979 *Commentary* essay "Dictatorships and Double Standards." Jeane Kirkpatrick, a Georgetown University political science professor, served on Ronald Reagan's Cabinet on the National Security Council, Foreign Intelligence Advisory Board, and Defense Policy Review Board, and she served as the 16th U.S. Ambassador to the United Nations (1981–85). In her previous celebrated essay, Kirkpatrick formulated what is known as the "Kirkpatrick doctrine," according to which right-wing authoritarian regimes which were allies of the West were distinct from and better than left-wing 'totalitarian' regimes, because pro-U.S. right-wing authoritarian regimes were putatively susceptible to an incremental transition to liberal democracy, and their enmity to communism served as the predominant piece of evidence for their political disposition.

ADVANCED LIBERALISM: THE GLOBAL MONOLOGUE PROJECT IN THE ERA OF ADVANCED MODERNITY

The end of World War II signaled the victory of liberalism over fascism, and the end of the Cold War signaled the victory of liberalism over communism. In the post-Cold War era, the Atlanticist geopolitical thought gave rise to the following two models for the management of world affairs:

1) Unipolarity: This model has been endorsed by the neoconservatives (such as Irving Kristol, Norman Podhoretz, etc.) and, generally, by leading members of the Republican Party of the U.S. According to the unipolarity model, the U.S. should be the center of the world system, like a liberal-democratic empire enjoying the privilege of world hegemony, whereas all other states should be organized around the U.S. on, more or less, the same strategic and ideological basis. In 1997, the Project for the New American Century (PNAC) was founded under the Chairmanship of William Kristol, former Chief of Staff to Vice President Dan Quale during the Presidency of George H. W. Bush. Kristol's father,

THE THREE BASIC POLITICAL THEORIES OF MODERNITY   125

Irving Kristol, is widely regarded as the "Godfather of Neoconservatism."
The goal of PNAC was to promote the argument that U.S. world leadership is beneficial to the U.S. and to the whole world, and, furthermore,
to explain what U.S. world leadership entails. On May 29, 1998, PNAC
sent a letter to the then Speaker of the House of Representatives, Newt
Gingrich, and to Senate Majority Leader, Trent Lott, repeating arguments
that PNAC members had already put forward in a letter that they had
sent to U.S. President Bill Clinton four months earlier. In those letters,
PNAC was expressing its members' concern that U.S. policy of containment of Saddam Hussein was failing, and it was arguing that the United
States and its allies in the Middle East would soon be facing a threat of
unprecedented magnitude since the end of the Cold War. In April 2011,
William Kristol wrote an editorial in the *Weekly Standard* arguing that
the United States' military interventions in Muslim countries (e.g., the
Gulf War, the Kosovo War, the Afghanistan War, and the Iraq War, etc.)
should not be characterized as "invasions," but rather as "liberations."[48]

2) Multilateralism: This model has been endorsed by the pluralism/
interdependence/neoliberal 'school' of International Relations, whose
founders are Joseph Nye, Jr. and Robert Keohane, and by leading members
of the Democratic Party of the U.S. According to the model of multilateralism, it is almost impossible for any state to achieve global hegemony in
the era of advanced modernity and globalization, and, therefore, the U.S.
should partly give up its hegemonic pretensions and share the rule of the
world with other powers, especially with those powers which are close to
the U.S. with regard to values and history, like Western Europe.

The models of unipolarity and multilateralism are associated with
different approaches to the concept of power. In his book *The Future of
Power*, Joseph Nye, Jr. has discerned 'hard power,' which is the ability to
get what you want through coercion and/or payment (i.e., through 'sticks
and carrots') and 'soft power,' which is the ability to get what you want
through attraction, which arises from the attractiveness of a country's
culture, institutions, and political behavior. In other words, according
to Nye's typology of power, hard power consists in commanding others
to "change their behavior against their initial preferences" and/or in the
ability to control agendas, whereas soft power consists in "the ability to
affect others' preferences so that they want what you want."[49] Military

48. Harland, *Democratic Vanguardism*, 197.
49. Nye, *Future of Power*, 11.

interventions and negative sanctions (taking away economic benefit) are characteristic examples of hard power. On the other hand, Nye provides several noteworthy examples of the extent and influence of U.S. soft power, such as the influence of American political ideals on Europe after World War II, the support that Radio Free Europe built for Western political and economic ideals in communist countries during the Cold War, the influence of American political ideals and lifestyle on non-Western countries, etc. Whereas the supporters of the unipolarity model emphasize the projection of hard power, the supporters of multilateralism emphasize the projection of soft power.

In 1928, Edward L. Bernays, nephew of the father of psychoanalysis Sigmund Freud, published his highly influential book *Propaganda*, from which Josef Goebbels, Hitler's Minister of Propaganda, took many of his ideas. In his *Propaganda*, Bernays argued that, if one understands the mechanisms and motives of the group mind, he can control and regiment the masses according to his own will, without the masses knowing it; furthermore, he made the following remarks: "The conscious and intelligent manipulation of the organized habits and opinions of the masses is an important element of democratic society. . . . Those who manipulate this unseen mechanism of society constitute an invisible government which is the true ruling power of our country."[50] In 1954, Bernays headed the propaganda operations of the CIA supported *coup* in Guatemala, framing it as an act of "liberation from Communism," even though it was a fascist regime protecting the interests of the United Fruit Company. Soft power is the most advanced form of Western propaganda theory.

The significance and the impact of soft power have been enhanced by the globalization of the international economy, and simultaneously U.S. soft power promotes the globalization of the international economy along the lines of liberal cosmopolitanism. The rapid globalization of the international economy, especially in the areas of production and finance, and the changing nature of the inter-state system in what Zbigniew Brzezinski has called a "complex post-hegemonic world"[51] contribute to the emergence of the Global (as opposed to International) Political Economy. Robert Cox has defined Global Political Economy as an economic space that transcends all country borders and simultaneously co-exists with an international economy that is based on transactions

50. Bernays, *Propaganda*, 9.
51. Brzezinski, *The West in the Complex Post-Hegemonic World*.

across national borders and is regulated by inter-state agreements and practices.[52] Thus, from the viewpoint of Global Political Economy, there are three different levels of economic space: supra-regional, national, and sub-regional; furthermore, there are at least three different levels of social organization: social forces, states/national societies, and global society. Cox describes this state of affairs as a "multi-level world" that challenges the state-centric Westphalian model of international relations.[53]

In the context of the global economy, neither the strong actors nor the weak ones are immune to the effects of globalization, since no state can exercise sufficient control over globalized production for world markets. Thus, in the context of the global economy, states become more like firms, in the sense that states can bargain, but they cannot determine results. The central policy question of Global Political Economy revolves around the manner in which and the extent to which states can maintain authority over their policy making process in the sphere of international economics.[54] According to Cox,[55] globalization consolidates the emergence of "the transnational managerial class," and, according to Susan Strange,[56] globalization consolidates the emergence of "an international business civilization."

As a result of globalization and the revolutions in the fields of telecommunications, transportation, and social media, humanity has entered an era of unprecedented global interconnectedness. Thus, as Zbigniew Brzezinski has pointed out, global political leadership has become much more "diversified" unlike what it was until the 1980s, and the whole world has become "politically awakened," in the sense that, everywhere around the world, politics is a matter of social engagement, and most people are consciously aware of the basic characteristics of the international system and of the basic political and economic events that happen around the world.[57] Therefore, the so-called neoliberals emphatically argue that humanity cannot be controlled by simply projecting hard power and that the neoconservatives' approach to power is outdated.

52. Cox, "Structural Issues of Global Governance," 260.
53. Ibid., 263.
54. Reich, *Work of Nations.*
55. Cox, "Structural Issues of Global Governance," 261.
56. Strange, "Name of the Game."
57. Brzezinski, "Global Political Awakening."

Following World War I, liberal elites sought to create a world order according to their own designs. Thus, as I will argue in chapter 5, U.S. President Woodrow Wilson proclaimed a right to "national self-determination," which became a means of creating nation-states that reflected the political values and institutions of Western nations, and, also, they were hegemonized by Western nations. In the first half of the twentieth century, liberal elites realized that, in order to control people, one must create institutions of control, such as the nation-states of Iraq, Saudi Arabia, Jordan, Lebanon, Syria, Kuwait, etc., which did not exist prior to World War I. By creating the previous nation-states, the West managed to disintegrate civilization zones, such as the Islamic civilization zone, and to acculturate and integrate non-Western societies into a political and economic system that was reflecting and serving the interests, the values, and the mentality of the Western world.

As I have already argued, before the end of the Cold War, the Atlanticist elite was seeking to control populations and individuals for its own desires, regardless of whether the political system was that of fascism, socialism, or liberal democracy. Members of the Atlanticist elite (mainly Zionists) managed to manipulate even the Bolshevik Revolution to their advantage. The Rothschild financial network had a long feud with the Tsars of Russia, because they were not co-operating with the Rothschilds. Moreover, in the American Civil War, Abraham Lincoln invited Tsar Alexander II to send the Russian fleet to the U.S. as protection in order to foil the plans of the Rothschilds, France, and Great Britain to intervene on the side of the South. Indeed, on September 24, 1863, the Russian Baltic fleet began to arrive in New York harbor, and, on October 12, 1863, the Russian Far East fleet began to arrive in San Francisco. Lincoln's Secretary of the Navy Gideon Welles wrote in his diary: "God bless the Russians!"[58] In 1904, in Russia's war with Japan, Jacob Schiff,[59] head of the New York Jewish banking house Kuhn, Loeb and Co., financed Japan, and, simultaneously, he made sure that Russia was deprived of access to credit resources, and, therefore, Russians were defeated by the Japanese.

58. Golder, "The American Civil War"; Kushner, "The Russian Fleet and the American Civil War."

59. Jacob Schiff was born in 1847 in Frankfurt, Germany, to Moses and Clara Schiff, members of a distinguished Ashkenazi Jewish rabbinical family. His father, Moses Schiff, was a broker for the Rothschilds. Jacob Schiff migrated to the United States after the American Civil War, and, from his base on Wall Street, he was the foremost Jewish leader from 1880 to 1920.

In 1917, the Rothschilds and the British geopolitical strategists stroke a fatal blow against Tsarist Russia through the Bolshevik Revolution.

The U.S. State Department, in its three-volume report on the origins of communism in Russia, published in 1931, reveals how Jewish-controlled German banks under the leadership of Max Warburg conspired as early as 1914 to send large payments to Lenin, Trotsky, and other Bolsheviks in their attempt to bring down the Tsar.[60] As part of this conspiracy, Jacob Schiff invested close to 20 million USD toward the establishment of Bolshevism in Russia, and he financed Trotsky's trip from New York to Russia. The Bolshevik Revolution had important political and geopolitical implications: it caused the replacement of the Tsarist regime, which had significant pre-modern characteristics and anti-modernist tendencies, by the Bolshevik regime, which was an offshoot of Western modernity;[61] it isolated Russia from geopolitically and economically significant areas in Central Europe, the Balkans, and the Middle East; and it deprived Russia of the ability to export its huge natural gas reserves internationally, thus facilitating the Atlanticist pole to dominate the oil-rich Middle East countries and to establish the petro-dollar system after the end of World War II.

After the victory of liberalism over fascism and communism, the U.S. neoliberals desire to impose a global political monologue, in the sense that, for them, it is not enough that governments of other nations serve U.S. interests. U.S. neoliberals not only want all other nations to serve U.S. interests, they also want all other nations to endorse the ideology and the values of the U.S. neoliberal elite, whose rhetoric is based on human rights, civil society, and the globalization of the international political economy. U.S. neoliberals believe that, in the era of globalization and massive political awakening, every traditional authoritarian regime (regardless of whether or not it is friendly toward the U.S.) entails significant political risks due to its weak popular legitimacy, and, therefore, they believe that, in the era of globalization and massive political awakening, the "Kirkpatrick doctrine" is of limited validity. Furthermore, U.S. neoliberals oppose all governments that are nationalist and/or aim at preserving great cultural traditions, since such governments do not facilitate the complete integration of humanity into the system of global

60. United States Department of State, *Papers Relating to the Foreign Relations of the United States, 1918: Russia.*

61. Jerry Hough and Merle Fainsod argue that, "even during the days of the desperate struggle for survival, the Bolsheviks seemed to demonstrate their dedication to modernity"; Hough and Fainsod, *How the Soviet Union Is Governed*, 89.

political economy that is promoted by the U.S. neoliberal elite. Thus, U.S. neoliberals aim at projecting their soft power on a global scale and at bringing about regime changes in several countries.

As a result of the soft-power doctrine and the neoliberals' ambition to establish a global political monologue, in the beginning of the twenty-first century, the U.S. started to withdraw its support from pro-U.S. authoritarian regimes, such as that of Hosni Mubarak in Egypt, even though the democratic elections that followed after the U.S.-supported Egyptian Revolution of 2013 brought Mohamed Morsi, a leading member of the Muslim Brotherhood, to power. Moreover, as a result of the soft-power doctrine and the neoliberals' ambition to establish a global political monologue, in 2011, the U.S. decided to overthrow Muammar Qaddafi's nationalist and socialist regime in Libya, even though Qaddafi had started to normalize Libya's relations with the U.K. and the U.S. since 1999, he condemned the September 11 attacks on the U.S. by Al Qaeda, he called for Libyan involvement in the War on Terror against jihadists, and he was always maintaining a tough stance on drug trade in West Africa. However, since Qaddafi was not a liberal, on April 30, 2011, NATO intervened in Libya in order to support rebel militia groups, even though the anti-Qaddafi forces included Salafists and terrorists belonging to the Al Qaeda in the Islamic Maghreb (an Algeria-based Sunni Muslim jihadist group). After the overthrow of Qaddafi's government and the lynch-mob murder of Qaddafi, carried out by U.S.-supported extremists, Libya slipped into chaos, and, on September 11, 2012, uncontrolled Libyan rebels who had previously been allied with the U.S. government in order to overthrow Qaddafi's regime, set the U.S. Consulate compound in Benghazi on fire; U.S. Ambassador Christopher Stevens and three other U.S. nationals were killed during the attack. On December 29, 2013, a lengthy front-page report in *The New York Times* provided additional confirmation that the attack on the U.S. Consulate in Benghazi, in September 2012, was the outcome of the Obama administration's use of jihadists in its war against the Libyan regime of Muammar Qaddafi. In particular, according to the previous *New York Times* article authored and signed by David D. Kirkpatrick, the attack was organized "by fighters who had benefited directly from NATO's extensive air power and logistics support during the uprising against Colonel Qaddafi."[62]

---

62. Kirkpatrick, "Deadly Mix in Benghazi."

Even though the Benghazi affair shows the risks of trying to buy durable loyalty and the difficulty of discerning friends from allies of convenience in non-Western countries, the Atlanticist elite has developed a scientifically rigorous methodology for the manipulation of the revolutionary phenomenon. In particular, in the U.S., there are institutes and private companies that train social rebels and activists in order to be used by the Atlanticist elite. For instance, Gene Sharp, the founder of the Albert Einstein Institution, a non-profit organization dedicated to advancing the study of non-violent action, and a professor emeritus of political science at the University of Massachusetts Dartmouth, has developed a methodology for training social rebels and activists who can bring about regime change without recourse to armed violence.[63] Moreover, in the U.S., a private company called Social Movement Laboratory, founded in 2005 by James D. Lomas, who has developed and taught social design courses at the University of California San Diego, offers consulting services to social rebels and activists.

In the Obama administration, there are extreme proponents of humanitarian interventionism, such as Susan Rice and Samantha Power. Susan Rice served as the 27th U.S. Ambassador to the United Nations during 2009–13, and, on July 1, 2013, U.S. President Barack Obama appointed her as the 24th National Security Advisor. On August 2, 2013, Obama appointed Samantha Power as the 28th U.S. Ambassador to the United Nations. Susan Rice and Samantha Power promoted the Obama administrations' policy of 'humanitarian war' in Libya. Before joining the Obama administration, Samantha Power worked for the International Crisis Group (ICG), an NGO supported by the Ford Foundation and George Soros's Open Society Institute. The ICG played an instrumental role in the dismantling of former Yugoslavia during the Clinton administration.

In the post-Cold War era, the globalist strategy of the Atlanticists and especially of the neoliberals is based on what I call 'advanced liberalism,' which is the highest stage of liberalism. The adherents of advanced liberalism argue that the model of liberal democracy is not just an ideology, but it is the only 'natural' and incontestable political system. In other words, in the era of advanced modernity, the political platform of the bourgeois liberals is not just an ideological option, but it is assumed to be a 'natural fact,' like the law of gravity; thus, liberalism evolved into

63. Sharp, *Politics of Nonviolent Action*.

'advanced liberalism,' which is a post-ideological phenomenon, or rather it is an attempt of an ideology to elevate itself to post-ideological status.

Liberalism 'liberates' the individual from every kind of collective identity and collective participation (e.g., traditional culture, religion, ethnicity, etc.), and it treats the individual as an ontologically sufficient foundation of values and truth. Thus, in the context of liberal globalization, the 'individual' as a historical subject is not simply a Western anthropological path and way of life, but it is a global duty. When man feels that he belongs only to the general collectivity of 'humanity,' or human species, and that all other partial collective identities are insignificant or, at best, one's private matters, a global imperial structure emerges, since citizens tend to accept the establishment of a global authority as the global guarantor of human rights.

Liberals' conception of global governance is based on a holistic and totalitarian reformulation of the terms under which political liberty is perceived. The institutions of global governance constitute an attempt to fill the political vacuum that is left by the decline of the nation-state in the context of the global market economy. Under these circumstances, the attempt to disintegrate every sovereignty-seeking collectivity into 'free individuals' is a political action. Therefore, Karl Polanyi has correctly argued that markets are socio-political constructs rather than simply rational interactions between economic agents.[64] Furthermore, the 'rights of the citizen' have the same conventional characteristics and the same individualistic orientation as any 'social contract' signed between a hegemon and his subjects. In the context of the emerging global community, into which the institutions of global governance and the 'citizens' of the world are symbolically and culturally integrated, the hegemon and his citizens organize their relations on the basis of norms which, like the Bill of Rights (1688), are the outcome of negotiations between the hegemon and the representatives of the social classes (or the 'peoples') of the imperium, and, furthermore, these norms have the form of 'concessions.'

In the stage of advanced liberalism, the attributes of good citizenship are derived from and based on legal instrumentalism, and they are politically insignificant. As a result of advanced liberalism's individualism, political freedom is fragmented into various particular freedoms, and, ultimately, it reduces to a 'private matter,' in the sense that it is not founded on a collectivity. Since, in the context of advanced liberalism, the multitude

64. Polanyi, *Great Transformation*.

does not constitute a form of socially determined political will, freedom is separated from the social field, in which it can be authentically exercised, and, thus, it is confined to the context of a submissive political relationship.

The spiritual conclusion of the aforementioned process is a type of self-complacent nihilism. In Latin, the word *nihilismus* consists of the negative prefix *ne* and the word *hilum*, which means cord. Thus, nihilism means lack of connection. When beings and things are not connected with each other, they do not constitute a *cosmos*, and, furthermore, they cannot be integrated into a spiritual hierarchy. A nihilist is a man who is spiritually unconnected, volatile, and, hence, spiritually unfounded. By transforming people into nihilistic individuals, advanced liberalism leads to the deconstruction of both logic and morality through postmodern-ism and post-industrial society. In the stage of advanced liberalism, ra-tionality, scientism, and positivism are severely criticized and discredited by postmodern scholars. For instance, Richard Rorty's book *Philosophy and the Mirror of Nature* is a 'deconstruction' of analytical philosophy, in the sense that it turns analytical philosophy against itself in order, ulti-mately, to justify a radical anti-foundationalist attitude typified by Rorty's description of his position as that of a "postmodern bourgeois liberal."[65]

Advanced liberalism leads to the total 'liberation' of the individual from logic and morality, and it confines humanity to a negative con-ception of liberty. In other words, advanced liberalism is concerned with 'freedom from,' but it is not concerned with the meaning or *telos* of freedom. Additionally, advanced liberalism rejects the very pursuit of the *telos* of existence, and it attempts to substitute lifestyle practices, Hollywood-Mass Media productions, technological gadgets, capitalist pursuits, financial imperatives, and activism focused on the rights of in-dividuals and imaginary minorities (e.g., the Gay-Lesbian-Transgender movement) for the *telos* of existence.

Finally, advanced liberalism leads to the creation of an Atlanti-cist empire, because it leads to the total individuation of the bearer of freedom, and, therefore, to an abstract conception of freedom; for in-stance, advanced liberalism abstracts freedom from the sphere of social relations. Through the universalization of the principle of 'human rights' (whose original goal was to undermine the societies of the Soviet Bloc), conscious beings are urged to advocate for the establishment of an 'ab-stract' international (but essentially Atlanticist) arbitration authority that

---

65. Rorty, "Postmodern Bourgeois Liberalism."

will be exclusively responsible for the world-wide dispensation of 'global justice' and will be directly legitimated by the physical 'individuals' and their rights. The previous 'liberation' vision of the Atlanticists was officially declared on September 11, 1990, by the then U.S. President George H. W. Bush in his address before a Joint Session of the Congress on the Persian Gulf Crisis and the Federal Budget Deficit. From the viewpoint of advanced liberalism, in 1990, the Atlanticist forces, acting on the basis of purely Anglo-Saxon traditions about the individual, society, and civilization, invaded Iraq in order to 'liberate' physical individuals living in a physical space that, due to local national mythology, is called 'Iraq,' from the Iraqi society and its political traditions. In general, through the ideology of 'human rights,' the Atlanticists aim at devaluating, manipulating, and, whenever deemed necessary, delegitimating every collective entity (such as culture, ethnicity, nation-state, religion, etc.) that comes between the physical individual and the globalist Atlanticist elite.

In the stage of advanced liberalism, liberalism has a right-wing apparatus, represented by liberal and modern Anglo-Saxon conservative parties, and a left-wing apparatus, whose ideology is known as third-way socialism or simply as the 'Third Way.' Thus, through its right-wing and left-wing political apparatuses, advanced liberalism aims at controlling the entire political spectrum and at eliminating or marginalizing every different political ideology. Third-way socialism or simply the 'Third Way' is an ideological trend of social democracy that aims at attaining a structural compromise between social democracy and advanced liberalism. The founder of third-way socialism is Anthony Giddens, Baron Giddens, a British sociologist who is known for his theory of "structuration" (an analysis of agency and structure) and his holistic approach to modern sciences.[66] Giddens served as Director of the London School of Economics from 1997 until 2003, and, in June 2004, he was given a life peerage as Baron Giddens and sits in the House of Lords for the Labor Party. The advocates of third-way socialism argue for a synthesis between liberalism and social democracy founded and centered on the ideological principles of the Enlightenment and on their opposition to pre-modern conservatism and to political extremes.

According to Anthony Giddens, third-way socialists promote a cooperation between social democrats and liberals in order to create a European society based on the ideology of 'human rights,' on the protection

66. Giddens, *Third Way*.

of private property rights, and on the existence of a pre-determined institutional framework within which governments will be obliged to function. In contrast to classical nineteenth-century social democrats and European communists, third-way socialists are positively disposed toward the United States, and they adhere to the Atlanticist geopolitical 'school.' Furthermore, third-way socialism helps the capitalist system to become morally and politically acceptable by all social classes, since third-way socialism cultivates the impression that the whole society participates, at least potentially, in the benefits of capitalism.

5

THE THREE BASIC THEORETICAL DEBATES IN INTERNATIONAL RELATIONS

THE FIRST GREAT DEBATE in the scholarly discipline of International Relations was that of idealism/utopianism versus political realism in the 1940s. The second great debate was behavioralism versus traditionalism in the 1950s and 1960s. In the late 1960s and throughout the 1970s, there was increasing criticism of political realism, which was the dominant paradigm. In particular, in the 1970s and in the beginning of the 1980s, the criticism of political realism was focused on its image of the world, its alleged state-centrism, its preoccupation with power relations, and its failure to address various kinds of processes domestically, transnationally, and beyond the political-military realm. Thus, the third great debate in the scholarly discipline of International Relations is known as the inter-paradigm debate among the following three paradigms: political realism, pluralism/interdependence, and Marxism/radicalism.

FIRST DEBATE: IDEALISM/UTOPIANISM VERSUS POLITICAL REALISM

The diplomatic tradition that was dominant in Europe from the seventeenth to the nineteenth centuries is known as *Realpolitik*. This tradition consists in two principles, which have been summarized by Henry A. Kissinger as follows: (1) the principle of *reason d'état* (state interest), according to which the interests of the state justify whatever means are necessary to pursue them, and "the success of a policy of reason d'état depends above all on the ability to assess power relationships"[1]; (2) the principle of the balance of power, which emerged from the principle of *reason d'état*: "states were no longer restrained by the pretense of a moral code. ... The stronger would seek to dominate and the weaker would resist by forming coalitions to augment their individual strengths,"[2] and, hence, if the coalition could check the aggressor, a balance of power emerged, but, if the coalition failed, some country would achieve hegemony. Thus, from the viewpoint of *Realpolitik*, the seeming anarchy of the international system gave rise to a self-equilibrated system, in the sense that, when any state threatened to become a hegemonic power in Europe, its neighbors formed a defensive coalition out of pure self-interest to deter the potential hegemon from actualizing his ambitions.[3]

The spirit of modern philosophy—especially Spinozism, Locke's empiricism, and Newton's world-conception—combined with the Enlightenment's faith in human reason were expressed in the field of International Relations through the concepts of 'balance of power,' 'national sovereignty,' and 'rationality.' Daniel Defoe (1660–1731), a young contemporary of John Locke, published several commentaries on international politics in his journal *Review*.[4] Defoe was an adherent of William of Orange, an early proponent and practitioner of balance-of-power politics, who had assumed the English throne in 1689. According to Defoe, although balance of power was "something we have made much ado about in the World," it was, nevertheless, "little understood"[5]; thus, he devoted many pages of his *Review* to the elucidation of balance-of-power politics.

Henry St. John, later Viscount Bolingbroke (1678–1751), a Tory politician, conducted methodical studies in European balance-of-power politics.[6] He had been Secretary of War under Queen Anne, and he played a key role in the Peace of Utrecht (1713), which signaled the end of French ambitions of hegemony in Europe expressed in the wars of Louis XIV and preserved the European system of balance of power.

1. Kissinger, *Diplomacy*, 63.
2. Ibid., 67.
3. Ibid., 69–70.
4. Roosen, *Daniel Defoe and Diplomacy*.
5. Defoe, *Review*, 263.
6. Plumb, *England*, 54.

The most influential proponent of balance-of-power politics in the eighteenth century was the Scottish philosopher David Hume, who wrote extensively on international politics. Hume's speculations on international politics are set out in his *History of England* and in his essays *Of the Balance of Trade* and *Of the Balance of Power*.[7]

Great Britain was most famous for its practice of a balance-of-power policy based on British empiricism, but France was the country in which the theory of balance of power was most systematically articulated. In 1700, François Fénelon (1651–1715) defended the balance-of-power principle on the basis of natural law in his essay *On the Necessity of Forming Alliances*.[8] In 1716, François de Gallières (1645–1717) wrote his seminal book *The Art of Diplomacy*, in which he argues that there is a self-equilibrating interstate system.[9]

A scientifically rigorous contribution to the international-political theory of the Enlightenment is due to Charles-Louis de Secondat Montesquieu, who was strongly influenced by Locke and Spinoza. His book *The Spirit of the Laws* is based on a mechanistic world-conception and on the principle of equilibrium.[10] Antoine Pecquet (1704–62) applied Montesquieu's political theory to the field of international relations. Pecquet's book *Spirit of Political Maxims* is an analysis of international relations pretentiously conceived as a sequel to Montesquieu's *The Spirit of the Laws*, and it provides an in-depth analysis of "the equilibrium of Europe."[11]

Furthermore, Montesquieu associated war with regime type. In his book *The Spirit of the Laws*, he argued that conflict and war are natural characteristics of political life, but also he asserted that monarchic regimes were prone to reinforce these characteristics of political life. As a consequence of Montesquieu's argument, if monarchic regimes are prone to war, then peace should be pursued through regime change (i.e., by establishing democratic republics). François-Marie Arouet Voltaire (1694–1778) realized and explicitly defended the previous implication of Montesquieu's political theory. In Voltaire's eyes, eighteenth-century

7. Van de Haar, "David Hume and International Political Theory."
8. Fénelon, "Alliances," 766 ff.
9. Keens-Soper and Schweizer, *Diplomacy*.
10. Pangle, *Classical Political Rationalism*.
11. Wright, *Balance of Power*.

wars were dynastic squabbles, and, in his *Philosophical Dictionary*, kings are held responsible for the evils of war.[12]

Like Voltaire, Charles-Irénée Castel, Abbé de Saint-Pierre (1658–1743) studied the question of war and peace in connection with regime types and especially in connection with the princes of Europe. Saint-Pierre's *Project for Making Peace Perpetual in Europe* is founded on the culture of the Enlightenment; in other words, on the theses that men, including princes, are endowed with reason and that reason will, sooner or later, force the princes of Europe to realize that their interests are better served by peace and order than by war. According to Saint-Pierre, this realization would rationally drive the rulers of Europe into closer co-operation and, finally, into a European confederation, i.e., a council or diet on which the ruling princes of all member states would be represented.[13] Additionally, Saint-Pierre endorsed the characteristic Enlightenment belief that trade promotes peace.[14]

On the other hand, Jean-Jacques Rousseau, in the context of his revolt against reason, rejected the argument that trade promotes peace, and he defended quite the opposite thesis.[15] Additionally, he rejected Saint-Pierre's argument that the kings of Europe would abandon war once they realized that peace was in their best interest, and he argued that kings are rational actors pursuing their 'interest,' but they would always define their 'interest' in terms of military achievements and enlargements of their domains.[16] According to Rousseau, rulers are greedy and they are motivated by the desires to extend their territorial power and to enhance their authority over their subjects. From Rousseau's viewpoint, the citizens are alienated, and, therefore, they contribute resources to support wars of conquest and the subjection of conquered peoples, without realizing that they thereby aggravate their own misery.

In his *Plan for Perpetual Peace*, Rousseau argues that the European balance of power is a system founded on common religion, international law, common standards, common letters, and on international trade.[17] From Rousseau's viewpoint, this equilibrium is more a product of na-

12. Voltaire, *Philosophical Dictionary*.

13. Archibugi, "Models of International Organization." Perkins, *Abbé de Saint-Pierre*.

14. Perkins, *Abbé de Saint-Pierre*.

15. Rousseau, *Discourses*, and *Social Contract*.

16. Rousseau, *Perpetual Peace*.

17. Ibid.

ture than the product of man's initiatives. Furthermore, according to Rousseau, geographical factors (e.g., mountains, seas, rivers, etc.) have naturally fixed the number and the size of European powers.[18] Thus, due to Europe's cultural geography, although rulers of individual states always act to extend their territorial power, balance obtains.[19]

Moreover, in his *Plan for Perpetual Peace*, Rousseau argues that the 'law of the strongest' only partially accounts for the relative order of the European international system. Balance-of-power arrangements can only explain the mechanical workings of the European international system. Rousseau argues that, in order to understand European politics, one must also realize that the foundation of the European international system is the Treaty of Westphalia (1648), which recognized the right of European rulers to act on the calculus of their own interest. Rousseau maintains that the authority of European rulers *within* states is not unlimited, and it keeps in check mutually competing individuals, but the relations *among* states constitute an anarchic system, in the sense that there is no higher authority to regulate the interaction of states. According to Rousseau, peace can be secured only if the states of Europe give up their sovereignty in favor of a higher, federal political entity, i.e., only if the states of Europe establish a social contract among them.[20]

In France and Great Britain, each of which was a big and unified state, the Enlightenment triggered social revolutions. On the other hand, in Germany, which was fragmented into many tiny states and principalities, apart from Prussia, which was ruled by the powerful regime of Frederick the Great, the Enlightenment gave rise to abstract ideas and to political theories that seek to transcend the level of the human individual. French and British Enlightenment emphasizes individuality on the basis of Cartesian and empiricist arguments, whereas German Enlightenment emphasizes individuality on the basis of Kantianism and Hegelianism.

In 1740, Crown Prince Frederick of Prussia published his treatise *Anti-Machiavel*, in which he attempted to refute the doctrines set out in Niccolò Machiavelli's book *The Prince*. In his book, Crown Prince Frederick of Prussia argues that he comes "to the defence of humanity against this monster who would destroy it," and he undertakes "to oppose reason and justice to inquiry and crime . . . so that the antidote may

18. Ibid.
19. Ibid.
20. Ibid.

be found next to the poison."[21] According to Frederick the Great, who was a proponent of 'enlightened despotism,' the 'enlightened despot' is a monarch who embraces the principles of the Enlightenment, especially its emphasis upon rationality, and he applies them to his territory. Thus, 'enlightened despots'—such as Frederick the Great, Charles III of Spain, Catherine II of Russia, Gustav III of Sweden, Joseph I of Portugal, Joseph II of Austria, Louis XVI of France, etc.—tend to allow religious toleration, freedom of speech and the press, and the right to hold property, and they foster the arts, sciences, and education. Thus, Frederick the Great declared: "My principal occupation is to combat ignorance and prejudice ... to enlighten minds, cultivate morality, and to make people as happy as it suits human nature, and as the means at my disposal permit."[22]

As I argued in chapter 3, Kant rejected pre-modern metaphysics, according to which equilibrium derives from and is founded on God, and he argued that human reason and human intentionality are ontologically sufficient foundations of international peace. Moreover, Hegel distanced himself from pre-modern metaphysics, and, as I argued in chapter 3, he articulated his own rationalist political theory through historicism. In the scholarly discipline of International Relations, political realism consists in a theory focused on power politics and balance-of-power arrangements, and it is philosophically founded on Cartesianism (especially on Spinozism) and British empiricism, whereas idealism/utopianism emphasizes abstract principles, and, depending on its variety, it is philosophically founded either on Kant or on Hegel.

The European system of balance of power dramatically collapsed in 1914, when World War I began. The inability of the European system of balance of power to safeguard a sort of equilibrium became clear due to the following reasons:

(1) The power of Germany increased at extremely high levels vis-à-vis the power of Great Britain.[23] In particular, at the beginning of the twentieth century, the growth of the German GNP was twice that of Great Britain. Moreover, in the middle of the nineteenth century, Great Britain had one-quarter of the world's industrial production, but by 1913 that had been reduced to 10 percent, whereas Germany's share had risen to 15 percent. Germany used its industrial strength in order to increase its military ca-

21. Fredrick II, *Anti-Machiavel*, 31.
22. MacDonogh, *Frederick the Great*, 341.
23. Nye, *International Conflicts*, 59–61.

pability. Great Britain reacted to the rise of Germany's power by changing its diplomacy. In particular, in 1904, Great Britain ceased to function as the balancer[24] of the European balance of power, and it established an alliance with France. In 1907, the Anglo-French partnership broadened to include Russia, thus giving rise to the Triple Entente. As a reaction to the Triple Entente, Germany tightened its relations with Austro-Hungary. These two alliances were becoming more and more rigid, and, therefore, the diplomatic flexibility which was underpinning the European balance was lost. The traditional European balance was based on shifting alignments which were not allowing any country to achieve hegemony. After 1907, this was not the case any more. The major powers were divided in two rigid alliances.

Two more factors contributed to the loss of flexibility in the early twentieth century balance of power. For about forty years, the great powers had not been involved in a major war in Europe, and, therefore, they had the impression that the established system could continue automatically deterring long and major wars. On the other hand, the diplomacy of all great powers was founded on a simplistic application of Darwin's principle of survival of the fittest in politics, and, therefore, the diplomacy of each and every great power was becoming more and more egocentric (i.e., more and more nationalistic) and short-sighted. Another factor which contributed to the loss of flexibility in the early-twentieth-century balance of power was the confusing and vague character of Germany's diplomacy. In particular, Germany was pursuing its "world ambitions" by antagonizing all other great powers at the same time.[25] As the British diplomat and historian Sir Eyre Crowe (1864–1925) has pointed out, Great Britain, France and Russia failed to understand on time the "world ambitions" of Germany, and they complacently believed that a long war was unlikely and that short wars won by the strong would not cause unwelcome consequences. However, in his 1907 *Memorandum on the Present State of British Relations with France and Germany*, Sir Eyre Crowe opposed appeasement of Germany by arguing that the policy of giving way to the blackmailer's

24. In the eighteenth and the nineteenth centuries, Great Britain was the one European country whose *reason d'état* did not require it to expand in Europe, and, therefore, it was perceiving its national interest to be in the preservation of the European balance of power. Kissinger, *Diplomacy*, 70.

25. Germany antagonized Great Britain by starting a naval arms race, it antagonized France over a protectorate in Morocco, and it antagonized Russia over issues in the Ottoman Empire.

menaces in order to satisfy him and secure thereby temporary peace leads to renewed molestation and higher demands.[26]

(2) Changes in the domestic society and politics of the Austro-Hungarian and the Ottoman Empires and of Germany undermined the efficiency of the European balance of power.[27] In particular, the Austro-Hungarian and the Ottoman Empires were multinational empires, and, therefore, their integrity was threatened by the rise of nationalism. The Treaty of London, which was signed on May 30, 1913 to deal with territorial adjustments arising out of the conclusion of the First Balkan War,[28] officially terminated the five-century rule of the Ottoman Empire in the Balkans.

In addition, German social problems were important contributors to the outbreak of World War I. According to Fritz Fischer, Germany was ruled by a domestic coalition of landed aristocrats and very large industrial capitalists.[29] This domestic political and economic elite followed expansionist policies in order to overcome the problems of the established socio-economic system without having to reform it substantially and in order to react against mounting socialism,[30] which was threatening the German political and economic establishment.

However, the aforementioned factors are not enough in order to articulate a complete explanation of the collapse of the European balance of power. The previous factors describe the collapse of the balance of power, but they do not really explain why that system collapsed. According to the above analysis, the European balance of power collapsed because: (1) the hegemonic tendency of Germany was not deterred by the creation of the adequate alliance, (2) the alliance system became rigid, and (3) domestic political and economic developments in certain great powers influenced their capabilities and the manner in which they defined and pursued their national interest. The previous factors describe *how* exactly the European balance of power collapsed, but they do not explain *why* this happened.

---

26. Nye, *International Conflicts*, 59.

27. Ibid., 62–63.

28. The First Balkan War broke out on October 8, 1912, when Bulgaria, Greece, Montenegro, and Serbia, having large parts of their ethnic populations under Ottoman sovereignty, attacked the Ottoman Empire.

29. Fischer, *Germany's Aims*.

30. In 1912, the Social-Democratic Party became the biggest party in the German Parliament.

The reason why the European balance of power collapsed is because *Realpolitik* (or the balance-of-power system) is inherently unable to provide a viable international peace. *Realpolitik* is philosophically founded on modern Western individualism, whose varieties I attempted to elucidate in chapter 3. Under *Realpolitik*, states' behaviors serve the logic of selfish historical goals, and they are based on the calculation of necessities of policy which arise from the unregulated competition among them. The calculation of necessities of policy can only temporarily harness the selfish soul of the state, and, therefore, it can only create a temporary and fragile balance between imperialist passion and rationality, because the calculation of necessities cannot endow states with that form of social consciousness which would enable states to create sustainable anti-hegemonic alliances and equilibria. According to the system of balance of power, the state, with its selfish goals and ambitions, is the ultimate criterion of balance-of-power politics. Since the state, with its selfish goals and ambitions, is the ultimate criterion of balance-of-power politics, *Realpolitik* continually increases the ego-centrism of the state, and, therefore, it continually decreases the ability of the state to create sustainable international alliances in order to keep the international system in equilibrium.

Woodrow Wilson (1856–1924), the American President during World War I, openly blamed balance-of-power politics for the war. According to Wilson, "the balance of power is the great game now forever discredited. It's the old and evil order that prevailed before this war. World War I was to do away with an old order, one that was unstable."[31] Woodrow Wilson correctly pointed out that balance-of-power politics is unstable, since, from the viewpoint of *Realpolitik*, the state makes war, and war makes the state.[32] However, Woodrow Wilson did not completely understand the contradictory nature of balance-of-power politics. Therefore, instead of emphasizing that balance-of-power politics weakens the social consciousness of states as members of the international system and, eventually, makes them too ego-centric to make the necessary collective decisions in order to avoid war and preserve order, Woodrow Wilson emphasized the need to strengthen the right of national self-determination beyond the limits imposed by a balance-of-power system. In other words, Wilson correctly argued that balance-of-power politics is not successful, even according to its own criteria (i.e., in preserving order), but Wilson's

31. Nye, *International Conflicts*, 74.
32. Tilly, *Coercion, Capital and European States*.

own proposal was the invigoration of the ego-centrism of the states and not the strengthening of their social consciousness.

Woodrow Wilson's political idealism/utopianism was philosophically inspired by Kantianism. Thus, whereas, in balance-of-power politics, alliances were created against any state which was becoming too strong, Wilson's doctrine of collective security was focused on the aggressive policies/intentions of a state rather than its capacity. However, in both cases, the individual state is the ultimate criterion of the international system. Wilson's doctrine of collective security was not aiming at restoring the centrality of medieval universals (God), but it aimed at promoting an idealistic approach to national self-determination and at establishing a Kantian system of morality. In Wilson's system, legal procedure, especially compliance with the Covenant of the League of Nations,[33] and arbitration within the framework of the League of Nations are regarded as ontologically sufficient foundations of world peace and as substitutes for the 'Absolute.'

Since the system of collective security which was established after the end of World War I failed to overcome the fundamental antinomy of *Realpolitik* (which dictates the need for international alliances and simultaneously weakens states' social consciousness, since, from the perspective of *Realpolitik*, the state is regarded as the ultimate criterion of the international system), it was unable to safeguard a viable international order. Thus, when Hitler's Germany decided to disregard the political pretexts of the League of Nations and execute a ruthless plan of national-interest maximization, the institutions of collective diplomacy proved to be unable to deter German expansionism, and they misguided Chamberlain's Great Britain, which followed a policy of appeasement toward Germany.[34] However, in contrast to Arthur N. Chamberlain's political calculations, appeasement was the wrong approach to Adolf Hitler, and, thus, World War II was not prevented.

BEHAVIORALISM VERSUS TRADITIONALISM

In modern International Relations, the two major contending approaches to the epistemology and methodology of International Relations are known as 'traditionalism' and 'behavioralism.' In the context of the

33. Wilson's doctrine of collective security was embodied in the Covenant of the League of Nations.

34. Bell, *The Second World War in Europe.*

epistemology and methodology of International Relations, traditionalism is an epistemological 'school' according to which the International Relations scholar should rest on his findings and interpretations and on historical analogies, and also he should trust his personal training and experience in order to glean from all the data the relative meanings that are contained in them. On the other hand, behavioralism is an epistemological 'school' according to which personal judgment (regardless of one's training and experience) is only a beginning, and the International Relations scholar is compelled to proceed beyond personal judgments in order to render his findings as scientifically objective as possible. Thus, the behavioralist prefers to use formal methods of analysis (logic and mathematics) whenever possible in order to build scientifically rigorous models of international systems or situations; Richardson's arms race model, Lanchester's model of battles, Decision Theory, Game Theory, Catastrophe Theory, Chaos Theory, and Artificial Intelligence are the most characteristic behavioralist approaches to the use of formal methods of analysis in International Relations.[35]

The antithesis between the epistemological 'schools' of traditionalism and behavioralism corresponds to the antithesis between anti-rationalist/anti-positivist philosophies and rationalist/positivist philosophies. Behavioralists argue that social behavior can be explained in similar ways to natural (i.e., inanimate) behavior (i.e., in terms of causal laws).[36] In the twentieth century, Carl G. Hempel, the principal proponent of the "covering law" theory of explanation, played a key role in the formation of 'logical empiricism,' and Nobel Prize-winning economist Milton Friedman was a pioneer of the application of 'logical empiricism' in economics.[37] On the other hand, the opponents of behavioralism, such as the British philosophers Robin G. Collingwood and Peter Winch, reject the idea of a scientific *explanation* of social behavior on the grounds that, unlike physical objects, human beings interpret their behavior, and, therefore, we have to *understand* behavior in terms in which the actors themselves understand it.[38]

The major defect of behavioralism is that, inspired by British empiricism and physiocracy, it assigns a passive role to human consciousness. John Searle has argued that, even though he admits that consciousness is

35. Bennett and Nicholson, "Formal Methods."
36. Nicholson and Bennett, "Epistemology of International Relations."
37. Nicholson, *Causes and Consequences.*
38. Hollis and Smith, *Explaining and Understanding.*

a higher state of the brain, man's conscious mental states and processes have a peculiar characteristic that is not possessed by other natural phenomena (i.e., subjectivity), and, therefore, conventional methods of biological and physiological research cannot be applied in the study of consciousness.[39] However, the so-called traditionalist epistemological 'school' as it is represented by Collingwood and Winch is based on nominalism and on Ludwig Wittgenstein's analytical philosophy, and, therefore, from the perspective of the arguments that I put forward in chapter 3, both the traditionalist and the behavioralist epistemological 'schools' are derived from the same Western principle, which is the spiritual core of Western civilization; namely, from the principle of individual truth, according to which consciousness (regardless of whether it is scientific or traditionalist) is an ontologically sufficient foundation of truth.

On the other hand, from the perspective of the arguments that I put forward in chapters 1 and 2, ancient and medieval Greek metaphysics leads to a teleological approach to the problem of knowledge. According to the arguments that I have put forward so far about Plato, Aristotle, and the Hesychasts, the study of human systems should be focused on the manner in which actors give meaning to their actions; that is, it should be focused on the *telos* of historicity.

In ancient Greek, *kairos* literally means the 'opportune moment,' a moment in which things are possible, and, in ancient Greek mythology, Kairos was a son of Zeus. Aesop[40] writes that Kairos was running swiftly, balancing on the razor's edge, he was bald, but there was a lock of hair on his forehead, so that, if one grasps Kairos from the front, he might be able to hold him, but, once Kairos has moved on, no one can pull him back. In his *Description of Greece*, 5.14.9, the famous Greek travelogue Pausanias writes that Ion of Khios (fifth-century B.C. poet) wrote a hymn to Kairos and that, quite close to the entrance to the stadium at Olympia, there was the altar of Kairos. In his *Descriptions*, 6, Callistratus (a Greek rhetorician who flourished in the third/fourth century A.D.) described a bronze statute of Kairos at Sikyon, and he mentioned that the lock of hair on Kairos's forehead indicated that he is easy to catch as he approaches, but, when he has passed by, the moment of action has likewise expired.

The notion of *kairos* helps us to transcend the antithesis between 'explanation' and 'understanding.' Through the notion of *kairos*, ancient

39. Searle, *Rediscovery of the Mind*, 90–93.
40. Aesop, *Fables*, 536.

Greeks recognized and respected the existential otherness of the reality of the world, but simultaneously they realized that man can act in order to pursue goals and, therefore, transform his existential conditions. According to Evanghelos Moutsopoulos, the notion of *kairos* (opportune moment) is combined with Aristotle's notion of *metron* (right measure), and it appears under the form of the temporal categories 'not yet' or 'too early' and 'never again' or 'too late.'[41]

From the perspective of Plotinus's *On Time and Eternity* and from the perspective of the Hesychasts' notion of man's participation in the uncreated energies of God, *kairos* is not merely a 'proper moment' to act according to one's intentionality, but it is the exclusive 'temporal point' at which the continuity of temporality is substituted by the discontinuity that is caused by the presence of 'eternity' in time, and, thus, time undergoes a fundamental qualitative change. In Neoplatonic sense, this process does not mean 'exit' from time, but rather the transfiguration of 'horizontal time' into 'vertical time.' In the context of Eastern Christianity's Hesychastic tradition, the church fathers spoke about the moment of enlightenment of the mind that comes as a result of a process of psychic cleansing that culminates in the vision of God as uncreated light. From the Hesychasts' perspective, *kairos* can be interpreted as the meeting point of *ens creatum* (created being) and *ens increatum* (uncreated being).

According to Plotinus and the Hesychasts, history is not a deterministic chain of events. Moreover, in his *Republic*, Plato argues that "the fault lies not with God, but with the soul that makes the choice."[42] Thus, historical action can transform the nature of time under the condition that man is oriented toward the idea. For this reason, classical Greek philosophers argue that man's participation in the universal meaning of beings and things is a creative act, and, more specifically, it is the essence of 'creativity.' As a consequence, the elucidation of human systems transcends both the traditionalist and the behavioralist epistemological 'schools,' and it consists in a methodical enquiry into the manner in which historical actors relate to time and eternity.

41. Moutsopoulos, "Kairos."
42. Plato, *Republic*, 617e.

THE TRIPLE INTER-PARADIGM DEBATE

In the scholarly discipline of International Relations, it is widely argued that there are three paradigms, three major 'schools.' The first is the realist paradigm, and it has two varieties: classical realism, and neorealism/ structural realism; the second paradigm is alternately called pluralism, interdependence, and world society, and, additionally, it is often regarded as the liberal paradigm (and it includes neoliberalism); the third paradigm is Marxism or more broadly radicalism.[43]

The level of analysis with which classical realism[44] is concerned is state-centric, but neorealism[45] recognizes and emphasizes the significance of structural causes. Classical realists, such as Edward H. Carr, Hans J. Morgenthau, and Reinhold Niebuhr, argue that, in international politics, states are the basic actors, and the machinations of international politics are reducible to human nature and to the behavior of the state, which, according to classical realists, is a rational actor seeking to maximize its own interest or national objectives in foreign policy.[46] However, neorealists/structural realists, such as Kenneth N. Waltz, argue that structural constraints (regardless of the state's strategy, ethos, and intentions) condition behavior in international relations. In particular, according to neorealism, the nature of the international structure is defined by its ordering principle (namely, anarchy, i.e., lack of world government) and by the distribution of capabilities (which gives rise to a specific balance-of-power arrangement). Both classical realists and neorealists agree that national interests exist objectively, international relations is the realm of recurrence (i.e., it is based on timeless laws), relations among states are basically conflictual/competitive, and national security is the top political issue in international relations. Furthermore, according to Michael Banks, political realism can be regarded as a "billiard ball model," where the 'billiard balls' represent states.[47]

The level of analysis with which pluralism/interdependence[48] is concerned is multi-centric, in the sense that this paradigm holds that, in international relations, there are numerous politically significant sub-

43. Kauppi and Viotti, *Global Philosophers*.

44. Rosenau, *Foreign Policy*.

45. Waltz, *Theory of International Politics*.

46. Viotti and Kauppi, *International Relations Theory*.

47. Banks, "The Inter-Paradigm Debate."

48. Rosenau, *Foreign Policy*.

state, trans-state, and non-state actors (e.g., multi-national corporations, international organizations, transnational NGOs, etc.). According to pluralism/interdependence, actors do not actually maximize their utility functions; foreign-policy making and transnational relations involve conflict, bargaining, coalition, and compromise, and they do not necessarily result in optimal outcomes.[49] Moreover, pluralism/interdependence makes the following assertions: perceptions and roles are characterized by subjectivity, academic analysis should aim at helping actors to find rational and optimal policy, the top international-political issues include several goals other than national security (e.g., welfare), international relations is not the realm of recurrence, but change and possibly 'progress' can happen in international relations, and, furthermore, relations among states are potentially co-operative, and non-state actors often mitigate conflict, and they increase the complexity of the international system. Michael Banks argues that pluralism/interdependence can be regarded as a "cobweb model," thus emphasizing transnationalism.[50] In the 1980s, pluralism/interdependence started evolving into what I earlier called advanced liberalism, which, in the scholarly discipline of International Relations, is often referred to as neoliberalism.

During the 1980s, realism became neorealism, which is focused on Waltz's concern with "a small number of big and important things," emphasizing a scientific study of international structure, and on Waltz's admission that "structures condition behaviors and outcomes, yet explanations of behaviors and outcomes are indeterminate because both unit-level and structural causes are in play."[51] Moreover, during the 1980s, pluralism/interdependence followed the path of scientific minimalism, too, and it became neoliberal institutionalism, which is focused on "how institutions affect incentives facing states," emphasizing "the pervasive significance of international institutions without denigrating the role of state power."[52] Thus, in the 1980s, in the scholarly discipline of International Relations, realism and liberalism were not mutually competitive paradigms any more, but, on the contrary, they shared a conception of science and a rationalist attitude toward international politics, and they both endorsed the neorealist premise of anarchy (as it has been formu-

49. Viotti and Kauppi, *International Relations Theory.*
50. Banks, "The Inter-Paradigm Debate."
51. Waltz, "Reflections," 343.
52. Keohane, *International Institutions and State Power,* 5, 11.

lated by Kenneth N. Waltz) and the neoliberal investigation of institutional issues and the evolution of co-operative systems (as it has been proposed by Robert Keohane). In other words, in the 1980s, the scholarly discipline of International Relations entered into a new phase of development characterized by the pursuit of a synthesis between neorealism and neoliberalism.[53]

The level of analysis with which the third paradigm (i.e., Marxism/radicalism) is concerned is global-centric, in the sense that, according to Marxism/radicalism, the basic international actors are the capitalist world economy and classes. From the viewpoint of Marxism/radicalism, the state represents class interests, relations within and among states are conflictual (because the class struggle is the main political pattern), the top international issues are economic factors, and, therefore, International Relations theory should be focused on patterns of dominance within and among states.[54] Michael Banks argues that the Marxist approach to international relations can be regarded as an "octopus model," the head of the 'octopus' being the capitalist world economy.[55] Moreover, according to Marxism/radicalism, economic structures are stable and consistent, but, in capitalism, political actors suffer by what Karl Marx has called "false consciousness," i.e., they are unable to see things, especially exploitation, oppression, and social relations, as they really are.

As a result of the emphasis that Marxist scholars place on the interplay between power relationships and "false consciousness," both Marxism and postmodernism can be placed in the same broadly called radical political space. Postmodernists' criticism of rationalist, Western, essentialist theories is an attack against Marxism, too, and some Marxists argue that postmodernism is ultimately reactionary and a plot of the establishment against Marxism. But, on the other hand, both postmodernism and Marxism are Western extreme contenders, and, from the 1980s onward, the borders between Marxism and postmodernism have become less rigid and more permeable, since postmodernism has started replacing classical Marxism, and several scholars have started theorizing a synthesis between Marxism and postmodernism.[56]

53. Baldwin, *Neorealism and Neoliberalism.* Buzan et al., *Logic of Anarchy.* Keohane and Martin, "Institutionalist Theory." Lamy, "Contemporary Mainstream Approaches."

54. Viotti and Kauppi, *International Relations Theory.*

55. Banks, "The Inter-Paradigm Debate."

56. Gibson-Graham et al., *Re/presenting Class.*

6

GEOPOLITICS

THE CONCEPT OF GEOPOLITICS

THE SCHOLARLY DISCIPLINE OF geography is concerned with the spatial analysis of the natural and human phenomena, area studies, the study of the man-land relationship, and research in the Earth sciences.[1] Political geography, in particular, is the scientific study of the state as a spatial phenomenon. On the other hand, geopolitics is the spatial study of inter-state relations and the changes in the political map as a whole.

The father of geography is the Greek mathematician, geographer, poet, astronomer, and music theorist Eratosthenes of Cyrene (c.276–c.195/94 B.C.). The founder of modern political geography was the German geographer Friedrich Ratzel. According to Ratzel, political geography is the study of the state as a "space organism."[2] Furthermore, Ratzel argues that space (*Raum*) and position (*Lage*) are the two principal determinants of the destiny of the state. From Ratzel's viewpoint, each state has its needs, but adequate living space (*Lebensraum*) for a state's population and the physical and human resources that are controlled by a state determine if a state will actually manage to evolve into a great world power. In general, according to Ratzel, the acquisition of adequate living space for a state's population necessitates territorial expansion, even if this implies recourse to war.

In the 1890s, the Swedish political scientist Johan Rudolf Kjellén coined the term 'geopolitics' (*Geopolitik*). Kjellén was strongly influenced

1. Pattison, "The Four Traditions of Geography."
2. Ratzel, *Politische Geographie*.

by Ratzel, and he defined geopolitics as a scholarly discipline that "conceives of the state as a geographical organism or as a phenomenon in space."[3] Ratzel, Kjellén, Alexander von Humboldt, and Karl Ritter are the founders of the German geopolitical thought, which, in the first decades of the twentieth century, was espoused and promoted by the German general and geopolitician Karl Ernst Haushofer, who was the mentor of Rudolf Hess, Adolf Hitler's Deputy Führer. Haushofer argued that Germany, being relatively small and densely populated, had to acquire additional *Lebensraum* in order to increase its power.[4] According to Haushofer's geopolitical analysis of Germany, Germany's power should be based on a strong and supportive *Mitteleuropa*, i.e., on the geopolitical expansion of Germany in Central Europe.

The extent to which and the manner in which geography affects politics are consequences of fundamental cultural choices that are made by policy-makers. For instance, a policy-maker can seek additional economic resources through territorial expansion (a geographical way) or, alternatively, through scientific progress[5] (a spiritual way). Moreover, one may conceive of the human being as a geographically and biologically determined being or, alternatively, as the royal species of the Earth and, therefore, as the master of geography and biology.

If we separate human life from spirit, specifically from everything that transcends material reality and is not reducible to merely biological factors, then geography takes precedence over ontology, ethics, institutions, and science (pure and applied), and the geography of the territory that is occupied by a political community molds political thought. Whereas the Bible states that "God created the heavens and the earth"[6] and that both the "land" and the "seas" are manifestations of God's will,[7] geopolitics divides the world into mutually conflicting geopolitical poles and interprets conflict and war as naturally (i.e., 'geographically') determined phenomena. Furthermore, in contrast to the Bible, which states that man was created in the image of God,[8] and in contrast to Plato's

---

3. Kjellén, *Der Staat als Lebensform*, 24.

4. Dickinson, *German Lebensraum.*

5. Paul M. Romer, Professor of Economics at Stanford University, argues that ideas and technological discoveries are the driving engines of economic growth. Romer, "Endogenous Technological Change."

6. Gen 1:1.

7. Gen 1:9–12.

8. Gen 1:26.

argument that man should be oriented toward the "this region beyond the skies," which is "the abode of the reality with which true knowledge is concerned, a reality without color or shape, intangible,"[9] geopolitics interprets man as a geographically and biologically determined being.

If we restrict our thought to geopolitics alone, then we assume that political actors have very elementary personalities. It is one thing to say that geography does not allow the human being to make arbitrary choices and another to claim that the history of a political community is determined by the geography of the territory that it occupies.

THE ATLANTICIST 'SCHOOL' OF GEOPOLITICS

A great pioneer of the Atlanticist 'school' of geopolitics was Alfred T. Mahan, a U.S. Navy flag officer, geostrategist, and historian, who has been called "the most important American strategist of the nineteenth century."[10] Mahan asserts that the key issues of geopolitics are the global dichotomy of land and sea power, and the importance of sea power for the security of the world's great maritime states, thus emphasizing the commercial usage of the sea in peace and the sea's control in war.[11] These themes were taken up by the English geographer Sir Halford J. Mackinder, the first Principal of University Extension College, Reading (which became the University of Reading) and Director of the London School of Economics. Mackinder is one of the most influential founders of geopolitics and geostrategy. According to Mackinder, the underlying theme running through world history is the conflict between the two geopolitical poles: sea power and land power.[12]

According to Mackinder's geopolitical terminology, there are two basic poles (i.e., the pole of sea power and the pole of land power) and the Earth's land surface is divided into the "World-Island" (which comprises the interlinked continents of Europe, Asia, and Africa, and it is the largest, most populous, and richest of all combinations of land power), the "Offshore Islands" (including the British Isles and the isles of Japan), and the "Outlying Islands" (including the continents of North America, South America, and Australia). Mackinder maintains that the natural

9. Plato, *Phaedrus*, 247c–e.
10. Keegan, *American Civil War*, 272.
11. Mahan, *Sea Power*.
12. Mackinder, "The Geographical Pivot of History."

repository for land power is the Eurasian "Heartland," or the "Pivot Area," which stretches from the Volga River to the Yangtze River and from the Himalayas to the Arctic; thus, it corresponds to the area ruled by the twentieth-century Russian Empire and after that by the Soviet Union except for its far eastern section. In his book *Democratic Ideals and Reality*, Mackinder put forward the following argument: "Who rules East Europe commands the Heartland; who rules the Heartland commands the World-Island; who rules the World-Island commands the world."[13] Moreover, Mackinder called the regions in Europe, Asia, and the Middle East that border the Heartland "the Inner or Marginal Crescent," and he placed the remaining land areas of the globe, which include Great Britain, Japan, Australia, North America, and South America, in the "Outer Crescent" of his geopolitical map.

Immediately after World War II, Nicholas J. Spykman, a Sterling Professor of International Relations at Yale University, refined Mackinder's strategy to adapt it to the conditions of the Cold War. Based on Mackinder's geopolitical divisions of the world, Spykman divided the world into the following geopolitical spaces: the "Heartland," the "Rimland" (which corresponds to Mackinder's "Inner or Marginal Crescent"), and the "Offshore Islands and Continents" (corresponding to Mackinder's "Outer Crescent"). According to Spykman, Mackinder had overrated the Heartland's power potential. From Spykman's viewpoint, the Heartland was not a region that would be unified by powerful transportation or communication infrastructure in the near future, and, therefore, it would be unable to compete with the United States' sea power. According to Spykman, the Heartland, could not offer the Soviet Union anything more than a uniquely defensive position. In his book *The Geography of the Peace*, Spykman argues that the key region of world politics was the Rimland (i.e., the intermediate region lying between the Heartland and the Marginal Crescent sea powers). Spykman noted that the Rimland (i.e., Western Europe, the Middle East, Southeast Asia, China, and the Far East) together with the offshore islands of Great Britain and Japan possessed greater industrial and manpower resources than the Heartland, and they wielded both land and sea power. Furthermore, Spykman noted that the three most recent aspirations to world hegemony (namely, Napoleon's France, Wilhelmline Germany, and Nazi Germany) all emerged from the Rimland and that, in each instance, a coalition of powers from different

---

13. Mackinder, *Democratic Ideals and Reality*, 194.

geopolitical spaces (from the Rimland, offshore islands, the Heartland, and America) was necessary in order for the strongest Rimland power to be defeated. In his book *America's Strategy in World Politics*, Spykman argued that the great geopolitical threat to the U.S. has been the possibility that the Rimland would be dominated by a single power, and he argued that "who controls the Rimland rules Eurasia."[14]

In the post-Cold War era, the U.S. geostrategist Zbigniew Brzezinski has emphasized that the geopolitical pole of sea power (i.e., the Atlanticist pole) must prevent Russia from re-unifying the Eurasian Heartland (i.e., the former Soviet space) and from achieving a geopolitically preponderant role in the Rimland.[15] In the post-Cold War era, under President Vladimir Putin, Russia strives to control the Heartland from within, i.e., it strives to geopolitically re-unify the former Soviet space; additionally, it strives to project its geopolitical power in the Rimland through the Russian gas pipelines to Europe. Thus, Brzezinski argues that Ukraine, Azerbaijan, South Korea, Turkey, and Iran are critically important geopolitical pivots and must be controlled by the Atlanticist pole in order to help NATO to control the Heartland from without.[16]

Furthermore, as I argued in chapter 5, after the end of the ideological war between the American camp and the Soviet camp, an ideologically unipolar world emerged by virtue of the global spread and domination of a Western, primarily American, model of liberal democracy, market capitalism, and utilitarianism. The previous model was methodically described and glorified by the American political scientist Francis Fukuyama in his controversial book *The End of History and the Last Man*. In that book, Fukuyama, in Hegelian fashion, declared "the end of history," in the sense that, according to his analysis, after the end of the Cold War, there was no alternative to the ideology of the American camp, and the whole world was ideologically united.

Fukuyama's argument about "the end of history" was narrow-minded, and soon it was refuted by the American political scientist Samuel Huntington, who argued that, even though the age of ideology had ended, the world had entered a new era of civilization clashes. In his famous 1993 *Foreign Affairs* article, Huntington put forward the following argument: "the fundamental source of conflict in this new world will not be

14. Spykman, *America's Strategy*, xxvii.
15. Brzezinski, *The Grand Chessboard*.
16. Ibid.

primarily ideological or primarily economic. The great divisions among humankind and the dominating source of conflict will be cultural."[17] In 1996, Huntington expanded the previous argument in his book *The Clash of Civilizations and the Remaking of World Order*.

Huntington divided the world into the following major civilization zones: Western civilization, Latin American civilization, the Christian-Orthodox world, the Eastern world (being a mix of the Buddhist, the Chinese, the Hindu, and the Japanese civilizations), the Muslim world, and the civilization of Sub-Saharan Africa. In his typology of civilizations, Huntington erroneously argued that Western civilization is the authentic heir to classical Greek civilization. As I argued in chapters 1–3, there are substantial differences between classical Greek civilization and Western civilization, and, in contrast to Huntington's profoundly misguided arguments about classical Greek civilization, the essence of Greek philosophy was preserved in Byzantium. Furthermore, in his typology of civilizations, Huntington seems to ignore that, in the Middle Ages, Slavic peoples adopted Byzantine Orthodox Christianity without having previously become partakers of Greek philosophy, on which the Greek church fathers had been based in order to form the dogmatology of Orthodox Christianity.

With regard to religion, the Slavic world is a spiritual descendant of Byzantium due to Orthodox Christianity, but, with regard to philosophy, the Slavic world is not a spiritual descendant of Byzantium. In the Slavic world (including Russia), the development of philosophy and even the manner in which several Slavic scholars have interpreted Plato's, Aristotle's, and Plotinus's philosophical works have been strongly influenced by the West, and they have been linked to the modernist policies of Tsar Peter the Great (1672–1725), who was an adherent of the Renaissance and a sympathizer of German Protestantism, and Empress Catherine the Great (1729–96), who was an adherent of the Enlightenment. Thus, several Slavic societies, including Russia, are characterized by an important dichotomy between their Byzantine Christian Orthodox tradition and their Westernized philosophical tradition. The previous cultural dichotomy of the Slavic world and especially of Russia has been addressed by the Russian novelist Fyodor M. Dostoyevsky. In the modern era, the Russian philosophical thought has been dominated by Enlightenment scholars, existentialists, Marxists, Neognostic mystics, and a few sympathizers of fascism, who are all representatives of the Western spirit.

17. Huntington, "The Clash of Civilizations?" 22.

Having been intellectually based on Western philosophy and on Western interpretations of classical Greek philosophy, many modern Russian philosophers are ignorant of the difference between the Greek *logos* and the Western *ratio*, a difference which I attempted to elucidate in chapters 1 and 2. Thus, many modern Russian philosophers think that, when one feels suffocated in rationalism, one's only significant philosophical alternatives are Heidegger's existentialism and Nietzsche's voluntarism. However, as I argued in chapter 3, in this way, they remain confined to the limits and the defects of Western individualism. Thus, in the nineteenth and the twentieth centuries, Russian political thought never managed to depart from Western political thought, since both Tsarist autocracy and Bolshevism are founded on Western political thought. Moreover, in the post-Cold War era, Russia remained intellectually anchored on the fundamental categories of Western political philosophy, on the Western theory of *Realpolitik*, and on the Western economic model of corporatism.

The strongest forces of resistance against the cultural Westernization of the Slavic world are the Slavs' popular traditions, and the Slavs' Hesychastic tradition, whose pioneers were the following Russian Neptic Fathers: Paisius Velichkovsky, Seraphim of Sarov, Abbott Nazarius of Valaam, Elder Theodore of Senaxor, Elder Zosima of Siberia, and Herman of Alaska. The previous Russian Neptic Fathers' theology was consciously and accurately founded on Byzantine Hesychasm, which was spread throughout the Slavic world in the fourteenth and the fifteenth centuries by the Byzantine Hesychast Gregory of Sinai, the Bulgarian Patriarch Evtimiy of Tarnovo (he was Patriarch of Bulgaria between 1375 and 1393), the Russian Hesychast Nil Sorsky (ca. 1433–1508), and other Slavic Hesychasts.

However, the Soviet regime cultivated a deviant kind of theological thought that led to the misinterpretation of Hesychasm by Russian churchmen in the context of the Soviet regime's attempt to Westernize the spirituality of the Russian people in order to assimilate it into Marxism–Leninism. Thus, for instance, in the book *The Russian Orthodox Church: Tenth to Twentieth Centuries*, edited by Alexander Preobrazhensky, Soviet authors portray the Russian Orthodox Church under the Soviet regime as renovating certain dogmatic traditions and embracing the "flexibility" necessary in theological dialogues with Roman Catholic and Protestant theologians for the sake of the Kremlin's ideology and diplomacy, and, furthermore, they argue that Orthodox Christian theology should subject to the communist dogma of "social determination."[18] During the Soviet era, the authentic tradition of Russian Hesychasm was preserved primarily by the "Catacomb Church" (which was founded in the 1930s by Metropolitan Cyril of Kazansk and Metropolitan Joseph of St. Petersburg) and by the Russian Orthodox Church Outside Russia.

Huntington's analysis of Orthodox Christianity has failed to address not only the aforementioned issues in the history of Slavic Orthodoxy but also the contradiction between the modern Greek state's Byzantine heritage and its policy of Westernization. The modern Greek state was established in 1830 as a protectorate of Western Great Powers (especially of Great Britain and France) in the Rimland. In the nineteenth century, the dominant ideology of the political, economic, and intellectual elites of Greece was founded on Rousseau, Voltaire, and German idealism and neoclassicism. After the assassination of the first head of the Greek government, Count Ioannis Kapodistrias, in 1831, the 1832 Treaty of London made Greece a monarchy. The foreign Patrons of Greece chose Otto Wittelsbach, Prince of Bavaria, as Greece's first king. King Otto's regime attempted to impose Western culture on the Greek society by controlling the University of Athens and the Church of Greece.[19] In particular, in 1833, the state Church of Greece, though officially maintaining the Christian Orthodox dogmatology, was irregularly (i.e., in violation of Christian Orthodox Canon Law) instituted and presided by the Protestant and liberal German statesman and legal historian Georg Ludwig von Mauer, who was a regent under King Otto from 1832 to 1834. Thus, even though with regard to religion and language, the modern Greek state is an heir to Byzantium, the Greek state is alienated from both ancient and medieval Hellenism.

EURASIANISM: THE RUSSIAN 'SCHOOL' OF GEOPOLITICS

In the previous section, I argued that Huntington's analysis of classical Greek civilization, Byzantium, and the Christian Orthodox world contains important mistakes. But, on the other hand, Huntington's work has significantly enriched geopolitical thought by emphasizing the role of

18. Preobrazhensky, *The Russian Orthodox Church*, 340–47.

19. The Bavarian regime combined soft and hard power, since it attempted to conquer the Greeks' hearts and minds, and also it destroyed many Greek Orthodox monasteries and besmirched many monuments and treasures of the Greek Orthodox spirituality.

civilization zones. This theme has been taken up by the Russian politologist and geopolitical thinker Alexander G. Dugin, the acknowledged father of the Eurasian Movement. In 2012, *The Fourth Political Theory* was the first book by Alexander Dugin to appear in the English language. In this book, Alexander Dugin expounds Eurasianism, which is at the core of the Russian 'school' of geopolitics.

During the Cold War, the academic discipline of Sovietology consisted in a methodical study of the Soviet Union. In the post-Cold War era, Eurasia is a term that refers to the entire post-Soviet space, including the Russian Federation. In other words, Eurasia is a region and not a country. In contrast to the Atlanticists' models of unipolarity and multilateralism, which are based on an Atlanticist monologue, Dugin's model of Eurasianism is a system of different civilizations, i.e., a system of different regional hegemonies. In particular, Dugin uses the German term *Grossraum*, which was coined by the German philosopher, jurist, and political theorist Carl Schmitt, and it means 'big space.' Eurasianism's vision of a multipolar world contains the following *Grossräume* ('big spaces'), i.e., regional hegemonies, which could give rise to a global system of balance of power: the North Atlantic, or Western civilization zone with its American component and its European component (however, some continental European powers, such as Germany and France, often tend to pursue a greater degree of political autonomy vis-à-vis the U.S.); Eurasia as a geopolitical space; the Islamic civilization zone; the Chinese civilization zone, consisting of China, Taiwan, and other Asian regions in which the Chinese influence is strong; a Latin American *Grossraum*, founded on Latin culture, Christianity, and local cultural traditions; a Hindu *Grossraum* centered on the Indian subcontinent; a Japanese system of regional hegemony; and an African Sub-Saharan *Grossraum*.

Dugin's multipolarity model is different from both the classical state-centric model of balance of power and the model of globalization, which is founded on the idea of global integration under a regime of global monologue. Dugin's model is a 'polylogue,' in the sense that it recognizes and gives voice to different human communities, each of which has its own relationship with temporality and spatiality, its own vision for the world, and its own cultural identity, instead of passively conforming to a globalist policy that is based on a Western monologue. Dugin has emphasized that a *Grossraum* is based on common values and the principle of historical affinity, and, therefore, it unites national governments into a common spiritual horizon, or a common destiny. In the 2010s,

Russian President Vladimir Putin made it clear that his geopolitical attitude consists in accepting the role of Eurasia as a geopolitical entity
and of Russia as the center of 'land power.' Moreover, the Eurasian Union
and the Collective Security Treaty Organization are founded on the
principles of Eurasianism.

Dugin's multipolarity/polylogue model signals a revolt against the
defects and the repressive nature of the Atlanticists' globalism, and it is
a thought-provoking response to the crisis of the post-Cold War world
order that led to what the French philosopher Myriam Revault d' Allones has called a "crisis without end."[20] According to Myriam Revault
d'Allones, the decade of 2000 is marked by the beginning of a global
crisis that affects finance, education, culture, the natural environment,
and human relationships. Furthermore, according to Myriam Revault
d'Allones, originally, the Greek word *krisis*, from which the English word
crisis is derived, means a decisive moment that, during the evolution of
an uncertain process, often associated with pity and fear, permits the de-
cision-maker to make a diagnosis of his situation and, therefore, to find
a solution to the drama of his suffering and attain *katharsis* (purgation of
emotions). But, Myriam Revault d'Allones argues, in the era of advanced
modernity, the nature of crisis is different, because the contemporary
man cannot envisage his orientation toward the future (i.e., he cannot
envisage an existential *telos*) and, therefore, he is incapable of making a
diagnosis that can lead him to his *katharsis*.[21]

The first step in order to overcome the kind of crisis to which Myriam Revault d'Allones refers is to decide to exist authentically and to seek
an ontologically grounded freedom, instead of conforming to an established monologue and surrendering to nihilism. The pursuit of authentic
existence underpins Dugin's multipolarity/polylogue model. But, in his
book *The Fourth Political Theory*, Dugin makes it amply clear that his
pursuit of authentic existence and his identitarian politics are founded on
Heidegger's theory of *Dasein* and on a constructivist approach to reality.
As I argued in chapter 4, Heidegger's theory of *Dasein*, constructivism,
and postmodernism are components of Western civilization's crisis, and,
therefore, the attempt to find a solution to Western civilization's crisis and
to create a better world order should be founded neither on the principle
of *Dasein* nor on constructivism, but, according to the arguments that I

20. D'Allones, *La Crise Sans Fin*.
21. Ibid.

put forward in chapters 1 and 2, it should be founded on the rediscovery of metaphysics, or ontology, and on the notion of 'personhood.'

Even though the notion of 'personhood' plays a fundamental role in Orthodox Christian theology in general and in Russian Hesychasm in particular, Eurasianism, instead of founding its multipolarity model on the notion of 'personhood,' proposes a multipolarity model founded on *Dasein* and constructivism, and, in this way, Eurasianism compromises with the Western tradition of individual truth and with Russia's philosophical dependence on the West. As I have already argued, Russia has an underlying philosophical deficit which stems from the fact that it adopted Orthodox Christianity from Byzantium without absorbing the philosophical preliminaries (i.e., the Greek philosophical underpinnings) of Orthodox Christianity, and, therefore, the Russian cultural elite has a serious difficulty in combining myth with *logos*. Russian philosophy tends to confuse Hesychastic metaphysics with mysticism (ecstasy), and it is intellectually inclined to existentialism and voluntarism. In the twenty-first century, Eurasianism as a geopolitical school disputes the dominant Atlanticist geopolitical theses (namely, unipolarity and multilateralism), but Eurasianism as a cultural identity is intellectually anchored on Western philosophy. Thus, not only does Eurasianism leave the aforementioned philosophical deficit of Russia intact, but also, due to its commitment to *Dasein* and constructivism, it entails the risk of giving rise to a world without any cohesive *logos* (such as the one described in the Bible by the metaphor of the Tower of Babel[22]) and of sinking Russia into a delirium of reactionary passion.

In order to understand why the Eurasianists' intellectual dependence on *Dasein* may lead the Russian geopolitical thought to a dead-end, it is useful to analyze the tragedy of Fyodor Dostoyevsky's heroes and to understand why Dostoyevsky's psychological thought is very appealing to Nietzsche and why Nietzsche's thought is very appealing to Dostoyevsky's intellectual epigones. In contrast to classical Greek philosophy, Dostoyevsky does not understand the soul as the link between the particular and the universal. Plato conceives of the soul as an immaterial idea and Aristotle conceives of the soul as a material species, and they both argue that man's participation in the reality of the soul is the ontological foundation of phenomena and discloses the purpose of phenomena. Moreover, in the context of the Orthodox Christian faith,

22. Gen 11:4–9.

the 'universal' is identified with the life of the church, which is something substantially different from psychological faith. Within the church, the soul experiences its existential otherness, and simultaneously communion is identified with truth. On the other hand, outside the church, in the context of psychological faith, God reduces to a cultural phenomenon which can educate an instinctive soul and transform it into a civilized soul, but it cannot endow man's soul with uncreated grace. In the context of church life, the universal is not something supra-rational, but it consists in a personal *Logos* who is completely open to the 'other.'

Dostoyevsky, like the existentialists, conceived of salvation as an individual mental change without being aware of the significance of the universal soul which is constituted by the church community. This aspect of Dostoyevsky's thought implies that the relation between Dostoyevsky's work and Orthodox Christian anthropology is dubious, and it explains why Nietzsche was fond of Dostoyevsky.[23] Similarly, Eurasianism is intellectually anchored on existentialism and, more specifically, on Heidegger's concept of *Dasein*, thus departing from the Orthodox Christian anthropology and from the Greek philosophers' sociocentric political thought. Hesychasm, in the history of which the Russian Hesychasts have played a key role and occupy a preeminent position, is centered on the concept of personhood, which can underpin a theory of multipolarity much more effectively than the concept of *Dasein*.

In contrast to the West's varieties of individualism, which I studied in chapter 4, and which are derived from the West's commitment to the thesis that consciousness is an ontologically sufficient foundation of truth, a 'person' is an individual-in-communion-with-a-truth-that-transcends-the-individual. A 'person' is an existential otherness that is socialized, and, hence, a 'person' is continually open to the 'other.' As I have already argued, Plato emphasizes man's participation in a truth that *ontologically* transcends him (i.e., in the world of ideas) and Hesychasm emphasizes that man can participate in a truth that *ontologically* transcends him (i.e., in God's uncreated energies). Therefore, from the perspective of classical Greek metaphysics and Hesychasm, 'truth' is identified with 'reality,' and it is ontologically autonomous from the 'subject,' but it is available to the human being, that is, the human being can participate in the truth (i.e., in God). In the context of Platonism and Hesychasm, man's participation in the truth is the foundation of both his existential otherness, or

23. Shestov, *Dostoevsky, Tolstoy, and Nietzsche.*

individuality (since the experience of participation in the truth endows man with a sense of individual value), and his socialization (since man is aware that he is not an ontologically sufficient foundation of truth, and he exists in communion with a truth that ontologically transcends him). As I will argue in chapter 8, the major goal of the "fourth political theory" that I propose is to transform political actors into 'persons,' and, therefore, to provide an ontologically grounded treatment for the development and invigoration of the social nature of the human soul.

THE EUROPEAN INTEGRATION PROJECT

The ideological and political origins of the European Union can be found in the work of Richard Nikolaus Eijiro von Coudenhove-Kalergi (1894–1972), who was an Austrian geopolitician and philosopher.[24] Moreover, he was the founder and President for forty-nine years of the Pan-Europa Movement. It is the oldest European unification movement, and it began with the publishing of Coudenhove-Kalergi's manifesto *Pan-Europa* (1923).

The fundamental principles of Coudenhove-Kalergi's[25] program for the European unification are the following:

1. Coudenhove-Kalergi considers the idea of a unified European federation to be the sixth historical attempt for the unification of a large number of nations into a single super-state. According to Coudenhove-Kalergi, the previous five attempts were made by Alexander the Great, Julius Caesar, Charlemagne, Pope Innocent II, and Napoleon I. Additionally, Coudenhove-Kalergi has argued that Russia should be a member of the unified Europe.

2. Coudenhove-Kalergi argues that the political and economic integration of Europe presupposes a common European culture, which would underpin the creation of a single European nation. From Coudenhove-Kalergi's perspective, the different European nations are artificial. Therefore, Coudenhove-Kalergi has argued that the different European national identities should be considered merely private matters for private individuals, and states should not be founded on national identities or traditions, thus becoming the components or 'regions' of the "United States of Europe."

24. Weigall and Stirk, *Origins and Development of the European Community*, 11–15.

25. Coudenhove-Kalergi, *Pan-Europe*.

3. According to Coudenhove-Kalergi, the problem of European nations' borders could be overcome through a new conception of the term 'citizen.' In particular, Coudenhove-Kalergi has argued that European citizens should support the transformation of nation-states into regions and, also, the transformation of national borders into regional ones, in the context of a unified European political entity.

Through the term 'common European culture,' Coudenhove-Kalergi promotes an ideal for the unification of Europe founded on coercive biological and rationalist principles, on Frederick the Great's authoritarian political legacy, and on a Zionist neo-mythology.[26] In particular, in his two major books, *Pan-Europa* and *Practical Idealism*, Coudenhove-Kalergi credits the Jews with most of the European civilizations' spiritual attainments, describes the Jews as "the spiritual master race," praises the ethos and the coercive political structures of Western feudal nobility, and he promotes his vision of one world government. Coudenhove-Kalergi argues that Ferdinand Lassalle, Albert Einstein, Henri Bergson, and Leon Trotsky are characteristic representatives of the "Jewish spiritual nobility," which he strongly praises. Moreover, he has divided European peoples into two categories: the "men of quantity" and the "men of quality," and he has argued that the "men of quality" have a "higher mission," and they come from the bloodline of Western feudal nobility and from what he calls the "Jewish spiritual nobility." Coudenhove-Kalergi's vision of a unified Europe is founded on the biological unification of the Eurasian space (i.e., on what Coudenhove-Kalergi has called the "Eurasian-Negroide race") and on a Judeo-Christian alliance and neo-mythology.[27]

Of all the empires, it was perhaps the Nazis who came closest to achieving the military conquest and occupation of Europe. In June 1940, Herman Göring, the "Reich Marshal of the Greater German Reich," was reviewing the final plans for the German invasion of Great Britain, and, additionally, he was discussing with Hitler a new plan to unite Europe not only through military means but also through a lasting political and economic union which the Nazis named the "European Economic Community." In 1942, a conference was held in Berlin to discuss the political

26. There is a close affinity between Coudenhove-Kalergi's vision of a unified Europe and the ideology of Asher Zvi Hirsch Ginsberg (known also as Ahad Ha'am), who was one of the central literal figures of Zionism. Moreover, Coudenhove-Kalergi's Pan-Europa Movement was generously funded by Jewish capitalists, such as Louis Rothschild, the bankers Paul and Max Warburg, and the stock-broker Bernard Baruch.

27. Coudenhove-Kalergi, *Praktischer Idealismus*.

and economic integration of Europe. In the 1940s, Great Britain suc-
cessfully resisted invasion and, also, proved to be the greatest obstacle to
Germany fulfilling its ambition to dominate Europe. By 1944, it was clear
that the fortunes of war had turned against Germany. Thus, on August 10,
1944, a secret meeting was held at the Maison Rouge Hotel in Strasbourg
among officials of the Nazi government and top German industrialists
and bankers in order to devise a plan for the protection of Nazi leaders and to answer the following question: how will Germany dominate
the peace when the Nazis lose the war?[28] In 1957, the Treaty of Rome
revived the idea of European Economic Community. The Treaty of Rome
created an international organization named European Economic Community (EEC), whose founding members were France, West Germany,
Italy, Belgium, Luxemburg, and the Netherlands. After the Treaty of
Maastricht (1992), the EEC became the European Union, which, in 2013,
consisted of twenty-eight member-states.

The European Economic Community/European Union has glorified
its Continental imperialist 'forebears' by instituting the "Charlemagne
Prize" and the "Coudenhove-Kalergi Prize" (Coudenhove-Kalergi was
the first recipient of the Charlemagne Prize in 1950). Moreover, the rationalist mentality of Continental Western philosophy, which underpins the
history of European absolutism, has been manifested in European Union's
political and economic institutions. The European Union methodically
promotes the deconstruction of the 'nation-state' in the spirit of Coudenhove-Kalergi's federalist ideology.[29] As a result of the Maastricht Treaty
(1992), the Amsterdam Treaty (1997), the Treaty of Nice (2001), and the
Treaty of Lisbon (2007), the essence of the political process in the European Union is hidden behind hermetically sealed doors and is primarily
determined by the wills and the commands of an elite of technocrats,
bureaucrats, and businessmen. In his thought-provoking book *The European Union and the End of Politics*, James Heartfield points out that the
European Union (EU) did not come about as a result of any democratic
drive to transcend nation-states and replace them with a pan-European

28. In 1943/44, the German spymaster Admiral Wilhelm Franz Canaris, having
appreciated that Germany was going to lose the war, set up the DVD, which in German stands for Deutsches Verteidigungs Dienst (German Defense Service). He and
his deputy, Generalmajor Erwin von Lahousen, were determined that Germany would
win the peace; in fact, this is the Nazi approach to the European integration project.
Story, *European Union Collective*.

29. Minassian, "Nouvelles Dynamiques Identitaires Contre Etats-Nations."

superstructure, but, on the contrary, the EU emerged as a result of the decline of traditional European democratic institutions.[30] Moreover, in his
book *Euro Exit*, Jean-Jacques Rosa, who was an economic advisor to the
French Prime Minister during 1997–99, explains the manner in which
and the reasons why European politicians and businessmen decided to
circumvent democratic consent in order to lock their societies into the
Eurozone and "reap the advantages of monetary cartelization."

Hand in hand with the EU bureaucrats' attempt to deconstruct European nation-states goes the attempt of Germany's national economic and
political elite to exploit the unified European geoeconomic space. In particular, Germany, which, throughout the twentieth century, was the major
source of Europe's problems, saw the European Union and especially the
Eurozone as a free trade zone in which Germany's imperialist ambitions
could be actualized. In the end of the twentieth century and in the beginning of the twenty-first century, Germany derives approximately 40
percent of its GDP from exports. Germany's national economy is too large
for its own consumption, and, therefore, Germany pursues an imperialist
economic policy through exports. For Germany, the European Union was
from the beginning the geoeconomic *Lebensraum* which German industrialists need in order to survive and continue growing. Germany took
full advantage of this situation by convincing EU member-states to lock
their economies into the Eurozone, which is founded on institutions and
principles that reflect and serve Germany's economic interests.

In 1999, the Eurozone imposed a central monetary policy on all
member-states whose formerly independent monetary policies were effectively rendered inoperative, but other elements of effective economic
integration (such as fiscal policy and effective labor mobility) were not
harmonized. Thus, in 1999, and in the first decade of the twenty-first
century, the Eurozone offered enormous benefits to Germany's export-
oriented industries by solving the problem of exchange rate instability
among the currencies of the member-states and by establishing a central
monetary authority—i.e., the European Central Bank (ECB)—controlling the Union's money supply, primarily in accordance with the commands of Germany.

Until the outbreak of the 2008 global financial crisis, problems of
regional imbalance could not be addressed in an institutional manner
by national representatives in the governing apparatus of the European

30. Heartfield, *The European Union and the End of Politics*.

Union. Furthermore, the ECB's rigid monetary policy, reflecting and serving Germany's interests, ignores that, even though running deficits for contra-cyclical purposes is not an effective option in general, running deficits for specifically targeted objectives (especially for projects that yield benefits over a much wider horizon than the expenditure horizon) is a viable and often necessary policy on the part of any regional (national) actor. According to Germany's geoeconomic strategy, the ECB should not only be independent of political control on a routine basis, but also the ECB should function irrespective of a strong political consensus to the contrary. After the outbreak of the 2008 global financial crisis, the member-states of the Eurozone that faced a debt crisis asked for more credit in order to finance programs of economic stimulus in the spirit of Franklin D. Roosevelt's policy of the "New Deal," but Germany's national economic and political elite and the German-dominated ECB imposed austerity programs that led Southern Europe (namely, Spain, Portugal, southern France, southern Italy, Greece, and Cyprus) to a long period of economic depression.

The 2008 global financial crisis made it dramatically clear that, for one more time, Western European powers were unable to create social unity in general and the unity of Europe in particular. Thus, faced with the 2008 global financial crisis, the European Union not only did not depart from its tradition of individual truth, but it enhanced economic nationalism, in the sense that, in the absence of a transnational value system and of a common European economic policy, every EU member-state started arguing for its own interests without caring about the Union itself as a transnational entity, and, additionally, the interests of the EU member-states substantially diverged from each other.

7

NOOPOLITICS

THE CONCEPT OF NOOPOLITICS

MAN IS NOT ONLY a being of the 'earth,' but he is also a being of the 'skies,' in the sense that human creativity, through science and technology, helps the human spirit to overcome the forces and the inertia of the material world and to pursue structural changes. Moreover, humans relate to beings and things mainly through meanings and significances and evaluate them. Thus, due to the previous reasons, politics is conducted not only on the earth, but also in the information field that is created by the communication among conscious beings. The conduct of politics on the earth is called geopolitics, whereas the conduct of politics in the information field that is created by the communication among conscious beings is called noopolitics. The term 'noopolitics' was invented by defense experts John Arquilla and David Ronfeldt in a seminal RAND Corporation study of 1999, and it often appears in connection with Joseph Nye's notion of 'soft power.'[1]

The levels at which noopolitics can be conducted are the following:

- *Cyberspace:* this is the global system of the Internet-connected computers, communications, infrastructures, online conferencing entities, databases, and information utilities. According to informatics experts Chip Morningstar and F. Randall Farmer, the core characteristic of cyberspace is the communication among conscious

1. Arquilla and Ronfeldt, *Noopolitik.*

beings and the social interactions involved rather than its technical implementation (i.e., the computational medium).[2]

- *Infosphere:* it encompasses the cyberspace and information systems that may not be part of the internet, such as the 'mediasphere' (broadcast, print, and other media), libraries, military information infrastructures (command, control, computer, communications, intelligence, surveillance, and reconnaissance systems), etc.[3] Intimately related to the conduct of noopolitics at the level of the infosphere are operations whose objective is the exercise of control over the mass media and the movie industry.

  For instance, in the mid-1990s, the CIA appointed veteran CIA operative Chase Brandon as an official public relations liaison with Hollywood, and other U.S. government agencies, such as the FBI, the Secret Service, and the Armed Services, have been lending their cooperation to the movie industry for a long time.[4] In her book *The CIA in Hollywood*, Tricia Jenkins has methodically studied the manner in which the U.S. projects its soft power through the global movie industry.

- *Noosphere:* this term, from the Greek word *nous* (mind), was coined by the Jesuit philosopher Pierre Teilhard de Chardin in 1925, and, according to Teilhard de Chardin, it describes a globe-circling realm of the mind, or a "thinking circuit."[5] The conduct of noopolitics at the level of the noosphere is based on the concept of 'soft power,' to which I referred in chapter 4, and on the concept of 'Human Terrain System,' known by the acronym HTS. The HTS is a U.S. Army training and doctrine command support program employing social scientists (anthropologists, sociologists, political scientists, linguists, and experts in regional studies) in order to provide military commanders and staff with an understanding of the local population ("human terrain") in the regions in which they are deployed.[6]

2. Morningstar and Farmer, "The Lessons of Lucasfilm's Habitat," 664–67.

3. Cooper, *Infosphere.*

4. Patterson, "Caring, Sharing CIA."

5. Teilhard de Chardin, *The Future of Man.*

6. Bartholf, "Requirement for Sociocultural Understanding"; Casey and McCulloh, "HTS Support"; Hall, "Social Science Research"; Reanier, "Geo-statistical Forecasting"; Sengova, "Bilingual Data Collection and Research Protocols"; Thorne, "Local Conflict Assessment Framework."

The U.S. military and intelligence services have been financing social scientific research since the 1920s. The work of the American cultural anthropologist Margaret Mead, author of the book *Coming of Age in Samoa: A Psychological Study of Primitive Youth for Western Civilization*, originally published in 1928, is a characteristic case in point. Mead was a researcher for the CIA-connected RAND Corporation, and she supported CIA funding of anthropological research via research grants from the U.S. Agency for International Development (USAID). For instance, in the context of the USAID/CIA projects with the codenames Phoenix, Prosyms, Sympatico, and Camelot, social scientists were employed in order to study "human terrains" (i.e., targeted local populations) in South Vietnam, Indonesia, Pakistan, Colombia, and Chile and determine the most effective ways in which U.S. Special Forces and intelligence agents could use indigenous peoples to further U.S. military goals. In the first two decades of the twenty-first century, the U.S. government funded big HTS projects in Iraq, Afghanistan, and the Pacific region. In the context of the Obama administration's strategic "pivot" from the Middle East to East Asia, the CIA, in cooperation with the Australian Security Intelligence Organization (ASIO) and the New Zealand Secret Intelligence Service (NZSIS), developed programs whose objective is the geopolitical containment of China, and, furthermore, HTS operatives developed programs whose objectives are to counterbalance the Chinese cultural influence over Fiji, Vanuatu, and Papua New Guinea, and to train mercenaries from Marshall Islands, American Samoa, Guamania, Kiribati, Micronesia, the Independent State of Samoa, and Fiji.

CYBERWAR AND NETWAR

According to John Arquilla and David Ronfeldt, "netwar refers to information-related conflict at a grand level between nations and societies."[7] The essence of netwar is the attempt to exercise a decisive influence on the target population's perceptions, and it may focus on public or elite opinion, or both. Netwar may involve public diplomacy measures, propaganda, psychological operations, political and cultural subversion, deception, interference with local media, infiltration of computer networks

---

7. Arquilla and Ronfeldt, *Cyberwar Is Coming!*, 28.

and databases, and efforts to promote a dissident or opposition movements through the Internet.[8]

On May 24, 2012, *The Telegraph* compared Google's annual Zeit-
geist conference with annual Davos World Economic Forum.[9] Google's
significance for the conduct of netwar was illustrated by Wael Ghonim,
Google's head of marketing for the Middle East and North Africa, who
administered the Facebook page that helped spark the 'Arab Spring' in
Egypt in 2011. In his book *Revolution 2.0*, Ghonim described in detail
the role that he and other activists, primarily young persons adept in the
use of social media, played in organizing massive street protests that triggered the downfall of Egypt's then-President Hosni Mubarak. In February
2011, speaking at the Mobile World Congress in Barcelona, Google CEO
Eric Schmidt addressed the topic of Wael Ghonim, and he stated that he
was "very, very proud" of the key role that Ghonim played in the Egyptian protests which eventually brought down the Mubarak government.

Cyberwar consists in military operations based on information-related principles.[10] The purpose of cyberwar is to disrupt if not destroy the
adversary's information and communications systems, thus turning the
"balance of information and knowledge" in one's favor.[11] Cyberwar may
involve diverse technologies for intelligence collection, processing, and
distribution, 'smart' weapon systems, and electronic warfare. On June 7,
2013, *The Guardian* published U.S. President Barack Obama's "Directive
20," by which he ordered his senior national security and intelligence officials to draw up a list of international targets for U.S. cyber-attacks.[12]
Moreover, China has extensive cyberwar capabilities.[13] In February 2013,
a U.S. private cyber security company, Mandiant, published a report
in which it claimed that the Shanghai-based Unit No. 61398 of China's
People's Liberation Army (PLA) is responsible for a wide range of cyber-
attacks against U.S. networks that resulted in the stealing of hundreds of
terabytes of data from several organizations since 2006.[14]

---

8. Ibid.
9. Warman, "Google."
10. Arquilla and Ronfeldt, *Cyberwar Is Coming!*, 30.
11. Ibid.
12. Greenwald and MacAskill, "Obama Orders US."
13. Ball, "China's Cyber Warfare Capabilities."
14. MANDIANT. 2013. *Exposing One of China's Cyber Espionage Units.*

PARAMILITARY NETWORKS AND POLITICAL CRIME

Paramilitary networks, 'false flag' operations (i.e., covert military/para-military operations designed to deceive in such a way that the operations appear as though they have been carried out by other actors than those who actually planed and executed them), and 'stay-behind' operations (in the context of which a country places secret operatives or organizations in its own territory for use in the event that an adversary may overrun the territory) play important roles in noopolitics.

One of the biggest 'stay-behind' operations was Operation Gladio ('Gladio' is the Italian form of 'gladius,' a type of Roman shortsword). Operation Gladio was the codename for a clandestine NATO 'stay-behind' operation in Europe during the Cold War. The purpose of Gladio was to maintain paramilitary networks that would continue anti-communist actions in the event of a Soviet invasion and conquest. Gladio operated under different codenames in Italy, Germany, France, Belgium, the Netherlands, Greece, Luxemburg, Great Britain, Norway, Portugal, Spain, Austria, Turkey, Denmark, Switzerland, and Sweden.[15] It was part of a series of national operations first coordinated by the Clandestine Committee of the Western Union (CCWU), founded in 1948, but, after the creation of NATO in 1949, CCWU was integrated into NATO's Clandestine Planning Committee founded in 1951 and overseen by SHAPE (Supreme Headquarters Allied Powers, Europe). CIA Director Allen Dulles played a key role in the creation of Gladio networks, and many of Gladio's operations were financed and supported by the CIA and by CIA-controlled networks of organized crime and terrorism.[16]

Neofascist extremists, such as the far-right Ordine Nuovo subversive organization, and the Italian Masonic Lodge "Propaganda Due" (P2) headed by Licio Gelli executed Gladio's "strategy of tension" in Italy in the 1960s and the 1970s. In Italy, Gladio's "strategy of tension" included the following operations: the 1964 silent *coup d' état* through which General Giovanni de Lorenzo, who was the head of the Italian SIFAR intelligence agency, forced the Italian socialist ministers to leave the government; the 1969 Piazza Fontana bombing; the 1970 failed *coup* attempt "Golpe Borghese"; the 1972 Peteano massacre; the 1973 bombing of the airplane Argo 16; the 1974 Piazza della Loggia bombing; the 1978 murder of the then Italian Prime Minister Aldo Moro, who was pursuing the so-called

15. Ganser, *NATO's Secret Armies.*
16. Ibid.

"historic compromise" between the Christian Democrats and Italian Communist Party (PCI); the 1980 Bologna massacre, etc.[17] Through the previous "strategy of tension," an Atlanticist elite aimed at terrorizing Italian citizens in order to stop the rise of left-wing political forces in Italy and to implement Henry Kissinger's anti-communist policy, since Kissinger had warned the then Christian Democrat Prime Minister of Italy, Aldo Moro, not to bring all Italian political forces into direct collaboration.[18] In 1978, Aldo Moro was kidnapped and assassinated by the Italian leftist terrorist organization called "Red Brigades," which worked closely with the Hyperion Language School in Paris. An Italian police report referred to the Hyperion Language School as "the most important CIA office in Europe".[19]

On October 24, 1990, the then Italian Christian Democrat Prime Minister Giulio Andreotti publicly recognized the existence of Gladio. On November 22, 1990, the European Parliament passed a resolution (Nr. C 324/201) condemning Gladio. In 2000, a Parliament Commission Report from the Italian political coalition "Gruppo Democratici di Sinistra l'Ulivo" concluded that the "strategy of tension" had been supported by the United States in order to stop the Italian Communist Party (PCI) and the Italian Socialist Party (PSI) from reaching executive power in Italy.[20]

THE DISTORTION OF THE SHARIA AND THE MANIPULATION OF ISLAMIC MOVEMENTS BY WESTERN ELITES

In Arabic, *Sharia* means law, and, more specifically, it refers to a legal system whose foundation and source are regarded to be God's will. In other words, it is not a man-made law, but it is a law which is extended with human effort from the original core which, according to Muslims, was revealed by *Allah*.

A Greek approach to the *Sharia* can be found in Sophocles's tragedy *Antigone*, in which Antigone defends 'divine law' (the Greek equivalent of *Sharia*), which expresses eternity, against King Creon's human (i.e., man-made) law, which expresses the will of an ephemeral political authority. Parmenides of Elea, an influential pre-Socratic philosopher, used

17. Ibid.
18. Rowse, "The Secret U.S. War"; Willan, "US 'Supported Anti-Left Terror.'"
19. Ibid.
20. Willan, "US 'Supported Anti-Left Terror,'" and *Puppetmasters*.

the term *themis* in order to refer to divine law as opposed to human or-
dinance. Moreover, in Homer's *Odyssey* and *Iliad*, the term *themis* (from
which is derived the Greek word *thesmōs*, which means institution) refers
to the administration of justice, in the sense that, according to Homer,
judges issue their verdicts based on institutions whose source is Zeus,
and they create additional rules from the core of Zeus's law.

In the Christian world, the concept of *Sharia* refers to the sovereignty of God. In his *Epistle*, James writes that "there is only one Lawgiver
and Judge" (Jas 4:12).

In general, law depends on metaphysics in order to have a firm foundation, i.e., a 'hard core' of absolute values and principles, from which
individual legal rules are derived, as in mathematics, where theorems are
derived from a 'hard core' of axioms. Without any metaphysical foundation, law depends merely on political expediencies and ephemeral social
contracts, and, ultimately, it leads to nihilism. Thus, the famous eighteenth-
century American statesman, philosopher, and inventor Benjamin Franklin declared: "Man will ultimately be governed by God or by tyrants."[21]

According to Islam, Allah did not send down one *Sharia* for all
mankind. In Surat Al-Ma'idah, 5:48, in the Qur'an, we read the following: "To each of you we have ordained a law and a way," meaning that,
even though God created us from a single Father (Adam) and a single
Mother (Eve), He did not create us all as a single people, but He ordained
that humanity should emerge as different nations and different tribes. As
Sheikh Imran N. Hosein has pointed out with regard to the previous text,
there is diversity among mankind as there is diversity among flowers, and
this diversity is meant to enhance the splendor of Allah's creation and to
function as a means by which men recognize each other.[22]

The essence of the *Sharia* is that Allah is 'sovereign' (*al-Malik*), and,
therefore, the state and all its institutions must submit to Allah's supreme
authority and supreme law. Hence, according to Islam, the argument that
the state, rather than Allah, is sovereign is *Shirk* (blasphemy). Thus, by
the term 'Caliphate,' Islam means a political subject that recognizes the
sovereignty of Allah and maintains the *Sharia* as the source and foundation of the legal system.[23]

21. Morley, *Power in the People*, xxi.
22. Hosein, *The Caliphate*.
23. Ibid.

In the nineteenth century, the West realized that the domination of Western civilization over the Islamic world and the integration of the Islamic world into the capitalist system presupposed the deconstruction of the Caliphate. Aiming at the deconstruction of the Caliphate and having realized that this strategy required that the *Hejaz* (i.e., the Islamic holy cities of Mecca and Medina) should be subjected to Western influence in order that the Caliphate might be weakened and eventually eliminated, Great Britain concentrated its diplomacy in World War I on wresting the *Hejaz* from the control of the Ottoman Empire and on spreading the ideology of nationalism throughout the Arabo-Islamic world. The previous objective of the British diplomacy was achieved when 'Sharif' Husain, the Ottoman-appointed 'Sharif' (ruler) of Mecca and an ancestor of Jordan's Royal House, was induced by the British to rebel against the Ottoman caliph and to establish an autonomous authority over the *Hejaz* under British protection. By 1916, the Ottoman caliph had lost control over Mecca and Jeddah, and, in 1919, he lost control over Medina, too, since Ottoman troops within the city of Medina were induced to rebel against Fakhri Pasha.[24]

On March 3, 1924, the Ottoman Caliphate was abolished, and, on March 7, 1924, 'Sharif' Husain, who had been exercising *de facto* local control over the *Hejaz* since 1916, claimed the Caliphate for himself, and he boasted of being *Hashemite* (i.e., belonging to the same clan to which Prophet Mohammed himself belonged). However, 'Sharif' Husain had committed a strategic mistake: he had ignored the British, under whose protection he was ruling over the *Hejaz*.

In the beginning of the twentieth century, the objectives of the British diplomacy in the Arabian Peninsula were the following: (1) The British wanted to wrest the *Hejaz* from the control of the caliph. (2) The British wanted a friendly regime in control of the *Hejaz* in order to be able to manipulate the politics of the Arabian Peninsula. (3) After the decline of the Caliphate, the Zionist Movement built a consensus with Great Britain in the pursuit of the creation of a Jewish state in the Middle East, and this objective was included in the Sykes-Picot Agreement (officially known as the Asia Minor Agreement), which was concluded on May 16, 1916 between Great Britain and France, defining their proposed spheres of influence and control in the Middle East should the Triple Entente succeeded in defeating the Ottoman Empire in World War I. Moreover,

24. Ibid.

this objective was made clear with the 1917 Balfour Declaration, a letter from the British Foreign Secretary Arthur J. Balfour to Baron Rothschild, a leader of the British Jewish community.

The claim to the Caliphate by 'Sharif' Husain was incompatible with the British diplomacy, because 'Sharif' Husain had a tendency to pursue an autonomous policy in the Arabian Peninsula, and he could invigorate the Caliphate. However, both the British and the Zionists wanted to deconstruct the Caliphate. Thus, Great Britain assisted Abd al-Aziz Ibn Saud to move against 'Sharif' Husain and to wrest control of the *Hejaz* from him. Ibn Saud was a 'puppet' of the British diplomacy. In particular, during 'Sharif' Husain's rebellion against the caliph and during the imposition of Hashemite rule over the *Hejaz*, Ibn Saud was receiving a monthly sum of £5,000 sterling from the British Treasury in return for his policy of neutrality, which was then serving the interests of Great Britain.[25] But when 'Sharif' Husain claimed the Caliphate for himself, Great Britain urged Ibn Saud to move his forces against 'Sharif' Husain.

In 1902, the Saudis captured Riyadh as a result of an alliance between a tribal chief and the religious leader of the Wahhabi religious sect. The alliance ensured that the *Najdi* Saudis would be under the control of the Wahhabis and would seek to enforce Wahhabism in the 'heartland' of Islam (i.e., in the *Hejaz*). Wahhabism is founded on a modern Islamic reformer called Ibn Abd al-Wahhab (d. 1792); it is a puritanical, formalistic, and fanatical perception of the *Sharia*, and its mentality resembles that of Oliver Cromwell's English Puritanism.

By withdrawing support from 'Sharif' Husain and assisting Ibn Saud to impose a Saudi-Wahhabi regime in the 'heartland' of Islam, Great Britain ensured that the Caliphate could never be revived and that the Arabs would be unable to deter the creation of the Jewish State of Israel. Moreover, the Wahhabis could not claim the Caliphate, since Wahhabism had little relevance outside Saudi Arabia. In 1924, within a few months, Ibn Saud conquered Mecca, and, ultimately, the Kingdom of Saudi Arabia was founded by Abd al-Aziz Ibn Saud in 1932.

The internationally renowned Muslim scholar Sheikh Imran N. Hosein has emphasized that it is only Orthodox Christianity, described in the Qur'an as *Rum*, with whom an Islamic alliance may be forged (Surat Ar-Rum). On the other hand, Sheikh Imran N. Hosein maintains, Western Christianity, which is not *Rum*, has already forged a Zionist alliance

25. Ibid., 20.

with Jews, and it was to that Zionist Judeo-Christian alliance that the Qur'an (Al-Maidah, 5:51) referred when it prohibited Muslims from ever maintaining friendship and alliance with such Jews and such Christians who, themselves, were friends and allies of each other.[26]

The Qur'an distinguishes between those Christians who forge a Judeo-Christian alliance and other Christians about whom, according to the Qur'an, Allah declared: "and you will most surely find those who show the greatest love and affection for the believers (i.e., Muslims) to be those who say 'We are Christians'" (Al-Maidah, 5:82). Moreover, Sheikh Imran N. Hosein has argued that the Ottoman conquest of Orthodox Christianity's capital city of Constantinople in 1453, the disgraceful conduct of the Ottoman Sultan Muhammad Fatih in converting the greatest Orthodox Cathedral *Hagia Sophia* into a mosque, and the Ottoman sultans' brutal policy[27] toward their Orthodox Christian subjects caused enduring Greek and Orthodox Christian bitterness for Islam and proved to be the most formidable obstacle to the realization of the Muslim–*Rum* (Orthodox Christian) alliance that is prophesized in the Qur'an (Surat Ar-Rum). Even though the Ottoman Empire has left a legacy of embitterment between Orthodox Christians and Muslims, the Qur'an venerates Jesus Christ as the Messiah, and Arabo-Islamic civilization has been strongly influenced by ancient Greek philosophy and science.

Islam is not indiscriminately opposite to Christianity. From Sheikh Imran N. Hosein's perspective, the Qur'an prohibits only the alliance between Muslims and those Western powers which have forged a Judeo-Christian alliance. Thus, according to Sheikh Imran N. Hosein, Wahhabism, Salafism, the Muslim Brotherhood, and the Al Qaeda have a distorted perception of the Sharia, and they are instruments in the hands of the West and Zionism[28] for the destruction of the Caliphate.

26. Hosein, *Jerusalem*.

27. Robert Byron and Roger Portal have described the Ottoman rule as a phenomenon of cultural decay. Byron, *Byzantine Achievement*. Portal, *Slavs*.

28. In his seminal book *The Invention of the Jewish People*, Shlomo Sand, Professor of History at Tel Aviv University, explained the manner in which Zionism created a Jewish nationalist mythology on which the State of Israel was founded in 1948. In the previous book, Sand argues that, before the birth of the Zionist Movement in the nineteenth century, the idea of Jews being obliged to return from exile to the "Promised Land" was alien to Judaism. In particular, the Revisionist Zionist Movement, which was founded in 1923 by Ze'ev Jabotinsky (1880–1940) and, in 2009, managed to rule Israel under Israeli Prime Minister Benjamin Netanyahu, is a British colonial creation, part of the 'divide and conquer' strategy that Great Britain and France imposed on the

Apart from Wahhabism, whose role I explained above, the Muslim Brotherhood is another creation of the Sykes-Picot Agreement and of British intelligence. The Muslim Brotherhood evolved, spread, and spawned a virulent network of radical jihadists, including the Al Qaeda. Following a 1954 Muslim Brotherhood-led attempt on his life, the then Egyptian Deputy Prime Minister Gamal Abdel Nasser ordered a crackdown on the organization, put President Muhammad Naguib under house arrest, and he assumed executive office. During the 1950s and 1960s, Nasser persistently implemented a strict policy against the Muslim Brotherhood, and, during the same period, Saudi Arabia hosted Arab Muslim Brotherhood exiles. The strong presence of Muslim Brotherhood exiles in Saudi Arabia spawned a new Salafist movement, which is a hybrid of Wahhabism and other post-1960s Islamic movements, and it has been associated with literalist and puritanical approaches to Islam. When the then Syrian President Hafez al-Assad launched his own harsh crackdown against the Syrian branch of the Muslim Brotherhood in the early 1980s, a new wave of Muslim Brotherhood exiles moved to Saudi Arabia.

In the 1970s and the 1980s, Bernhard Lewis, who was a senior 'Arabist' of the British intelligence, a University of Princeton historian, and a leading Zionist, was advising successive U.S. administrations on how to play the 'Islamic card' as a tool in order to bring down the Soviet Union. Moreover, in 1976, France, Egypt, Saudi Arabia, Morocco, and Iran (under the Shah) established the Safari Club, which was a coalition among various intelligence agencies in order to fight communism and, more specifically, the Soviet Union. With the official blessing of the then head of the CIA, George H. W. Bush, Saudi intelligence chief, Kamal Adham, transformed a small Pakistani merchant bank, the Bank of Credit and Commerce International (BCCI), into a huge, clandestine financial network through which the Safari Club was being financed.[29] Following Nixon's resignation as President, the CIA was embroiled in domestic scrutiny over the Watergate scandal and a Congressional investigation into covert CIA activities. Thus, under U.S. President Gerald Ford, George H. W. Bush worked closely with Kamal Adham in order to conduct important CIA covert operations through the Safari Club. Kamal Adham had previously acted as a communication channel between the U.S. State Secretary Henry Kissinger and the Egyptian President Anwar Sadat. The

Middle East after the end of World War I.

29. Scott, *The Road to 9/11*, 62–63.

Safari Club was largely organized by the then head of French intelligence, Alexandre de Marenches.[30]

When Jimmy Carter became President in 1977, Zbigniew Brzezinski became National Security Adviser, and Samuel Huntington became Coordinator of National Security and Deputy to Brzezinski. In 1978, Brzezinski argued that an "arc of crisis" was stretching from Indochina to southern Africa and that the particular area of focus was consisting of the nations that were stretching across the southern flank of the Soviet Union from the Indian subcontinent to Turkey, and southward through the Arabian Peninsula to the Horn of Africa.[31] Moreover, according to Brzezinski, the "center of gravity" of the aforementioned "arc of crisis" was Iran, but the thirty-seven-year reign of Shah Mohammed Reza Pahlavi was almost over. Reza Pahlavi's reign, which had been extremely benevolent to the U.S., ended in February 1979 by months of civil unrest and revolution. With rising discontent in the region, Brzezinski argued that Islamic forces should be used against the Soviet Union, and George Ball, who was the head of a special White House Iran task force under Brzezinski, recommended that the U.S. government should drop support for the Shah of Iran, and it should support the fundamentalist Islamic opposition of Ayatollah Khomeini.[32] Covertly, the U.S. helped a radical Shia government under Ayatollah Khomeini to come to power in Iran, the "center of gravity" of the aforementioned "arc of crisis," and, soon afterward, in April 1980, the U.S., implementing its own 'divide and conquer' strategy, induced the Sunni regime of Iraqi President Saddam Hussein to invade Iran, thus stirring up a war in the region.[33]

In 1978, as Taraki's socialist government came to power in Afghanistan, almost immediately the U.S. began covertly funding rebel groups through the CIA.[34] On July 3, 1979, U.S. President Carter signed the first directive for secret aid to the opponents of the pro-Soviet regime in Kabul, and, that very day, Brzezinski wrote a note to the U.S. president in which he explained to him that the U.S. aid to Islamic fundamentalists in Afghanistan was going to induce a Soviet military intervention.[35] For a

30. Ibid., 62.
31. Garthoff, *Détente and Confrontation*, 730.
32. Engdahl, *A Century of War*, 171. Scott, *The Road to 9/11*, 67.
33. Scott, *The Road to 9/11*, 89.
34. Kalugin, "How We Invaded Afghanistan."
35. Brzezinski, "Interview," 76.

long period of time, in Afghanistan and the Soviet Muslim Republics, the dominant form of Islam had been local and mainly Sufi. But, during the Afghan War of the 1980s, British and U.S. intelligence agencies deepened their alliance with the Muslim Brotherhood, and this spawned Al Qaeda and several groups that were foreign fighters brought to Afghanistan as "mujahideen" trained and armed to fight the 'godless' Soviet regime. Robin Cook, a former British MP and Minister of Foreign Affairs, wrote that Al Qaeda, "literally 'the database,' was originally the computer file of thousands of mujahideen who were recruited and trained with help from the CIA to defeat the Russians."[36]

The Soviet invasion in Afghanistan prompted the U.S. national security establishment to undertake a colossal covert operation, in the context of which the CIA Director William J. Casey cooperated with Saudi Prince Turki bin Faisal, who was the Director General of Saudi Arabia's intelligence agency, and with the Pakistani intelligence agency (ISI) in order to create a foreign legion of jihadists, an idea that had originated in the Safari Club.[37] More than 100,000 jihadists were trained in Pakistan between 1986 and 1992, in camps overseen by the U.S. and the British intelligence agencies, which were training future Al Qaeda and Taliban fighters in bomb-making and terrorism.[38] Osama bin Laden was a major sponsor of jihadists in Pakistan, he was recruited by the CIA in 1979 in Istanbul, he had the close support of Prince Turki bin Faisal (i.e., the head of Saudi intelligence) and he developed ties with Hekmatyar in Afghanistan.[39] After the Soviet invasion in Afghanistan in 1979, the CIA began funding Hekmatyar's Hezb-e Islami mujahideen organization through the Pakistani intelligence agency.

The Libyan Islamic Fighting Group (LIFG), an arm of the Al Qaeda created by Afghan fighters who returned to Libya after the Soviet withdrawal from Afghanistan, is exemplary of the spreading neo-Salafist problem that emerged out of the Western plan to play Islamic movements against the Soviet Union. After the end of the Cold War and the dissolution of the Soviet Union in the early 1990s, the West in general and the United States in particular became the new target of the radicalized Muslims.

36. Cook, "Struggle against Terrorism."
37. Scott, *The Road to 9/11*, 122.
38. Ibid., 123.
39. Maurus and Rock, "The Most Dreaded Man"; Reeve, *New Jackals*, 168.

In the early 1990s, a Pashtun community known as the Taliban was a powerful military and political force in Afghanistan. In 1994 and 1995, the Taliban acquired a strong alliance with Pakistan's intelligence agency, and, between 1994 and 1996, the U.S. supported the Taliban through Pakistan and Saudi Arabia, because Washington viewed the Taliban as a force that could balance Iran in Central Asia and as a pro-Western movement.[40] Moreover, in the post-Cold War era, the neoconservative Jamestown Foundation, the Caucasus Fund of Georgia (a group affiliated with the Jamestown Foundation), and other groups funded by the U.S. Agency for International Development (USAID) and by George Soros's Open Society Institute attempted to destabilize the Russian Federation by radicalizing the Muslim inhabitants of the Caucasus region and inducing them to declare independence from Moscow and to forge close ties with the U.S.-controlled Wahhabi governments of Saudi Arabia and Qatar.[41]

THE NOOPOLITICS OF THE INTERNATIONAL ECONOMIC SYSTEM

For half a century prior to World War I, and again for a brief period in the 1920s, most of the major trading nations were on the gold standard, i.e., each of them was defining its monetary unit in terms of a certain quantity of gold and was standing ready to convert gold into paper money and paper money into gold at the rate stipulated in its definition of the monetary unit, while gold was being freely exported and imported. Thus, during the previous period of time, given that each nation was defining its monetary unit in terms of gold, exchange rates were fixed.

After World War II, a new monetary system emerged, known as the Bretton Woods system, since, in July 1944, 730 delegates from all forty-four Allied nations participated in the Bretton Woods Conference (officially known as the United Nations Monetary and Financial Conference), which took place at the Mount Washington Hotel, situated in Bretton Woods, New Hampshire, United States, to regulate the post-war international monetary and financial order. The Bretton Woods Agreement paved a way for the International Monetary Fund (IMF) to be established in 1945 with the explicit function of maintaining the rules of the new system and

40. Dreyfuss, *Devil's Game*, 279–80.
41. Laughland, "Chechens' American Friends."

of operating as the main instrument of public international management. The IMF commenced its financial operations on March 1, 1947.

The Bretton Woods system is a 'pegged rate' currency regime, in the sense that members were required to establish a parity of their national monetary units in terms of the reserve currency (a 'peg') and to maintain exchange rates within plus or minus one per cent of parity by intervening in their foreign exchange markets. The U.S. dollar became the reserve currency, thus taking the role that gold was playing before World War II, and, additionally, the U.S. dollar was the only currency backed by gold. The Articles of Agreement of the IMF prohibited the use of gold as money, since they prohibited any link between gold and paper currencies other than the U.S. dollar (Article 4, Section 2(b) of the Articles of Agreement of the IMF).

The IMF is the administrative center of a new international monetary system which was founded on the difference between 'domestic' paper currency, which was accepted as a medium of exchange in the country in which it was issued, and 'foreign exchange' paper currency, which was the medium of exchange for international trade. Thus, for instance, if a German wanted to sell goods in Greece, the Greeks had to find foreign exchange to pay for their purchases. However, such foreign exchange was limited to either specific European paper currencies or to the U.S. dollar. As a result of the previous system, the demand for few, specific European currencies and for the U.S. dollar increased dramatically, and, therefore, such currencies became known as 'hard' currencies. So long as the alliance of Western financial elites could maintain demand for their paper currencies, all that they had to do was to continue printing such money and, thus, creating financial wealth from nothing, or rather from the noopolitical domination of a Western financial elite over the rest of the world.

Furthermore, in the context of the Bretton Woods system, the value of Western currencies could be increased in relation to other currencies by coaxing or forcing devaluation of targeted currencies. The devaluation of a currency triggers a significant transfer of wealth from the masses to the financial elite, causes reductions in real wages, and it economically enslaves those who have taken hard currency loans from the IMF and from major European commercial banks and find themselves in ever-increasing difficulty to repay those interest-bearing loans. In the 1940s, the IMF was instituted as the administrative center of an international monetary regime in which targeted countries were trapped with huge loans, were forced to transfer their economic wealth to their big lenders, and, ultimately, they were impoverished as they were struggling to repay loans with devalued money. The manner in which financial elites play this evil game has been exposed by John Perkins in his book *Confessions of an Economic Hit Man*, and by Naomi Klein in her book *The Shock Doctrine*.

Finally, the new international monetary system of paper money facilitated the banking system to speculate by lending money it did not possess and to create and trade extremely risky financial instruments, such as 'credit default swaps,' Repos, 'futures,' 'options,' etc. In his 2002 letter to the shareholders of Berkshire Hathaway, the leading American investor Warren E. Buffett characterized the previous financial instruments as "financial weapons of mass destruction." In 2014, the Office of the Comptroller of the Currency advised banks to avoid some of the riskiest junk loans to companies, and it expressed concern about the false accounting practices that take place by means of financial derivatives.[42] For instance, in 2010, the court-appointed examiner of Lehman Brothers' bankruptcy, Anton R. Valukas, Chairman of Jenner and Block LLP, issued a 2,200-page report documenting that Lehman Brothers was systematically using Repos and other financial derivatives in order to move bad debts off its balance sheet just long enough in order to remedy its quarterly financial reports, and, thus, it was systematically engaged in balance sheet manipulation. Moreover, at the end of 2012, the JP Morgan Chase had a $69.5 trillion gross notional derivatives exposure, and Deutsche Bank had $72.8 trillion gross notional derivatives exposure, whereas the entire GDP of Germany was 2.7 trillion euros.

The domination of a global financial elite over the international economy was significantly precipitated by U.S. President Richard Nixon's decision to unilaterally challenge the direct convertibility of the U.S. dollar to gold in 1971. By 1971, the United States' gold stock had fallen to about half its 1960 level, and foreign banks held more U.S. dollars than the U.S. held gold, leaving the U.S. vulnerable to a run on its gold. The Nixon Administration put an end to the existing Bretton Woods system of relatively fixed exchange rates, ushering in the era of freely floating exchange rates and, thus, the triumph of paper money. Moreover, during the Clinton administration, the 1999 Gramm–Leach–Bliley Act eliminated legal barriers among commercial banks, investment banks,

---

42. Roumeliotis, "Exclusive: U.S. Banking Regulator."

securities firms, and insurance companies, thus formally instituting the so-called "casino capitalism."[43]

On December 5, 2001, Lynn Turner, former chief accountant of the U.S. Securities and Exchange Commission (SEC) told the *New York Times* that "the amount of gimmickry and outright fraud dwarfs any period since the early 1970s . . . and the 1920s, when the rampant fraud helped cause the crash of 1929."[44] On September 6, 2011, Janet Tavakoli, President of Tavakoli Structured Finance, published an article entitled "Fraud as a Business Model" in the American online news aggregator and blog *Huffpost Business*. In that article, Tavakoli argued that financial deregulation, cheap money from the Fed, failure to enforce remaining financial regulations, crony capitalism, hubris, speculation, leverage, and fraud were the key factors that contributed to the 'financial bubble' that caused the 2008 global financial crisis.

On November 18, 2012, the Financial Stability Board (FSB), which was established after the 2009 G-20 London summit in April 2009, published its annual *Global Shadow Banking Monitoring Report*, in which it stated that, in 2011, the size of the total shadow banking system grew to $67 trillion, which is equivalent to 111% of the aggregated GDP of all countries in the study; in 2011, the U.S. had the largest shadow banking system, with assets of $23 trillion, followed by the euro area ($22 trillion) and the U.K. ($9 trillion), and, therefore, credit intermediation through non-bank channels had become a source of "systemic risk."[45] On a quarter by quarter basis, during the audit time, banks and big corporations, including the *Fortune* 1,000 companies, shift their liabilities into the shadow banking system, consisting "in credit intermediation involving entities and activities outside the regular banking system," and then, once the auditor has left, they can bring them back onto the books. The shadow banking system destabilizes the economic system and underpins financial fraud. Thus, in 2008, the Bank for International Settlements (BIS) (i.e., the central bankers' bank) 'slammed' the Fed, the European Central Bank (ECB), and other major central banks for blowing the 'financial bubble' that caused the 2008 global financial crisis, failing to

43. Giroux, *Zombie Politics*.
44. Berenson, "Watching the Firms."
45. O'Donnell and Miedema, "Shadow Banking."

regulate the shadow banking system, and then using gimmicks which only worsen the financial situation.[46]

The well-known Spanish sociologist Manuel Castells has called the global financial market an "automaton," and he has warned humanity that the nightmarish scenario of machines taking control of the human world tends to become a reality as "an electronically based system of financial transactions," in the context of which people mechanically conform to the out-of-control financial "automaton."[47] The domination of the digitalized structures of financial markets and banks over the world economy and the political superiority of robotized technocratic entities (such as the Troika, i.e., the European Commission, the International Monetary Fund, and the European Central Bank, which, after the 2008 global financial crisis, outrightly became the supreme economic authority in several European Union member-states, e.g., in Greece, Spain, Portugal, Ireland, Cyprus, etc.) have given rise to a superstructure which imprisons its subjects in a world that resembles the "Matrix" described in the 1999 science-fiction action film *The Matrix* written and directed by the Wachowski Brothers. In the era of "casino capitalism" and "network society," the West's multifaceted spiritual tradition of individual truth, liberalism's individualist agenda, and physiocratic economic thought have merged and culminated into what Castells has called a financial "automaton," which is even more suffocating than Spinoza's deterministic universe (in fact, it is not a matter of coincidence that, in the era of advanced liberalism and globalization, Spinozism gains increasing popularity among Western intellectuals).

46. Evans-Pritchard, "BIS Slams Central Banks."
47. Stalder, *Manuel Castells*, 54.

8

THE FOURTH POLITICAL THEORY
A THEME IN NEED OF A FOCUS

THE QUEST FOR THE FOURTH POLITICAL THEORY:
WHAT THE FOURTH POLITICAL THEORY SHOULD NOT BE

In HINDSIGHT, THE END of the twentieth century marks the absolute pre-ponderance of what I have called the "first political theory" (chapter 4), i.e., liberalism, which defeated the other two major political ideologies of modernity, i.e., fascism (in the 1940s) and Marxism (in the 1990s). The defects of what I have called "advanced liberalism" (chapter 4), the deep crisis that is associated with the institution of liberal globalization in the twenty-first century, and the geopolitical and noopolitical issues that I studied in chapters 6 and 7 have led several Western scholars, such as Alain de Benoist, Alain Soral, Christian Bouchet, and Laurent James, to seek a "fourth political theory" in order to counter the liberal monologue.

Alain de Benoist,[1] an influential French philosopher and a founder of the "Nouvelle Droite" (New Right), has published several attacks on globalization, unrestricted mass immigration, and liberalism as being fatal obstacles to Europe's attempt to exist authentically. In the context of his criticism of liberal globalization, Benoist opposes Christian-ity as inherently intolerant, theocratic, and bent on persecution, and he argues that Europe must return to its pre-Christian roots, using the Indo-European model (such as Nordic, Celtic, Greek, and Roman civi-lizations) as an alternative to capitalism and communism. In particular,

---

1. Benoist, *Being a Pagan*; Benoist *Beyond Human Rights*; Benoist *The Problem of Democracy*.

he has asserted the superiority of 'faith' to 'law,' the superiority of 'myth' to 'logos,' the superiority of 'will' to 'pure reason,' and the superiority of 'image' to the 'concept.'[2]

Alain Soral,[3] a Franco-Swiss essayist, journalist, film maker, and boxing coach, has published several polemical essays on capitalism, Islamic and gay 'communitarianism,' feminism, and Zionism. His ideology is a mix between social and economic ideas from 'Left' and values like 'nation' and 'morality' from 'Right.' Moreover, Alain Soral's criticism of modernity is founded on 'traditionalism.' Traditionalism is a twentieth-century anti-modern movement that emerged from the occultist *milieu* of late nineteenth-century France and was fed by the widespread loss of faith in progress that followed the First World War.[4]

Working first in Paris and then in Cairo and being intellectually founded on Hindu religious texts, the French author René Guénon (1886–1951) rejected modernity as a dark age, and sought to reconstruct the "Perennial Philosophy," by which he meant a system of fundamental truths that, according to him, underpin all the major world religions.[5] In 1910, Guénon was initiated into Sufism, and he obtained the name Sheikh Abd al-Wahid Yahya. In fact, traditionalism comprises several esoteric and sometimes very influential religious groups in the West and in the Islamic world. Furthermore, Julius Evola (1898–1974), who was a renowned Italian Dadaist artist, idealist philosopher, mystic, anti-modernist, and scholar of world religions and the occult, attempted to guide fascism along traditionalist lines.[6]

The New Right and traditionalism treat religion as a means for preserving the established system of social hierarchy and for controlling the distribution of power. In essence, such intellectuals as Benoist, Soral, Guénon, and Evola endorse Marx's argument that religion is "the opium of the people,"[7] but, in contrast to Karl Marx and the Enlightenment, they support religion *qua* "the opium of the people." From the perspective of New Right and traditionalist intellectuals, religion is dangerous and upsetting only when it functions as an ultimate purpose (i.e.,

2. Ibid.

3. Naulleau and Soral, *Dialogues Désaccordés*; Soral, *Sociologie du Drageur*, and *Chroniques d' Avant-Guerre.*

4. Sedgwick, *Against the Modern World.*

5. Ibid.

6. Ibid.

7. Pals, *Eight Theories of Religion*, chapter 4.

as an end-in-itself), because then it does not function as an instrument in the hands of the social establishment, and it proclaims the potential divinity of the human being independently of all historically determined hierarchies and identities.

Christian Bouchet, a leading French national-revolutionary affiliated with France's right-wing nationalist party "Front National," has argued that the European national-revolutionary movement is the European counterpart of the national liberation movements in the Third World, and its objectives are to revive what has been destructed by the French Revolution and to promote a radical attack on political centrism as being an underpinning of the liberal monologue.[8] Bouchet's primary sources of inspiration are the works of Julius Evola and René Guénon. At the geopolitical level, Bouchet argues for the creation of a geopolitical axis Paris-Berlin-Moscow, and, at the economic level, he espouses Keynesianism, and he argues that the state should direct capitalism.[9] Bouchet has accomplished a PhD in anthropology in the University of Paris Diderot about the occultist Aleister Crowley (1875–1947), and, according to Nicholas Goodrick-Clarke, he has been associated with Nazi mysticism.[10]

Laurent James, an influential French philosopher, scholar of esotericism, and the editor of the website *Parousia*, is focused on traditionalism, and he has published several attacks on what he has called a postmodern "anti-world." According to Laurent James, the postmodern "anti-world" can be defeated only by mysticism and by the revival of Pagan traditions. Moreover, Laurent James promotes a neo-Templar mythology, in the context of which the medieval order of the Knights Templar is presented as the culmination of Celtic Christianity and as a powerful link among Celtic Europe, Rome, and the Near East.

The aforementioned arguments against liberal globalization are strongly influenced by the philosophical legacy of Nietzsche and Heidegger, whose works I studied and criticized in chapter 3, and they merely constitute particular aspects of the Western tradition of individual truth, to which I often referred in this book. Alain de Benoist, Alain Soral, Christian Bouchet, and Laurent James criticize only one particular aspect of the historical manifestation of the Western tradition of individual truth, specifically liberalism, but they do not transcend the

8. Bouchet, *Directi*, and *Karl Maria Wiligut*.

9. Ibid.

10. Goodrick-Clarke, *Hitler's Priestess*.

Western tradition of individual truth *per se*, and, therefore, spiritually, their anti-liberal and anti-globalization attitude and liberal globalism are two sides of the same coin.

The manifestation of the Western tradition of individual truth through liberalism consists in a type of human being who wants to be self-actualized by continually bringing about changes, i.e., by creating new forms that reflect his intentionality and manifest his capabilities and power. Thus, the liberal individual treats 'innovation' and 'entrepreneurship' as ends-in-themselves. The liberal individual wants to change everything in his external existential conditions in order to leave his *ego* and inner life unchanged. Thus, the distinctive characteristic of the liberal individual is vanity. Furthermore, conservatism, as it is understood in modern West, is nothing more than an attempt to enhance the ability of the liberal individual to control risks, and, therefore, ultimately, conservatism is simply a manifestation of limited imagination.

The manifestation of the Western tradition of individual truth through socialism/communism consists in a type of human being who wants to give permanent solutions to historical problems and petrify institutions in order to conceal his inferiority complex *vis-à-vis* those whom he sees as historically superior and to justify his socio-economic ineffectiveness. In other words, the socialist/communist individual appeals to utopianism and to mediocrity in order to redistribute power away from those actors who are more socio-economically effective toward those actors who are less socio-economically effective. Thus, the distinctive characteristic of the socialist/communist individual is envy.

The political history of modern West moves like a pendulum between the liberal individual and the socialist/communist individual, and, additionally, there are different combinations between the ethos of the liberal individual and the ethos of the socialist/communist individual, such as fascism. The attempts that have been made by Alain de Benoist, Alain Soral, Christian Bouchet, and Laurent James to articulate a "fourth political theory" constitute a continuation of the West's tradition of individual truth by means of a political theory whose objective is to defend the Western individual against the failures of liberalism. Furthermore, Benoist's, Soral's, Bouchet's, and James's revolt against modern rationalism does not signal a departure from the core of Western thought, since, as I argued in chapters 2 and 3, within the framework of Western civilization, rationalism, mysticism, romanticism/German idealism, and neoclassicism co-exist as different aspects and manifestations of the same principle, namely, of the principle of individual truth.

Finally, and most glaring of all, Benoist's, Soral's, Bouchet's, and James's attempts to create a fourth political theory are founded on a superficial and misguided approach to the history of European civilization. In particular, Alain de Benoist, Alain Soral, Christian Bouchet, and Laurent James seem to be totally ignorant of the spiritual division of Europe into two different civilization zones, specifically into the Greco-Byzantine East and the Latino-Frankish West, and of the substantial differences between the Greco-Byzantine East and the Latino-Frankish West.

In the prehistoric era, the relationship between the Greeks and the Celts was already intimate and strong, and, in general, the civilization of prehistoric Europe was founded on the Mycenaean civilization.[11] In his *Geographica*, Strabo writes that Marseille, which was founded in the sixth century B.C. by Greeks from Phocaea, was schooling the Galatae (Celts and Gauls) to be fond of the Greek civilization and to write even their contracts in Greek, and it was one of the most important educational centers in the Roman Empire.[12] In his *De bello gallico*, Gaius Julius Caesar writes that the Helvetti (a Gallic tribe occupying most of the Swiss plateau) were writing in Greek characters, and, also, the Druids, i.e., the priests of the Celts, were using Greek characters in their public and private transactions.[13]

The intimate and strong relationship between the Greeks and the Romans is an ancient phenomenon, too. Rome was founded by the Etruscans and by the Greek inhabitants of Kimi (current Cuma) and Sicily. The Latin alphabet is derived from the Greek one, and the first known Roman author is the Greek dramatist and epic poet Livius Andronicus (third century B.C.). Moreover, during the classical era, the Romans adopted the Greek religion.

But, after the era of Alexander the Great (fourth century B.C.), the Greek East and the Latin West started following mutually different and diverging cultural paths. In the fourth century B.C., Alexander the Great unified the Greek world, and he decided to move his forces eastward, thus hampering the Greeks' cultural interaction with the Romans and the Celts. During the Hellenistic period (i.e., the period between the death of

11. Hawkes, *Prehistoric Foundations of Europe*.
12. Strabo, *Geographica*, IV, 181.
13. Julius Caesar, *De bello gallico*, I, 29:1, and VI, 14:4.

Alexander the Great in 323 B.C. and the annexation of the classical Greek heartland by Rome in 146 B.C.), the Greek culture was dynamically interacting with Eastern traditions (primarily Jewish, Persian, and Egyptian ones). When the Roman Emperor Theodosius the Great (346–95 A.D.) divided the Roman Empire between his two sons, Arcadius in the East and Honorius in West, the Adriatic Sea became the official border between 'East' and 'West.'

As I argued in chapters 1 and 2, the difference between the Roman legal tradition and the Greek philosophical tradition and, additionally, the change of the Roman Empire's capital from Rome to Constantinople contributed to the widening of the cultural gap between the Greek East and the Latin West. Moreover, as I argued in chapter 2, the previous cultural gap became even wider as a result of the antithesis between scholasticism and Hesychasm. Thus, according to the arguments that I put forward in chapters 1–3, regardless of many Western scholars' appeal to classical Greek philosophy, the Greek East's *logos* is substantially different from the Latino-Frankish West's *ratio*, and the way in which the Greek East understands 'myth,' 'faith,' 'idea,' 'truth,' and 'freedom' is substantially different from the way in which the Latino-Frankish West and modern European philosophers understand 'myth,' 'faith,' 'idea,' 'truth,' and 'freedom.' Finally, in chapter 2, I elucidated the substantial differences between the Greek East's Christianity and the Latino-Frankish West's Christianity.

As I have already argued, in the Greek East, *logos* and myth are united. In the Greek East, the knowledge of truth consists in man's participation in the Absolute, which Plato calls the world of ideas, and which the Hesychasts call the uncreated energies of God, and, therefore, it is not primarily based on rational accountability, but on psychic cleansing. From the previous perspective, Greek philosophy and Hesychasm transcend the subject–object dichotomy, without espousing either of them, and without pursuing any structural synthesis between the subject and the object. The Greek philosophy and Hesychasm transcend the subject–object dichotomy by accepting the ontological reality of Truth, or the Absolute, and by arguing that humans can participate in the energies of the Absolute according to their free will and according to the degree of their psychic cleansing. From the previous perspective, the ontological reality of Truth does not coincide with the thesis that the Absolute is an objective substance which, in Kantian fashion, commands unconditionally.

From the viewpoint of Greek philosophers, the first step of philosophy consists in one's awareness that being constitutes a signification, and, therefore, the truth of an entity transcends its material substance. In other words, philosophy would be impossible if we decided to separate the object from its significance. Given that truth transcends essence, the *logos* that discloses truth is myth (i.e., it refers to the source of the significance of beings and things). The objectivist approaches to truth are related to and derive from Western rationalism, which, in turn, is derived from medieval scholars, and they are alien to classical Greek thought. Moreover, both the negation of metaphysics and the tradition of Western humanism (which is centered on historical action) are irrelevant to classical Greek philosophy and its objectives.

Western anti-rationalist scholars, including existentialists, romantics, and postmodernists, have failed to realize that an ontologically grounded truth implies and underpins a deterministic world order *only if* one assumes that necessity is the primary force in the functioning of the world. On the other hand, in his *Laws*, Plato emphasizes that the principle of necessity is not self-existent, but it complies with God, and, furthermore, as I argued in chapter 2, the Hesychasts emphasize that cosmic laws are God's *wills*. Thus, classical Greek philosophy and Hesychasm differ from both Western rationalist thought and Western anti-rationalist thought. In contrast to Western thought, Greek philosophy and Hesychasm refuse to treat truth as a creation of man, and, instead, they understand the knowledge of truth as an ontological shift from an individualist existential state to an existential state in which being is united with its significance.

In contrast to scholasticism, the Hesychasts are focused on man's deifying experience of one's participation in God's uncreated energies, while maintaining that God's essence is totally unknowable. As I argued in chapter 2, God deifies man and is conjoined to the true members of His church in the context of a mystical union between humanity and divinity, not in super-essential essence, but through the grace of adoption, the uncreated deification. In addition, according to Gregory Palamas, deification is not just an existential *event*, but it is a *continual process*, a progressive itinerary toward the perfection of man's *noetic* nature. Thus, even though Greek philosophy and Hesychasm do not espouse Western philosophical realism, they do not espouse subjectivism/constructivism either, since the purpose of Greek philosophy and Hesychasm is man's participation in the Absolute, and not the creation of subjective forms.

METAPHYSICAL REPUBLICANISM:
A CANDIDATE FOR THE FOURTH POLITICAL THEORY

As I argued in chapters 1 and 2, according to classical Greek philosophy and Hesychasm, no relationship with beings and things themselves can lead one to the knowledge of truth. According to the previous metaphysical thesis, the knowledge of truth consists in the knowledge of the significance and, hence, of the existential *telos*, of beings and things. Thus, given the indeterminacy of significations, metaphysics proves to be the foundation of spiritual freedom. Nothing is what it is independently of the significance that is attributed to it by the human mind, and, additionally, in the language of the Hesychasts, God is the positive void from which all significations are derived. This is the meaning of the biblical statement that God created mankind in His own image (Gen 1:27).

From the aforementioned metaphysical perspective, history (namely, the field of human creativity, e.g., economic wealth, science, technology, institutions, military capabilities, art, etc.) is neither abolished nor disdained, but it is integrated into a spiritual hierarchy and a teleological perspective. In his *Symposium*, Plato argues that *poiesis*, or true creation, is the passage from non-being into being.[14] For instance, a sculpture exists because it is a material manifestation of the corresponding kind or species, and, therefore, its *poiesis* (creation) consists in the passage from formlessness into form. A sculpture is a creative act because it is a consequence of a conception and an imitation (in Greek: *mimesis*) of the corresponding species. In this case, imitation is *poiesis*, not because it represents something, but because it materializes a species, and, thus, it illustrates the truth of being (i.e., the absolute purpose of being). On the other hand, when imitation consists merely in representation, one ends up with a technically elaborate yet spiritually fruitless variety of imitation; this variety of imitation was cultivated and promoted during the Renaissance, as a result of Renaissance scholars' own interpretation of classical Antiquity and Christianity. In contrast to representational art in general and to Renaissance art in particular, ancient Greek art and Byzantine art understand an image as a link between the object imaged and its archetype (i.e., as an animated symbol).

In his creative activity, man is guided by the species, like the *Demiourgos* (divine Craftsman) in Plato's *Timaeus*. Man cannot create *ex nihilo* (out of nothing), but this does not imply that the creative activity

14. Plato, *Symposium*, 205c.

of man lacks originality. In the field of human creativity, originality consists in the disclosure and interpretation/reinterpretation of empirical data. Nevertheless, man does not create species. Species *qua* truth is not a human creation, but it is continually being disclosed, interpreted, and reinterpreted by humanity.

Species *qua* truth is a divine creation *ex nihilo*, as it is argued by Plato in his *Republic*, where we read that a carpenter's task is to create an empirical bed, which is an imitation of the idea of a bed, a painter's task is to create an image of an empirical bed, and God's task is the creation of the real bed-in-itself (i.e., the idea of a bed).[15] When man's creative activity imitates God, it is *poiesis*, and, in this sense, it can be understood as the passage from non-being into being, since it produces a meaningful world from formless matter. From the previous perspective, 'creation' does not consist in a new form that replaces a previous one, but it consists in the awareness of the continuity of purpose, or *telos*, which guides each and every act, and *telos* is man's ontological perfection. Without the previous awareness of the creativity of continuity in the context of *poiesis*, man would be confined to the biological cycle of life.

As a result of the aforementioned arguments, in his *Statesman*, Plato concludes that the acquisition of political power presupposes a deep awareness of historicity. The dialogue *Statesman* is not concerned with the issue of regime change, which plays a central role in Plato's *Republic*, but it is centered on an attempt to understand historicity through the awareness of the difference between eternity and time. According to Plato, a real statesman is one who is aware that, even though he is committed to historical action, he has to transcend the realm of history, for the purpose of his rule is *poiesis*. Thus, in his *Statesman*, Plato poses the following question: "Take the case of all those whom we conceive of as rulers who give commands: shall we not find that they all issue commands for the sake of producing something?"[16] A real statesman acts within a world marked by necessities, but the *telos* of his political activity is the eternal Good. Thus, for such a statesman, legal order is subject to the Good, which should not be conceived of as a petrified institution, but as an active *telos* which underpins a type of creativity that combines prudence with boldness. From this perspective, the *theocentric* character of classical Greek philosophy and of the Byzantine civilization is different from both *theocracy*, which understands

15. Plato, *Republic*, 597b–c.
16. Plato, *Statesman*, 261a–b.

the *telos* of being as a petrified institution, and Western *humanism*, which subordinates the significance of beings and things to historical becoming. Ancient and medieval Greek theocentrism implies that existence is not a value in itself and that time is not a self-moving dimension of existence. Hence, according to ancient and medieval Greek theocentrism, the meaning of being cannot be completely determined by logic, and, as a consequence, it is not a closed system.

From the perspective of classical Greek philosophy and Hesychasm, every intentional act is caused by a meaning, which is its purpose, but, if the meaning of an act is merely a practical goal (i.e., another act) then it is not an authentic meaning, and no act that is caused by an inauthentic meaning is creative. If every act is subject to and caused by practical reason, then practicality itself is meaningful only if its meaning transcends practice or action. Thus, every secular philosophy of action is inherently defective, and the fallacy of secularism has eventually caused the crisis of modernity. Practical reason is an intellectual fruit of modernity, and it contrasts mainly with grace, which is a force that transcends causality. God offers His grace to those men who abandon all rational certainties, and the space of grace is the society of people who are united in the same *Logos*. Therefore, the ultimate goal, or *telos*, of political action is not an institutional issue, but it consists in an attempt to change man in order to make him capable of overcoming his inner contradictions and communicating harmoniously with his fellow humans and with the world at large. This is the essence of what I call metaphysical republicanism.

Metaphysical republicanism rejects the reduction of *logos* to the logic of historical conditions. If *logos* is reduced to the logic of historical conditions, then man's existential conditions can be changed only in a rationally determined way, and time is identified with natural time (which is characterized by necessity, as opposed to eternity, which is characterized by freedom). If spirituality is identified with historicity, then the meaning of every being or thing is restricted to its practical utility. On the other hand, from the perspective of metaphysical republicanism, the meaning of eternity is the irreducibility of spirit to practicality. Additionally, from the perspective of metaphysical republicanism, historicity is supra-rational. If metaphysical republicanism espoused a rationalist approach to historicity, then it would pursue a biological or a state-centric way of achieving social unity. Both biological and state-centric types of social unity are totalitarian. The biological way of achieving social unity is founded on material processes of adaptation, and it is politically manifested through the total adjustment of all forms of social life to geopolitical and geoeconomic conditions, thus leading to fascism/ national-socialism. The state-centric way of achieving social unity is founded on what bureaucrats and the 'politburo' define as a 'historical necessity', thus leading to Bolshevism or Maoism. Bolshevism consists in a rationalist and, hence, iniquitous interpretation of the Russian people's eschatological visions and communal traditions (i.e., it consists in an attempt to achieve a metaphysical goal by means of legal institutions). Similarly, Maoism is a rationalist and, hence, iniquitous interpretation of the Chinese people's great metaphysical tradition. Thus, metaphysical republicanism opposes all three basic political ideologies of modernity, namely, liberalism, communism, and fascism.

METAPHYSICAL REPUBLICANISM AS A HEROIC IDEAL

From the perspective of the metaphysical arguments that I defend in this book, a true hero is a person who has the boldness, the prudence, and the perseverance to seek the ultimate meaning of existence, regardless of the particular historical conditions in which he exists, and, therefore, a true hero does not conform to the values and imperatives of historical becoming. A true hero has the boldness, the prudence, and the perseverance to maintain his spiritual autonomy from historicity. True heroism is a way of life, and not merely a phenomenon associated with war. If a hero were merely a person who fights gallantly, then heroism would be meaningless during periods of peace.

A true hero neither disdains history nor ignores his historical responsibilities and constraints, but he undertakes his historical responsibilities creatively and not passively. As Thomas Jefferson wrote to Elbridge Gerry in 1801, "unequivocal in principle, reasonable in manner, we shall be able I hope to do a great deal of good."[17] A true hero refuses to subject spirit to historicity. Thus, in 1816, Thomas Jefferson wrote to John Adams the following: "True wisdom does not lie in mere practice without principle."[18] From the viewpoint of a true hero, the end does not justify the means, and there is no element of heroism in crime. Furthermore, from the viewpoint of a true hero, there is a clear-cut distinction between terrorism and freedom-fighting movements, there is a clear-cut distinc-

17. Jefferson, *Writings*, vol. 10, 255.
18. Ibid., vol. 15, 75.

tion between legitimate and illegitimate exercise of political power, and there is a clear-cut distinction between justice and injustice.

In the political sphere, a true hero rejects political realists' power monism, since political realists, such as Morgenthau, Kissinger, and Waltz, cannot answer the following question which was originally posed by Plato in his *Republic*: "was this how you meant to define what is right, that it is that which *seems* to the stronger to be his interest, whether it really is or not?"[19] Evading the previous Platonic question and espousing power politics, ancient Athenians destroyed the Melians during the Peloponnesian War (431–404 B.C.), but, immediately after the destruction of Melos, the decline of Athens began. Evading the previous Platonic question, Demosthenes (384–322 B.C.) wrote his "Olynthiac Speeches," in which he argued that policy-makers must make decisions instead of debates and that every policy must be judged on results and not on moral principles, but Demosthenes's political pragmatism did not help Athens, since history vindicated Philip II of Macedon and Alexander the Great, instead of Demosthenes. Evading the previous Platonic question, Niccolò Machiavelli wrote *The Prince*, in which he argued that his political methodology is based on pragmatic and utilitarian approaches to politics, but, eventually, Machiavelli realized that the political model which he had proposed in *The Prince* had to be amended, and, therefore, he wrote the book *Discourse on the First Ten Books of Titus Livy*, in which he qualified and moderated many of the arguments that he had previously put forward in *The Prince*.[20] Evading the previous Platonic question, several Western governments have been destructive for both the West and the rest of the world, because, as I argued in chapter 7, in the twentieth and the twenty-first centuries, several clandestine and subversive operations of Western intelligence agencies and the 'pragmatic' compromise of Western governments with corrupt financial elites on the management of the world economic system went out of control, and, eventually, they damaged the West itself, too.

During the Cold war, the political cynicism and selfish strategy of the Western liberal elites, the penetration of Western European political principles, such as *Realpolitik* and authoritarianism, into the U.S. political system, and the massive employment of former Nazi scientists

19. Plato, *Republic*, 340c.
20. Bondanella and Musa, *Portable Machiavelli*.

and propaganda experts by the CIA[21] after the end of World War II rendered the U.S. incapable of resisting the temptation to imitate political practices and tactics of fascist and communist regimes in the name of power politics. In other words, during the Cold War, the U.S. political establishment made it amply clear that it was determined not to let the opponents/antagonists of the U.S. to retain a monopoly on amoralism and on any advantages that may be derived from amoralism. Thus, during the Cold War, the U.S. international strategy incorporated the following sub-strategies, which had originally been developed by Western European powers and the Soviet Union: the global drug offensive, the international terrorism offensive, international criminalism (i.e., the exploitation of organized crime in the interests of strategy), the doctrine of "friendly tyrants,"[22] and the Gramsci[23] dimension (cultural subversion). In addition, the history of the Cold War shows that, regardless of the pietist rhetoric of several Western policy-makers, the Western or Atlanticist political establishment was not less 'godless' than the Soviet political establishment. In fact, if we bear in mind that the only sinners to whom Jesus Christ said "woe to you"[24] were the hypocrites, then we can conclude that the kind of godlessness that characterizes the Western political establishment is even worse than that which characterizes the Soviet political establishment.

Hans Morgenthau argues that, in order to understand the behavior of states, it is necessary to have previously understood and explained individual behavior.[25] Additionally, he argues that "politics, like society in general, is governed by objective laws that have their roots in human nature."[26] However, because Morgenthau does not want to assert that international politics is a mechanistic field, he adopts a Cartesian-like view of 'methodological doubt'; namely, he maintains that, despite the fact that one can develop an objective understanding of these universal, timeless laws of international politics, there exist two major obstacles to the production of objective knowledge in the social sciences. First, the ideological beliefs that the social scientist has absorbed through a process

21. Lasby, *Project Paperclip.*
22. Pipes, *Friendly Tyrants.*
23. Gramsci, *Prison Notebooks.*
24. Matt 23:13.
25. Morgenthau, *Scientific Man versus Power Politics*, 43.
26. Morgenthau, *Politics among Nations*, 4.

of socialization make him conduct research with certain preconceptions; namely, the mind of the social scientist is "molded by the society which he observes."[27] Furthermore, even if a social scientist were able to obtain a picture of society which is not distorted by his 'ideological lenses,' Morgenthau argues that "one of the main purposes of society is to conceal these truths from its members."[28] On the other hand, Morgenthau argues that the previous obstacles to objective knowledge can be overcome, and he acknowledges the "existence and accessibility of objective truth."[29] In particular, Morgenthau argues that the acquisition of objective knowledge is achieved through the possession of an accurate theory.

Although Morgenthau argues that an international-political theory should be consistent within itself and with facts, the pursuit of unitary understanding ('power politics') and the tension between the abstracted (necessity in the form of power politics) and the unabstracted (the realm of freedom and morality which have been separated from politics by Morgenthau) undermine the empirical relevance of his theory and the cognitive significance of his theorems. As far as the human nature is concerned, Morgenthau adopts a pluralistic view of man, since he recognizes both ethical and rational dimensions.[30] But, on the other hand, he regards the "will-to-power" as the defining characteristic of politics and as the element with respect to which one can distinguish politics from economics, religion, and law. For, Morgenthau asserts the autonomy of politics as a distinct form of social life, which is characterized by the "will-to-power." Thus, having restricted himself to the abstraction of the 'political man' from the real man and of 'political life' from real life, having made those assumptions and those assumptions alone, Morgenthau's results do not constitute a general theory, and, in terms of operationally meaningful theorems, they are puny indeed. Morgenthau's arguments make it difficult to distinguish between explanation and prescription. For instance, does the behavior of the 'political man' analyzed by Morgenthau reflect the actual state of affairs or Morgenthau's prescriptions and ethos, and how can that behavior explain *reality* since it is supposed to characterize the 'political man' (i.e., an abstract entity)? Morgenthau, the acknowledged father of political realism, is unable to answer the previous ques-

27. Morgenthau, *Politics in the Twentieth Century*, 258.
28. Ibid., 259.
29. Ibid., 267.
30. Morgenthau, *Scientific Man versus Power Politics*, 5.

tions. Morgenthau, having committed himself to the necessity of power politics, is ignorant of ontology, and, therefore, he is oblivious of the dialectic of reality and construes 'generalization' in an ahistorical fashion.

The Platonic question that I mentioned at the beginning of this section ("was this how you meant to define what is right, that it is that which *seems* to the stronger to be his interest, whether it really is or not?") haunts the entire political history of Europe, even though political realists desperately try to evade it. From the perspective of metaphysical republicanism, political authority should be founded on a moral aristocracy (i.e., on a philosophical attitude toward politics). According to the ethos of classical Greek philosophers and Byzantines, aristocracy is manifested through service to society. In other words, the level of one's nobility is determined by what he can offer to society (i.e., by his capability of serving others). Thus, in his *Republic*, Plato emphasizes that whoever is devoted to serving the public interest abstains from daily worries, selfish thoughts, and individual agenda.

Jesus Christ has emphasized that greatness is in serving, and he has explicitly condemned authoritarianism (Mark 10:40–42; Matt 18:4; Luke 22:26). The Kingdom of Christ is founded on the principle that whoever desires to be great among his fellow humans shall be their servant; therefore, it is dramatically opposite to the mortal, earthly governments which are characterized by the exercise of authoritarian power over their subjects (Mark 10:40–42). Moreover, Jesus Christ explicitly condemned religious and political authoritarianism by saying to his disciples: "Watch out for the yeast of the Pharisees and that of Herod" (Mark 8:15).

The moral aristocracy that underpins metaphysical republicanism has also been emphasized by early Christian church fathers and Byzantine political philosophy.[31] Isidore of Pelusium (died ca. 450 A.D.) was a prominent early Christian church father, who is famous for his letters written to Cyril of Alexandria, Emperor Theodosius II, and a host of others, and for his close friendship with John Chrysostom, Archbishop of Constantinople. In his second, third, and twelfth *Epistles*, Isidore of Pelusium argues that a prince must have a deep sense of justice, that both priesthood and kingship set themselves the same objective (namely, the salvation of their subjects), and, additionally, that salvation is won not by force but by gentle persuasion and free will. In his thirty-fifth *Epistle*, Isidore of Pelusium advises Emperor Theodosius II to distribute wealth

---

31. Dvornik, *Early Christian and Byzantine Political Philosophy*.

as it should be, because "not even a king is saved by his great power, nor does one avoid the irreverence of idolatry who avoids the generous disposal of wealth."

In his *Homily on Wealth and Poverty*, 40, John Chrysostom urges us to reconsider the notions of 'poverty' and 'affluence,' and he argues that we should never consider wealthy people healthy, since they are "always yearning and thirsting after other people's poverty," and they are unable to enjoy any abundance. Thus, in his *Homily on Wealth and Poverty*, 40, John Chrysostom poses the following question: "if one cannot control his own greed, even if he has appropriated everyone's property, how can he ever be affluent?" Moreover, in his *Homily on Psalm 14: Against Usury*, Basil the Great reminds Christians of the following biblical principles: "In depicting the character of the perfect man, of him, that is, who is ordained to ascend to the life of everlasting peace, the prophet reckons among his noble deeds his never having given his money upon usury. This particular sin is condemned in many passages of Scripture."

METAPHYSICAL REPUBLICANISM AND TRADITION

Metaphysical republicanism emphasizes the value of tradition, but it differs from 'traditionalist conservatism' as the latter is understood in post-World War II Western societies.[32] In eighteenth-century Western Europe, traditionalism developed in response to English Civil War and the French Revolution. From the perspective of traditionalist conservatism, 'tradition' consists in a set of concrete answers that were given in the past, in the context of substantially different social conditions. Thus, traditionalist conservatism often consists in an obsessive formalism. In the context of traditionalist conservatism, tradition reduces to a fixation on a particular segment of historical space-time, and thus, it transforms a particular way of life into a mold.

The conservatism of traditionalist conservatives is merely a consequence of poor imagination. On the other hand, from the perspective of metaphysical republicanism, tradition does not consist in concrete answers that were given in the past, but it consists in a way of asking questions and in specific questions that manifest one's motives and values. The kind of questions that one asks disclose one's priorities, motives, and values. If we define tradition as a set of fundamental questions that

32. Frohnen et al., *American Conservatism*; Oldmeadow, *Traditionalism*.

manifest a human community's priorities, motives, and values, and not as a set of concrete answers, then a metaphysical republican is a sincere supporter and guardian of the spiritual freedom and the historical creativity of posterity.

From the viewpoint of metaphysical republicanism, tradition is a presupposition of freedom, in the sense that, by emphasizing and preserving specific existential *questions* and, therefore, a specific value system, but not concrete *answers*, tradition safeguards man's freedom from the impersonal and coercive logic of historicity and, also, from obsolete answers to traditional questions. Thus, metaphysical republicanism rejects both innovation as an end-in-itself (i.e., mechanistic models of 'progress') and fixation on a particular set of answers to traditional questions. For instance, if one insists on using Damascene swords in twenty-first-century battlefields, then one has a spiritually sterile conception of tradition, but, if one retains the ethos that was underpinning the use of Damascene swords in medieval societies (namely, the values of strength and struggle for freedom), then one has a spiritually fruitful conception of tradition. Similarly, if one insists that, in the twenty-first century, people should be forced to conform to particular dressing codes that were created centuries ago in the context of substantially different social conditions, then one understands tradition in a spiritually sterile way, but, if one retains the underlying ethos and purposiveness of old dressing codes (namely, expressing respect for the human body, discerning between the two genders, discerning among different social roles, etc.), then one has a spiritually fruitful conception of tradition.

Furthermore, according to metaphysical republicanism, conservatism should be inextricably linked to a strong sense of moral responsibility and respect for everything that has some value. Thus, from the perspective of metaphysical republicanism, a conservative is a person who 'keeps,' 'preserves,' and 'guards' certain things, not due to a pathological lack of imagination, but due to a strong sense of moral responsibility and respect for everything that has some value and, therefore, deserves to be preserved. In other words, from the perspective of metaphysical republicanism, conservatism implies keen conscience and affection.

FROM INTERNATIONAL RELATIONS TO
INTER-CIVILIZATIONAL RELATIONS:
THE THREE BASIC COSMOGENETIC SYSTEMS

From the viewpoint of metaphysical republicanism, the study of civilizations and of the relations among them is the cornerstone of international-
political studies. Moreover, civilizations can be categorized into different
types which can be called cosmogenetic systems. Each cosmogenetic
system corresponds to an archetypal man and to an archetypal society.
A civilization is a product of a specific cosmogenetic system, but it may
include elements from different cosmogenetic systems. There are three
basic cosmogenetic systems: Occidentalism, Orientalism, and Hellenism.

Occidentalism

By the term Occidentalism, I refer to the family of civilizations that
constitute the historical and spiritual entity which is called the 'West.' In
chapters 2 and 3, I elucidated the fundamental principles of the 'West.'
The cornerstone of Occidentalism is the thesis that truth is structurally
united with the individual. In other words, the major distinctive characteristic of Occidentalism is individualism, which, as I argued in chapters
2 and 3, can be expressed in different forms. In particular, in chapter 2,
I studied the individualistic character of Occidentalism in the context
of Western Christianity, and, in chapter 3, I studied the individualistic
character of Occidentalism in the context of modern philosophy and
postmodernity. Moreover, in chapters 4–6, liberalism (namely, the preeminent form of individualism in Anglo-Saxon political thought) was
methodically scrutinized.

Given the major role that the nation-state has played in the development of the scholarly discipline of International Relations, it is important
to mention that, as I already argued in chapter 3, the concepts of nation
and nationalism in the modern sense (i.e., distinguished from simple 'patriotism') are historically linked to individualism as a value. The 'nation'
is a type of social organization that corresponds to the realm of individualism as a value. The history of nationalism is inextricably linked to the
history of individualism, and, additionally, the 'nation' is a type of society
that consists of men who see themselves as individuals.

In the history of the nation-state, one can realize that there are
two basic ways in which the nation-state can attain its institutional

unification: one way is based on the national assembly, and another way is based on the ruler's power. For instance, the institutional unification of the French nation-state was attained through the French Revolution, which was politically focused and centered on the national assembly ("Assemblée nationale constituante"). In other words, the French nation-state was institutionally unified by the National Assembly of 1789. On the other hand, the German nation-state was institutionally unified, not by the Frankfurt National Assembly of 1848–49, but by the powerful Prussian King Frederick the Great 'through fire and iron.' Thus, Germany has given rise to a peculiar type of individualism. In the context of German civilization, the scholar assigns to himself a role of national significance. A paradigmatic 'German scholar' is simultaneously related to the communal culture and to the rest of the world, and, in particular, like a prince or a parliamentarian, he represents Germany in the external world, i.e., he acts as an intermediary between the German nation and the external world. For instance, in the sixteenth century, Martin Luther acted as a representative of German civilization.

German individualism is founded on the relationship between the 'German scholar' and the 'German nation.' Furthermore, German individualism is in conformity with the Reformation (as opposed to French individualism, which is in conformity with the French Revolution), and it is an introversive and idealistic type of individualism, a type of individualism that is based on *Bildung* (individual culture), and, for the Germans, *Bildung* (i.e., the self-constitution of the individual through education) is founded on one's participation in the national community. Thus, German civilization is characterized by a peculiar combination of individualism and holism, in the sense that, in German civilization, the sphere of communal organization is primarily characterized by holism, whereas the sphere of individual culture is primarily characterized by individualism. Thus, when the Germans' individualism increases dramatically, it is historically expressed through aggressive nationalism and through the political sickness of totalitarianism. Nazi Germany is a characteristic case in point.

Orientalism

By the term Orientalism, I refer to the family of civilizations that constitute the historical and spiritual entity which is called the 'East.' The major constituent parts of Orientalism are the Hindu civilization zone, the Chinese civilization zone, and the Islamic civilization zone. Oriental-ism has two complementary distinctive characteristics: society imposes relations of tight interdependence among its members, thus giving rise to coercive relations which are contrary to individualism, and, on the other hand, Oriental systems of mysticism allow a mystic to pursue his independence from his social environment through the renunciation of the world. Thus, Oriental mystics can be characterized as 'otherworldly individuals' in order to be distinguished from Western 'worldly indi-viduals.' However, due to their individualistic character, many 'schools' of Oriental mysticism are popular in the West.

In the context of Hindu political thought, holism is founded on the concepts of *dharma* (right, duty) and *danda* (force, punishment). According to Hindu political thought, human society is an integral part of the universe, which, for the Hindus, is characterized by *rta*, which is an inviolable cosmic order brought about by the operation of laws that represent divine intelligence. Hindu political thinkers argue that human society reproduces the cosmic order when all men keep to their proper place and discharge their relevant *dharma*. The major sources of *dharma* are the Vedas, the Smritis, and *Vyavahara* (custom). Furthermore, ac-cording to Hindu political thinkers, men can fall victim to illusions and temptations, and, therefore, *danda* becomes necessary to keep them on the right path. Thus, from the perspective of Hindu political thought, governing people consists in using *danda* to maintain *dharma*.[33] Howev-er, Hindu mystics may follow an individualistic path which is *samnyasa*. In Sanskrit, *samnyasa* means renunciation or abandonment, and it is composed of the term 'sam,' which means 'collective,' the term 'ni' which means 'down,' and the term 'asa,' which means 'to throw' or 'to put,' so that a literal translation of *samnyasa* would be 'laying everything down.' Of the 108 *Upanisads* which are contained in the *Muktika*, twenty-three are focused on *samnyasa* as the path to *moksa*, meaning liberation.[34] Moreover, Buddhism represents an important stage in the development of Hindu political thought, since it rejected the caste system, founded monasteries, it articulated a non-theological religion, and it enjoyed the support of inferior social classes (e.g., traders, craftsmen, merchants, and foreign settlers), thus invigorating the individualistic traits of Hindu civilization.

33. Ghoshal, *Hindu Political Theories*; Kane, *History of Dharmasastra*.
34. Olivelle, *Samnyasa Upanisads*.

In the context of Chinese political thought, holism is founded on the following political traditions: Confucius's theory of virtue, which emphasizes rule by moral example rather than by military supremacy or according to hereditary succession, Han Fei Tzu's Legalism (or 'school of the method'), which emphasizes the rule of law and administrative efficiency, and Tung Chung-shu's attempt to amalgamate Confucian political and moral philosophy with the metaphysical and cosmological speculations which are contained in the *Book of Changes* (*I Ching*), according to which the universe is an organic entity in which *yin* (representative of all that is dark, submissive, and female) and *yang* (representative of all that is bright, aggressive, and male) and derivatively the five elements (water, fire, wood, metal, and earth) are dialectically interrelated and subject to a predetermined order. Thus, Han Confucianism, of which Tung Chung-shu is the preeminent representative, grafted Confucian political and ethical notions on an organic conception of society, and it adopted an eclectic attitude toward the incorporation of Legalist practices in the administration of the empire.[35] However, the religious and political teachings of Taoism, whose preeminent representatives are Chuang Tzu and Lao Tzu, pave a mystical way to individualism through renunciation which, in this case, has the form of inaction: since the *tao*, or way (a term used by Confucians), is all encompassing and beyond human comprehension, and its movement proceeds unchecked by the activity of man, the Taoist mystic finds enlightenment in inaction. In the context of Taoism, inaction leads to the relativization of social life, and it allows the Taoist mystic to take distance from the social world.

In the context of Islamic political thought, holism is founded on the concept of the Caliphate, to which I referred in chapter 7. In the Islamic world, the religious and juristic genre is available in two versions: Sunni Islam holds that political and religious authority should be vested in the person of an imam-caliph elected by the *Ummah* (community), whereas Shia Islam (whose main groupings are the Twelvers, the Ismailis, and the Zaidis) limits the legitimacy to Muhammad's son-in-law and cousin Ali, who was ruling over the Islamic Caliphate from 661–65 A.D. In the political sphere, both the Sunni and the Shia emphasize the maintenance of the *Sharia* and of social order, and they are deeply concerned with justice, which they understand as the maintenance of things in their proper station and the regulation of practical life in accordance with

---

35. Ames, *Art of Rulership*; Hsiao, *Chinese Political Thought*.

the requirements of social order.[36] However, Islamic mystics—i.e., the Sufi orders (e.g., Alevi, Bektashi, Mevlevi, Ba'Alawi tariqa, Rifa'i, Chisti, Naqshbandi, Shadhili tariqa, etc.)—follow an individualistic approach to Islam, emphasizing the transmission of the divine light from the teacher's heart to the heart of the student, independently of the worldly society and its values; additionally, despite the Islamic tradition's general discomfort with parable, allegory, and metaphor, many Sufi masters make extensive use of parable, allegory, and metaphor.[37] As Henri Corbin has pointed out, "creative imagination" plays a central role in the work of many Sufi masters.[38] In the eighth and the ninth centuries A.D., great Sufis argued that they achieved the illumination of their individual souls by individual exertion, mortification, and austerity. Thus, there are several Sufi paths, or 'orders,' each of which reflects the mentality and the intellectual attainments of its founder.

Hellenism

By the term Hellenism, I refer to a spiritual tradition which originated in Plato's philosophy as I expounded it in chapter 1 and was further developed by Hesychasm as I expounded it in chapter 2. As I argued in chapters 1 and 2, the distinctive characteristics of this spiritual tradition are the principle of man's participation in the Absolute and its sociocentric way of thinking.

Hellenism is substantially different from both individualism and holism. Thus, from the perspective of Hellenism, true knowledge is not exhausted in the knowledge of the essence or the nature of things, but it primarily consists in the disclosure of the *logoi* of things, i.e., of the manner in which things are interconnected within the *Logos* (what Plato calls the world of ideas and what the Hesychasts call the divine *Logos*). It is participation in the *Logos* which makes beings 'be'; no being exists separated from its *logos*. Being without *logos* is insignificant and inconceivable. The substance of a being has no true being apart from its relationship with the *Logos*. Therefore, *Logos* is the metaphysical foundation of society, and society is an ontological category. 'To be' and 'to be social' (i.e., in communion with the universal *Logos*) are one and the same thing.

---

36. Bosworth *et al.*, *Encyclopedia of Islam*.
37. Abun-Nasr, *Muslim Communities*.
38. Corbin, *L'École Shaykhie*.

Therefore, in Hellenism, there is no such thing as absolute individual, conceivable in itself. Furthermore, as I argued in chapter 1 and 2, Plato and Aristotle have conceived of *eros* (love) as an epistemology, and, similarly, the Hesychasts' epistemology is founded on divine love, too. As a consequence, the ontological category of society stems from a concrete and free mind, and not from any natural necessity.

In the context of Hellenism, man exists on account of a person and not on account of substance. 'Person' means an existential-otherness-in-social-relationships. The Hellenic person is not constrained by his substance, since it is his relationship with *Logos* that enables his substance to exist. In addition, the Hellenic person is not constrained by the structure of his relationship with *Logos* either, because his relationship with *Logos* is an erotic one, and, therefore, far from suppressing the existential otherness of man, it is characterized by freedom of will. Furthermore, the Hellenic person never renounces the world, because he understands the world as a structure of *logoi*.

Hellenism's sociocentric approach to the world has been further supported by quantum physics, which has scientifically disclosed the logical constitution of matter: matter is not constituted simply by atoms of matter itself, but it is constituted by behavioral qualities, or energies.[39] From the perspective of Hellenism, the world is neither a morally 'neutral' object to be exploited by *homo economicus* nor something that must be renounced. Thus, Hesychastic asceticism is substantially different from an Oriental mystic's path of renunciation. A Hesychast affirms the goodness of creation (in accordance with Gen 1:31), prays for the entire world, participates in the communal life of the church, and, far from being antisocial, through Christocentric love and prayer, he participates in the afflictions of the world and aims at directly socializing with God, understanding God as the source of the significance of all beings and things.

As I argued in chapter 2, the Hesychasts understand the world as a structure of *logoi*, and, therefore, they never fight against the body, but they aim at liberating the body from the law of sin (i.e., from impersonal, uncontrolled impulses and instincts and from selfishness) and at establishing there the mind as an overseer. Additionally, as I explained in chapter 2, the Hesychasts emphasize the difference between the terms 'mind' (*nous*) and 'intellect' (rational faculty), and, in contrast to Oriental mysticism, the Hesychasts' notion of stillness implies that it is the

39. Dirac, *Quantum Mechanics*.

mind, and not the intellect, that must be detached from the world of the senses. For the Hesychasts, the mind is naturally oriented toward the divine *Logos*, and, therefore, it should be detached from the world of the senses, and it should function as the repository of uncreated grace in man, whereas the intellect's natural function is to organize sense-data into rational systems, and, therefore, the intellect should not be detached from the world of the senses.

Hellenism as a cosmogenetic system belongs neither to the 'East' nor to the 'West,' and, furthermore, it is not associated with the ideology of any particular nation-state. As far as the Greek nation-state is concerned, I have already argued that it was created in the nineteenth century on the basis of Western political principles and geopolitical calculations, the ideology of Greek nationalism has been founded on German neoclassicism, on French Enlightenment scholars, and on British geopolitical thought, and, in the twentieth century, Greece became an integral and passive member of NATO and the European Union, which are purely Western institutions. In other words, since its creation in 1830, the modern Greek nation-state is deeply alienated from (and often culturally opposite to) what I have described as Hellenism. In the twenty-first century, Hellenism as a cosmogenetic system is available to be adopted by any human community that seeks to overcome the antithesis between holism and individualism and to create a civilization founded on the metaphysics of personhood.

In the sphere of political theory, the cosmogenetic system of Hellenism underpins what I have called metaphysical republicanism. In the sphere of geopolitics, in particular, the cosmogenetic system of Hellenism leads to a multipolar system as it was defined in chapter 6. The cosmogenetic system of Hellenism implies support for Eurasianism only as far as the issue of multipolarity is concerned, since, in the context of the cosmogenetic system of Hellenism, multipolarity is philosophically founded on the concept of personhood (i.e., on the ontology of particularity as I defined it earlier in this book), and not on Heidegger's concept of *Dasein*.

As I have already argued, in the international sphere, metaphysical republicanism implies the transformation of international-political actors into international-political *persons*, and, therefore, it underpins the transformation of the international system into an international *society*. According to Hedley Bull, an international society exists when international-political actors are "conscious of certain common interests and common values," and "they conceive themselves to be bound by a common set of rules in their relations with one another, and share in the working of common institutions."[40] In the sphere of international politics, personhood implies that every international-political actor experiences and maintains his existential otherness, but, simultaneously, he is aware that he is ontologically dependent on a truth that transcends him; also, he has a strong sense of moral responsibility toward the entire humanity, specifically toward people whom he does not personally know and even toward people who have not been born yet. Thus, the theory of metaphysical republicanism which I proposed in this chapter endows Bull's theory of international society with ontological and moral underpinnings.

Western Europe in general and the European Union in particular are the cradle of what I have called Occidentalism, and, therefore, in the extent to which they conform to the tradition of individual truth, they are unable to create a true society, and they can only create national and international systems founded on ephemeral functional compromises or conventions among individual entities. When they attempt to attain a higher level of social unity, they, ultimately, give rise to authoritarianism and totalitarianism, since a system whose members are 'individuals' and not 'persons' can pursue a form of social unity only by suppressing individuality (i.e., through authoritarianism and totalitarianism). Thus, if one is confined to Occidentalism, liberalism seems to be preferable to fascism and Marxism, since, at least, liberals and especially libertarians admit the inability of Occidentalism to create a true society, and they try to adjust to this situation.

Asia is the cradle of what I have called Orientalism, and, therefore, in the extent to which Asian nations adhere to the tradition of holism, they tend to confine people to structures that are characterized by what I earlier called traditionalist conservatism (which is merely a consequence of limited imagination and reactionary formalism), and, also, they impede the spiritual maturity and freedom of individual human beings as historical actors. Thus, for instance, in several Asian countries, intellectually and aesthetically rich systems of spirituality coexist with material poverty and rigid exploitative relations.

Hellenism and especially the concept of personhood, as I defined them in the present book, can create a sustainable international society, because they combine the West's pursuit of individual freedom with the

40. Bull, *Anarchical Society*, 13.

East's pursuit of close social relations, without, however, adhering to either holism or individualism. Thus, Hellenism and especially the concept of personhood can endow an international order with the values and principles that are the necessary underpinnings for creating an international society. Furthermore, Hellenism and especially the concept of personhood can be adopted by both Russia and the United States in order to help both of these superpowers to extricate themselves from the intellectual shackles of Occidentalism's individualistic schools of thought and Orientalism's holistic traditions.

Russia is a 'natural' heir to Byzantium and, hence, to Hellenism. In the tenth century, Vladimir I of Kiev and all Russia was baptized into the Orthodox Christianity, and he adopted Byzantine Christianity as the official religion of Russia. In the ninth century, Cyril and Methodius, who were Byzantine Greek monks and brothers born in Thessaloniki, devised the Glagolitic alphabet, which is the oldest known Slavic alphabet. From the tenth century A.D. until the fall of Constantinople in the fifteenth century, the Varangian Guard (i.e., a Russian military Order which was first formed under the Byzantine Emperor Basil II in 988) was an elite unit of the Byzantine Army. In the fifteenth century, Sophia-Zoe Palaiologina, a niece of the last Byzantine Emperor Constantine XI Palaiologos, married Ivan III, who was then the Grand Prince of Moscow and All Rus. Thus, Sophia-Zoe Palaiologina became the Grand Duchess of Moscow, and the double-headed eagle, which was the official state symbol of the late Byzantine Empire and especially of the Palaiologues (the last Greek-speaking Byzantine dynasty to rule from Constantinople), was adopted by the Russian Empire. Nevertheless, as I have already argued, due to its philosophical deficit, due to the gradual Westernization of the Tsarist regime, and due to Bolshevism, Russia never managed to realize itself as an heir to Byzantium. In the twenty-first century, the biggest historical challenge for Russia is to consciously accept its role as an heir to Byzantium, to understand and absorb the philosophical and spiritual essence of the Eastern Roman Empire, and, furthermore, to articulate a Neobyzantine diplomacy focused on the concept of personhood and on the sociocentric values which I have studied in the present book.

The United States is a potential heir to Hellenism, too, since, in the eighteenth century, the United States was founded on the values of freedom and hope, and the Founding Fathers of the United States sought to create a "New World" that would be free from the negative historical legacy, the failures, and the defects of Western Europe, and it could function as a beacon of noble values. As Carl J. Richard has argued, the Founding Fathers of the United States wanted to emulate their Greek heroes: "to leave the empire and start anew would be to embrace the exciting possibility of creating a society so elevated and virtuous as to inspire future Plutarchs to immortalize the nation."[41] Nevertheless, due to the cultural domination of Occidentalism over America, and due to the fact that, in the twentieth century, the U.S. political elite adopted Western Europe's old political mentalities (e.g., *Realpolitik*, economism, and traditional Western imperialism), the United States has not managed to come up to the expectations and visions of its Founding Fathers. Instead, the United States has replicated fundamental defects of Western Europe's political system, and it has been trapped in the power games of Zionism and Wahhabism, which are by-products of Western Europe's colonial policies and imperialist ethos.[42]

In addition, due to their superpower status, both Russia and the United States need a *logos* that has universal relevance and, therefore, can philosophically underpin the creation of an international society, which is an essential presupposition for the effective management of those issues which necessarily have an impact on all parts of the globe and, therefore, require global solutions. Thus, Carl J. Richard has pointedly argued that "perhaps it is now time for the American public not only to return to the founders—to explore the totality of their lives— . . . but also to return to the great fountainhead of knowledge at which the founders filled their own buckets."[43]

Whereas the Eastern Roman Empire (Byzantium) was always capable of ensuring social unity, even though it was a multiethnic empire, the Western European great powers have always had serious difficulty in creating sustainable social structures and attaining social unity. For instance, from the seventeenth century until the end of World War II, every part of the world was either directly ruled by a Western European power or influenced by the policy of Western European powers, but, even as Western European powers expanded geopolitically and geoeconomically, there was an endless, unsettleable disorder, often manifested in wars, inside Western Europe. In other words, even when it was geopolitically and geoeconomically controlling the world, Western Europe was unable to

41. Richard, *The Battle for the American Mind*, 64.
42. Scheuer, *Imperial Hubris*, and *Osama Bin Laden*.
43. Richard, *The Battle for the American Mind*, 181.

create the unity of Europe. Eventually, the failure of Western European powers to create the unity of Europe cost them the world. The unprecedented savagery of World War I and World War II was the culmination of a long legacy of wars among Western European powers, and it signalled the end of the Western European powers' geopolitical and geoeconomic preponderance over the world.

In the aftermath of the two World Wars, and faced with the issue of nuclear arsenals, the United States and the Soviet Union suspended the sovereignty of European powers and cultivated a sense of moral responsibility toward the entire humanity. Thus, throughout the Cold War (namely, from 1945 until 1989), the United States and the Soviet Union managed to prevent a new great European war by behaving with prudence and by departing from the methodologies and the mentalities of the European diplomats of 1914 and 1939. However, for reasons that I have already explained, neither the United States nor the Soviet Union managed to create a true society. In 1991, the Soviet Union was dissolved. Moreover, whereas the Eastern Roman Empire (Byzantium) lasted for approximately one thousand years, and, it was an object of international admiration and envy throughout its long history, the United States managed to retain the role of international hegemon for just twenty years after the end of the Cold War, and, by the end of the twentieth century, the United States had already become an object of vigorous international criticism and, also, in several parts of the world, an object of contempt and hatred.

From a 'World Order' to a 'World Society'

In the twenty-first century, the United States of America and the Russian Federation need new ways of thinking and acting in order to handle important domestic, international, and global affairs, and, certainly, they should not confine themselves to the political and diplomatic legacy of Western Europe. For this reason, in the present book, I propose a new way of thinking about the metaphysics of world order in the hope that it will be philosophically fruitful, and it will guide political action in an effective way. In the present book, I endorse the Platonic[44] thesis that the Good (i.e., the absolute, universal good) consists in the participation of each particular good (what Plato calls 'idea') in the good-in-itself (God). Thus, 'being' means 'good,' and 'evil' means the negation of good.

44. Plato, *Republic*, VI.

From the perspective of Hesychasm, which underpins my theological arguments throughout the present book, the previous Platonic thesis corresponds to the Hesychasts' thesis about the participation of the created world in the uncreated grace of God.

On the other hand, the distinctive characteristic of modernity is the decision of modern philosophy to separate the notion of being from the notion of good. Thus, Hume's relativism rejects the objectivity of value; values reduce to subjective judgments. According to the Bible, values stem from the goodness of the cosmos (Gen 1:31), but, in the context of modernity, values cease to be cosmic elements. Kant argues that the only real good is man's good will, which is founded on man's sense of duty, which, in turn, is a categorical imperative. John Stuart Mill,[45] on the other hand, equates 'good' with 'pleasure', thus contributing to the further individualization of the notion of good. The fundamental weakness of Western European civilization is its inability to create social unity (without of course imposing authoritarian/totalitarian regimes), since, as I argued in chapter 3, modern (and postmodern) philosophy is founded on the principle of individual truth and on the separation of the notion of being from the notion of good.

In the political sphere, the Platonic and Hesychastic theses which I defend in this book lead to an ontologically grounded sociocentric theory of national and international politics. From the perspective of the arguments that I put forward in this book, man can participate in the good-in-itself, and his participation in a particular culture or a particular nation corresponds to his participation in a particular good. Thus, no particular culture and no particular nation-state are absolute values. Furthermore, neither cultures nor nation-states are ontologically self-sufficient. The endless, dynamic pursuit of the good-in-itself, specifically the progress of historical entities in the realm of the good-in-itself, transforms historical entities into 'persons' (i.e., into individuals-in-communion-with-the-good-in-itself), thus giving rise to an ontologically grounded world society.

---

45. Sabine and Thorson, *Political Theory*, 638 *ff.*

BIBLIOGRAPHY

For the study of ancient Greek and Roman scholars, I used Loeb, Oxford University Press, and Penguin editions. For the study of the Bible, I used the *Septuagint* edition by Alfred Rahlfs, the *Novum Testamentum Graece* editions by Nestle-Aland, and the New International Version. For the study of the Greek church fathers, I used the *Patrologia Graeca* (*P.G.*) by Jacques-Paul Migne, and, for the study of the *Hesychasts*, in particular, I used the *Philokalia* editions by Perivoli tis Panagias Publishers (Thessaloniki). For the study of Byzantine historians and Ecclesiastical history, I used F. Cairns, Loeb, Penguin, and Teubner editions. For the study of the Latin church fathers, I used the *Patrologia Latina* (*P.L.*) by Jacques-Paul Migne.

Abun-Nasr, Jamil N. *Muslim Communities of Grace: The Sufi Brotherhoods in Islamic Religious Life.* New York: Columbia University Press, 2007.

Ames, Roger T. *The Art of Rulership: A Study in Ancient Chinese Political Thought.* Honolulu: University of Hawaii Press, 1983.

Amin, Samir. *Imperialism and Unequal Development.* New York: Monthly Review, 1977.

Archibugi, Daniele. "Models of International Organization in Perpetual Peace Projects." *Review of International Studies* 18 (1992) 295–317.

Aris, Reinhold. *History of Political Thought in Germany from 1789 to 1815.* London: Routledge, 1965.

Arquilla, J., and David Ronfeldt. *Cyberwar Is Coming!* Santa Monica: RAND, 1993.

———. *The Emergence of Noopolitik: Toward an American Information Strategy.* Santa Monica: RAND, 1999.

Bahrim, Dragos. "The Anthropic Cosmology of St. Maximus the Confessor." *Journal for Interdisciplinary Research on Religion and Science,* 3 (2008) 11–37.

Baldwin, David A. *Neorealism and Neoliberalism: The Contemporary Debate.* New York: Columbia University Press, 1993.

Ball, Desmond. "China's Cyber Warfare Capabilities." *Security Challenges* 7 (2011) 81–103.

Banks, Michael. "The Inter-Paradigm Debate." In *International Relations: A Handbook of Current Theory*, edited by Margot Light and A. J. R. Groom, 7–26. London: Pinter, 1985.

Barry, Kieren. *The Greek Qabalah: Alphabetic Mysticism and Numerology in the Ancient World*. York Beach, ME: Weiser, 1999.

Barry, Norman P. *Hayek's Social and Economic Philosophy*. London: Macmillan, 1979.

Bartholf, Mark. "The Requirement for Sociocultural Understanding in Full Spectrum Operations." *Military Intelligence Professional Bulletin* 37 (2011) 4–10.

Beinhocker, Eric D. "Reflexivity, Complexity, and the Nature of Social Science." *Journal of Economic Methodology* 20 (2013) 330–42.

Bell, Philip M. H. *The Origins of the Second World War in Europe*. Harlow, UK: Pearson Education, 2007.

Benjamin, Cornelius A. "Coherence Theory of Truth." In *Dictionary of Philosophy*, edited by Dagobert D. Runes, 58. Totowa, NJ: Littlefield, Adams, and Co., 1962.

Bennett, P., and Michael Nicholson. "Formal Methods of Analysis in IR." In *Contemporary International Relations: A Guide to Theory*, edited by A. J. R. Groom and Margot Light, 206–15. London: Pinter, 1994.

Benoist, Alain de. *Beyond Human Rights*. Translated by Alexander Jacob. 2004. Reprint. London: Arktos, 2011.

———. *On Being a Pagan*. Translated by Jon Graham. 1981. Reprint. Atlanta: Ultra, 2004.

———. *The Problem of Democracy*. Translated by Sergio Knipe. 1985. Reprint. London: Arktos, 2011.

Berenson, Alex. "Watching the Firms that Watch the Books." *The New York Times*, December 5, 2001. No pages. Online: http://www.nytimes.com/2001/12/05/business/05INVE.html?pagewanted=1

Berkeley, George. *Philosophical Works; Including the Works on Vision*. London: Dent, 1975.

Bernays, Edward L. *Propaganda*. New York: Ig, 1928.

Bickerman, Elias J. *The Jews in the Greek Age*. New York: The Jewish Theological Seminary of America, 1988.

Biedermann, Hans. *Dictionary of Symbolism: Cultural Icons and the Meanings Behind Them*. New York: Meridian (Penguin Group), 1994.

Blowers, P., and Robert Wilken, eds. and trans. *On the Cosmic Mystery of Jesus Christ: Selected Writings from St. Maximus the Confessor*. New York: St Vladimir's Seminary Press, 2003.

Bondanella, P., and Mark Musa, eds and trans. *The Portable Machiavelli*. New York: Penguin, 1979.

Bosworth, Edmund C., et al. *Encyclopedia of Islam*. Leiden: Brill, 1960.

Bouchet, Christian. *Direction: Les Nouveaux Nationalistes*. Paris: Éditions Dualpha, 2001.

———. *Karl Maria Wiligut: Le Raspoutine d' Himmler*. Paris: Avatar Éditions, 2007.

Brandom, Robert B. *Tales of the Mighty Dead: Historical Essays in the Metaphysics of Intentionality*. Cambridge: Harvard University Press, 2002.

Breazeale, D., and Tom Rockmore, eds. *Fichte, German Idealism, and Early Romanticism*. Amsterdam: Rodopi, 2010.

Brockhaus Deutsche Geschichte. *Deutsche Geschichte in Schlaglichten*. Leipzig: Brockhaus Gmbh, 2007.

Brouwer, Luitzen E. J. "Life, Art, and Mysticism." *Notre Dame Journal of Formal Logic* 37 (1996) 389–429.

Brower, J., and Kevin Guilfoy, eds. *The Cambridge Companion to Abelard*. Cambridge: Cambridge University Press, 2004.

Brown, Chris. *International Relations Theory: New Normative Approaches*. New York: Harvester-Wheatsheaf, 1992.

Brzezinski, Zbigniew. "The Global Political Awakening." *The New York Times*, December 16, 2008. No pages. Online: http://www.nytimes.com/2008/12/16/opinion/16iht-YEbrzezinski.1.18730411.html?_r=0

———.*The Grand Chessboard: American Primacy and Its Geostrategic Imperatives*. New York: Basic, 1997.

———. "Interview." *Le Nouvel Observateur*, January 15–21, 1998, 76.

———. *Out of Control: Global Turmoil on the Eve of the 21st Century*. New York: Collier, 1993.

———.*The Role of the West in the Complex Post-Hegemonic World*. Lecture during the evening opening gala of the European Forum for New Ideas on September 26, 2012. Warsaw: EFNI Press Release, 2012.

Bull, Hedley. *The Anarchical Society: A Study of world Order in World Politics*. London: Macmillan, 1995.

Buzan, Barry, et al. *The Logic of Anarchy: Neorealism to Structural Realism*. New York: Columbia University Press, 1993.

Byron, Robert. *The Byzantine Achievement*. Mount Jackson, VA: Axios, 2010.

Cairnes, John E. *The Character and Logical Method of Political Economy*. London: Macmillan, 1888.

Casey, K., and Ian McCulloh. "HTS Support to Information Operations: Integrating HTS into COIN Operations." *Military Intelligence Professional Bulletin* 37 (2011) 28–32.

Clarke, Peter. *Liberals and Social Democrats*. Cambridge: Cambridge University Press, 1981.

Colish, Marcia L. *The Mirror of Language: A Study in the Medieval Theory of Knowledge*. Lincoln, NE: University of Nebraska Press, 1968.

Conway, Daniel W. "Genealogy and Critical Method." In *Nietzsche, Genealogy, Morality: Essays on Nietzsche's Genealogy of Morals*, edited by Richard Schacht, 318–33. Berkeley: University of California Press, 1994.

Cook, Robin. "The Struggle against Terrorism Cannot Be Won by Military Means." *The Guardian*, July 8, 2005. No pages. Online: http://www.theguardian.com/uk/2005/jul/08/july7.development

Cooper, Jeffrey R. *The Emerging Infosphere: Some Thoughts on Implications of the "Information Revolution."* McLean, VA.: Center for Information Strategy and Policy, Science Applications International Corporation, 1997.

Copi, I. M., and Carl Cohen. *Introduction to Logic*. 12th ed. New Jersey: Pearson Education/Prentice-Hall, 2005.

Corbin, Henri. *L' École Shaykhie en Théologie Shi'ite*. Tehran: Taban, 1967.

Coudenhove-Kalergi, Richard N. *Pan-Europe*. New York: Knopf, 1926.

———. *Praktischer Idealismus*. Vienna: Paneuropa, 1925.

Courtonne, Yves, ed. *Saint Basil: Lettres*, vol. III. Paris: Les Belles Lettres, 1966.

Cox, Robert W. "Structural Issues of Global Governance: Implications for Europe." In *Gramsci, Historical Materialism and International Relations*, edited by Stephen Gill, 259–89. Cambridge: Cambridge University Press, 1993.

Cunningham, Conor. *Darwin's Pious Idea: Why Ultra-Darwinists and Creationists Both Get It Wrong.* Grand Rapids: Eerdmans, 2010.

———. *Genealogy of Nihilism: Philosophies of Nothing and the Difference of Theology.* London: Routledge, 2002.

Cunningham, C., and Peter M. Candler, eds. *Belief and Metaphysics.* London: SCM, 2007.

D' Allones, Myriam R. *La Crise Sans Fin: Essai sur l' Expérience Moderne du Temps.* Paris: Seuil, 2012.

Dawson, Jr., John W. *Logical Dilemmas: The Life and Work of Kurt Gödel.* Wellesley, MA: Peters, 1997.

Déat, Marcel. *Le Parti Unique.* Paris: Aux Armes de France, 1943.

Defoe, Daniel. *Review of the State of the English Nation.* New York: Columbia University Press, 1938.

D'Entrèves, Alessandro P., ed. *Aquinas: Selected Political Writings.* Oxford: Blackwell, 1948.

Descartes, René. *Discourse on Method, Optics, Geometry, and Methodology.* Translated by P. J. Olscamp. Reprint. Indianapolis: Bobbs-Merrill, 1965.

———. *Meditations on First Philosophy: With Selections from the Objections and Replies.* Translated by Michael Moriarty. Reprint. Oxford: Oxford University Press, 2008.

———. *Passions of the Soul.* Translated by Stephen H. Voss. Reprint. Indianapolis: Hackett, 1989.

Di Bella, Stefano. *The Science of the Individual: Leibniz's Ontology of Individual Substance.* Dordrecht: Springer, 2005.

Dickinson, Robert E. *The German Lebensraum.* Harmondsworth, UK: Penguin, 1943.

Dirac, Paul A. M. *The Principles of Quantum Mechanics.* Oxford: Oxford University Press, 1958.

Dreyfuss, Robert. *Devil's Game: How the United States Helped Unleash Fundamentalist Islam.* New York: Metropolitan, 2005.

Dugin, Alexander. *The Fourth Political Theory.* Translated by Mark Sleboda and Michael Millerman. Reprint. London: Arktos, 2012.

Duverger, Maurice. *Introduction à la Politique.* Paris: Gallimard, 1964.

Dvornik, Francis. *Early Christian and Byzantine Political Philosophy*, 2 vols. Washington, DC: Dumbarton Oaks Center for Byzantine Studies, 1966.

Eliade, Mircea. *The Myth of the Eternal Return; Or, Cosmos and History*, 2nd ed. Translated by Willard R. Trask. Reprint 1949. Princeton: Princeton University Press, 1965.

Emmanuel, Arghiri. *Unequal Exchange: A Study of the Imperialism of Trade.* New York: Monthly Review, 1972.

Engdahl, William. *A Century of War: Anglo-American Oil Politics and the New World Order.* London: Pluto, 2004.

Engels, Friedrich. *Dialectics of Nature.* Translated by Clemens Dutt. Reprint. New York: International, 1940.

Evans, Gillian R., ed. *Bernard of Clairvaux: Selected Works.* New Jersey: Paulist, 1987.

Evans-Pritchard, Ambrose. "BIS Slams Central Banks, Warns of Worse Crunch to Come." *The Telegraph*, June 30, 2008. No pages. Online: http://www.telegraph.

co.uk/finance/markets/2792450/BIS-slams-central-banks-warns-of-worse-crunch-to-come.html

Fénelon, François de Salignac de la Monthe. "On the Necessity of Forming Alliances, Both Offensive and Defensive, against a Foreign Power which Manifestly Aspires to Universal Monarchy". In *A Collecion of Scarce and Valuable Tracts on the Most Interesting and Entertaining Subjects*, 2nd ed., edited by Walter Scott and John S. Sommers, vol. XIII, 766–70. London: Cadell, Davies, 1815.

Fichte, Johann G. *The Science of Knowledge*. Translated by Peter Heath and John Lachs. Reprint. Cambridge: Cambridge University Press, 1982.

Fischer, Fritz. *Germany's Aims in the First World War*. Translated by C. A. Macartney. Reprint. New York: Norton , 1967.

Fischer, Klaus P. *Hitler and America*. Philadelphia: University of Pennsylvania Press, 2011.

Foucault, Michel. *Discipline and Punish: The Birth of the Prison*, 2nd ed. Translated by Alan Sheridan. Reprint. New York: Vintage, 1995.

———. *Language, Counter-Memory, Practice*. Translated by Donald F. Bouchard and Sherry Simon. Reprint. New York: Cornell University Press, 1977.

———. *Power/Knowledge*. Translated by Colin Gordon et al. Reprint. New York: Pantheon, 1980.

Fredrick II (King of Prussia). *Anti-Machiavel*. Translated by Paul Sonnino. Reprint. Athens, OH: Ohio University Press, 1981.

Frohnen, Bruce, et al., eds. *American Conservatism: An Encyclopedia*. Wilmington, DE: ISI, 2006.

Frost, Mervyn. *Towards a Normative Theory of International Relations*. Cambridge: Cambridge University Press, 1986.

Fukuyama, Francis. *The End of History and the Last Man*. New York: Avon, 1992.

Ganser, Daniele. *NATO's Secret Armies*. Oxford: Cass, 2005.

Garthoff, Raymond L. *Détente and Confrontation: American–Soviet Relations from Nixon to Reagan*. Washington, DC: The Brookings Institution, 1994.

Gelzer, Heinrich. *Byzantinische Kulturgeschichte*. Tübingen: Mohr (Siebeck), 1909.

Ghonim, Wael. *Revolution 2.0*. New York: Houghton Mifflin Harcourt, 2012.

Ghoshal, Upendra N. *A History of Hindu Political Theories*. Calcutta: Oxford University Press, 1966.

Gibson-Graham, J. K., et al., eds. *Re/presenting Class: Essays in Postmodern Marxism*. Durham, NC: Duke University Press, 2001.

Giddens, Anthony. *The Third Way: The Renewal of Social Democracy*. Cambridge: Polity, 1998.

Giroux, Henry A. *Zombie Politics and Culture in the Age of Casino Capitalism*. New York: Lang, 2011.

Gödel, Kurt. "Some Basic Theorems on the Foundations of Mathematics and Their Implications." In *Kurt Gödel: Collected Works*. Edited and translated by Solomon Feferman et al., vol. III. Reprint. Oxford: Oxford University Press, 1995.

Golder, Frank A. "The American Civil War through the Eyes of a Russian Diplomat." *American Historical Review* 26 (1921) 454–63.

Goodman, Lenn, E., ed. *Neoplatonism and Jewish Thought*. New York: State University of New York Press, 1992.

Goodrick-Clarke, Nicholas. *Hitler's Priestess: Savitri Devi, the Hindu-Aryan Myth and Neo-Nazism*. New York: New York University Press, 1998.

Gramsci, Antonio. *Selection from the Prison Notebooks.* Translated by Quintin Hoare and Geoffrey N. Smith. New York: International, 1971.

Gregor, A. James. *Giovanni Gentile: Philosopher of Fascism.* New Jersey: Transaction, 2009.

Greenwald, G., and Ewen MacAskill. "Obama Orders US to Draw Up Overseas Target List for Cyber-Attacks." *The Guardian,* June 7, 2013. No pages. Online: http://www.theguardian.com/world/2013/jun/07/obama-china-targets-cyber-overseas

Guthrie, William K. C. *Orpheus and Greek Religion: A Study of the Orphic Movement.* Princeton: Princeton University Press, 1993.

Habermas, Jürgen. *The Theory of Communicative Action, Volume Two: Lifeworld and System,* 3rd ed. Translated by Thomas McCarthy. Boston: Beacon, 1987.

Hall, Melvin. "Integrating Social Science Research into Military (Division) Staff Planning." *Military Intelligence Professional Bulletin* 37 (2011) 72–76.

Hamilton, Alastair. *The Appeal of Fascism: A Study of Intellectuals and Fascism 1919–1945.* New York: Macmillan, 1971.

Hanna, P., and Bernard Harrison. *Word and World: Practices and the Foundation of Language.* Cambridge: Cambridge University Press, 2004.

Hampson, Norman. *The Enlightenment.* London: Penguin, 1968.

Harland, Michael. *Democratic Vanguardism: Modernity, Intervention, and the Making of the Bush Doctrine.* Plymouth, UK: Lexington, 2013.

Harris, Henry S. *Hegel's Development: Toward the Sunlight 1770–1801.* Oxford: Oxford University Press, 1972.

Hawkes, Charles F. C. *The Prehistoric Foundations of Europe to the Mycenaean Age.* London: Methuen and co., 1973.

Heartfield, James. *The European Union and the End of Politics.* Alresford, UK: Zero, 2013.

Hegel, Georg W. F. *Lectures on the Philosophy of World History.* Translated by Hugh B. Nisbet. Reprint. Cambridge: Cambridge University Press, 1975.

——— . *Phenomenology of Spirit.* Translated by A. V. Miller. Reprint. Oxford: Clarendon, 1977.

——— . *Philosophy of Right.* Translated by T. M. Knox. Reprint. Oxford: Oxford University Press, 1942.

Heidegger, Martin. *The Basic Problems of Phenomenology.* Translated by Albert Hofstadter. Reprint. Bloomington, IN: Indiana University Press, 1982.

——— . *Being and Time.* Translated by John Macquarrie and Edward Robinson. Reprint. Oxford: Blackwell, 1962.

Hobbes, Thomas. *Leviathan.* Reprint. Harmondsworth, UK: Penguin, 1968.

Hollis, M., and Steve Smith. *Explaining and Understanding International Relations.* Oxford: Clarendon, 1991.

Hosein, Sheikh Imran N. *The Caliphate, the Hejaz, and the Saudi-Wahhabi Nation-State.* New York: Masjid Darul Qur'an, 1996.

——— . *Jerusalem in the Qur'an.* New York: Masjid Dar-al-Qur'an, 2003.

Hough, J. F., and Merle Fainsod. *How the Soviet Union Is Governed.* Cambridge: Harvard University Press, 1979.

Hsiao, Kung-Chuan. *A History of Chinese Political Thought; Vol. 1: From the Beginnings to the Sixth Century A.D.* Princeton: Princeton University Press, 1979.

Hume, David. *Enquiries Concerning Human Understanding and Concerning the Principles of Morals.* Reprint. Oxford: Clarendon, 1975.

Huntington, Samuel. "The Clash of Civilizations?" *Foreign Affairs* 72 (1993) 22–49.

———. *The Clash of Civilizations and the Remaking of World Order*. New York: Simon and Schuster, 1996.

Husserl, Edmund. *Ideas: A General Introduction to Pure Phenomenology*. Translated by W. R. Boyce Gibson. Reprint. Oxford: Routledge, 2002.

Ivanov, Sergey A. *Holy Fools in Byzantium and Beyond*. Oxford: Oxford University Press, 2006.

Jaeger, Werner W. *Paideia: The Ideals of Greek Culture*, 3 vols. Translated by Gilbert Highet. Reprint. Oxford: Oxford University Press, 1945.

Jenkins, Tricia. *The CIA in Hollywood: How the Agency Shapes Film and Television*. Austin: University of Texas Press, 2012.

Jefferson, Thomas. *The Writings of Thomas Jefferson*, 20 vols. Edited by Andrew A. Lipscomb and Albert E. Bergh. Washington, DC: The Thomas Jefferson Memorial Association of the United States, 1903–4.

Johansen, Thomas K. *Aristotle on the Sense-Organs*. Cambridge: Cambridge University Press, 2007.

Johnston, Douglas, ed. *Faith-Based Diplomacy: Trumping Realpolitik*. Oxford: Oxford University Press, 2003.

Jolley, Nicholas, ed. *The Cambridge Companion to Leibniz*. Cambridge: Cambridge University Press, 1995.

Jung, Carl G. *Aspects of the Feminine*. Translated by R. F. C. Hull. Reprint. Princeton: Princeton University Press, 1982.

———. "The Relations between the Ego and the Unconscious." In *The Portable Jung*, edited and translated by Joseph Campbell, 70–138. New York: Penguin, 1976.

Kalugin, Oleg. "How We Invaded Afghanistan." *Foreign Policy*, December 11, 2009. No pages. Online: http://www.foreignpolicy.com/articles/2009/12/11/how_we_invaded_afghanistan

Kane, Pandurang V. *History of Dharmasastra*, 8 vols. Pune: Bhandarkar Oriental Research Institute, 2006.

Kant, Immanuel. *Three Critiques: Critique of Pure Reason, Critique of Practical Reason, Critique of Judgment*. Translated by Werner S. Pluhar. Reprint. Indianapolis: Hackett, 2002.

Kauppi, M. V., and Paul R. Viotti. *The Global Philosophers: World Politics in Western Thought*. New York: Lexington, 1992.

Keegan, John. *The American Civil War: A Military History*. New York: Random House, 2009.

Keens-Soper, H. M. A., and Karl W. Schweizer, eds. *The Art of Diplomacy: François de Gallières*. Lanham , MD: University Press of America, 1994.

Keohane, Robert O. *International Institutions and State Power: Essays in International Relations Theory*. Boulder: Westview, 1989.

Keohane, R. O., and Lisa L. Martin. "The Promise of Institutionalist Theory." *International Security* 20 (1995) 39–51.

Kierkegaard, Søren A. *Concluding Unscientific Postscript to Philosophical Fragments*. Translated by Howard V. Hong et al. Reprint. Princeton: Princeton University Press, 1992.

———. *Fear and Trembling*. Translated by Alastair Hanay. Reprint. London: Penguin, 1985.

————. *Philosophical Fragments*. Translated by Edna H. Hong. Reprint. Princeton: Princeton University Press, 1985.

————. *The Seducer's Diary*. Translated by Howard V. Hong et al. Reprint. London: Penguin, 1992.

————. *Stages on Life's Way*. Translated by Howard V. Hong et al. Reprint. Princeton: Princeton University Press, 1988.

Kington, Tom. "Recruited by MI5: The Name's Mussolini. Benito Mussolini." *The Guardian*, October 13, 2009. No pages. Online: http://www.theguardian.com/world/2009/oct/13/benito-mussolini-recruited-mi5-italy

Kirkpatrick, David D. "Deadly Mix in Benghazi: False Allies, Crude Video." *The New York Times*, December 29, 2013. No pages. Online: http://www.nytimes.com/projects/2013/benghazi/#/?chapt=0

Kirkpatrick, Jeane. "Dictatorships and Double Standards." *Commentary* 68 (1979) 34–45.

Kissinger, Henry A. *Diplomacy*. New York: Simon and Schuster, 1994.

Kjellén, Rudolf. *Der Staat als Lebensform*. Leipzig: Hirzel, 1917.

Klein, Naomi. *The Shock Doctrine: The Rise of Disaster Capitalism*. New York: Holt, 2007.

Kornbluth, Peter. "CIA Acknowledges Ties to Pinochet's Repression: Report to Congress Reveals U.S. Accountability in Chile." *The National Security Archive* September 19, 2000. No pages. Online: http://www2.gwu.edu/~nsarchiv/news/20000919/

————. *The Pinochet File: A Declassified Dossier on Atrocity and Accountability*. New York: New, 2003.

Kristeller, Paul O. *The Classics and Renaissance Thought*. Cambridge: Harvard University Press, 1955.

Kushner, Howard I. "The Russian Fleet and the American Civil War: Another View." *The Historian* 34 (1972) 633–49.

Lamy, Steven L. "Contemporary Mainstream Approaches: Neo-Realism and Neo-Liberalism." In *The Globalization of World Politics: An Introduction to International Relations*, edited by John Baylis and Steve Smith, 124–41. Oxford: Oxford University Press, 2008.

Laqueur, Walter, ed. *Fascism: A Reader's Guide; Analyses, Interpretations, Bibliography*. Harmondsworth, UK: Penguin, 1979.

Lasby, Clarence G. *Project Paperclip: German Scientists and the Cold War*. New York: Scribner, 1975.

Laughland, John. "The Chechens' American Friends." *The Guardian*, September 8, 2004. No pages. Online: http://www.theguardian.com/world/2004/sep/08/usa.russia

Lenin, Vladimir. *Collected Works*. 2nd English ed., vol. 38. Translated by Clemens Dutt. Reprint. Moscow: Progress, 1965.

Lévi-Strauss, Claude. *The Raw and the Cooked*. Translated by John and Doreen Weightman. Reprint. Chicago: University of Chicago Press, 1969.

Liddell, H. G., and Robert Scott, eds. *A Greek-English Lexicon*. Oxford: Clarendon, 1996.

Locke, John. *An Essay Concerning Human Understanding*. Oxford: Clarendon, 1975.

————. *Two Treatises of Government*. Reprint. Cambridge: Cambridge University Press, 1970.

Louth, Andrew. "Holiness and the Vision of God in the Eastern Fathers." In *Holiness: Past and Present*, edited by Stephen C. Barton, 217–38. London: T. & T. Clark, 2003.

———. *St. John Damascene: Tradition and Originality in Byzantine Theology*. Oxford: Oxford University Press, 2002.

MacDonogh, Giles. *Frederick the Great: A Life in Deed and Letters*. New York: St. Martin's Press, 2001.

Mackinder, Halford J. *Democratic Ideals and Reality: A Study in Politics of Reconstruction*. London: Constable and Co., 1919.

———. "The Geographical Pivot of History." *Geographical Journal* 23 (1904) 421–44.

Mahan, Alfred T. *The Influence of Sea Power on History: 1660–1783*. London: Samson Low, 1889.

Makkreel, Rudolf A. *Imagination and Interpretation in Kant*. Chicago: University of Chicago Press, 1990.

MANDIANT. *Exposing One of China's Cyber Espionage Units*. Alexandria, VA: The Mandiant Intelligence Center, 2013.

Manning, David J. *Liberalism*. London: Dent and Sons, 1976.

Marx, Karl. "1859 Preface to *A Contribution to the Critique of Political Economy*." In *The Marx-Engels Reader*, edited and translated by Robert C. Tucker, 3–6. Reprint. New York: Norton, 1974.

———. *Capital*, vol. I. Translated by Ben Fowkes. Reprint. New York: Penguin, 1990.

———. *The Economic and Philosophic Manuscripts of 1844 and the Communist Manifesto*. Translated by Martin Milligan. Reprint. New York: Prometheus, 1988.

———. *Selected Writings*. Edited and translated by David McLellan. Reprint. Oxford: Oxford University Press, 1977.

Martin, Gottfried. *Leibniz: Logic and Metaphysics*. Manchester: Manchester University Press, 1964.

Maurus, V., and Marc Rock. "The Most Dreaded Man of the United States, Controlled a Long time by the CIA." *Le Monde* September 14, 2001. No pages. Online: http://www.wanttoknow.info/010914lemonde

McCabe, Mary M. *Plato's Individuals*. Princeton: Princeton University Press, 1999.

McCarthy, James G. *The Gospel according to Rome: Comparing Catholic Tradition and the Word of God*. Eugene, OR: Harvest House, 1995.

McGinn, B., and Willemien Otten, eds. *Eriugena: East and West*. South Bend, IN: Notre Dame University Press, 1994.

McGrade, Arthur S. *The Political Thought of William of Ockham*. Cambridge: Cambridge University Press, 1974.

McGuckin, John A. *St Gregory of Nazianzus: An Intellectual Biography*. New York: St. Vladimir's Seminary Press, 2001.

McKeon, Richard. *The Philosophy of Spinoza: The Unity of His Thought*. New York: Longmans, Green and Co., 1928.

Mead, Margaret. *Coming of Age in Samoa*. New York: HarperCollins, 2001.

Meredith, S.J., Anthony. *Gregory of Nyssa*. London: Routledge, 1999.

Meyendorff, John. *The Orthodox Church*. New York: St Vladimir's Seminary Press, 1981.

Minassian, Gaïdz. "Nouvelles Dynamiques Identitaires Contre Etats-Nations." *Le Monde*, September 6, 2013. No pages. Online: http://www.lemonde.fr/idees/article/2013/09/06/nouvelles-dynamiques-identitaires-contre-etats-nations_3472561_3232.html

Moody, Ernest. *The Logic of William of Ockham*. New York: Sheed and Ward, 1935.

Moran, D., and Timothy Mooney, eds. *The Phenomenology Reader*. London: Routledge, 2002.

Morgenthau, Hans J. *Politics among Nations: The Struggle for Power and Peace*. Revised by Kenneth W. Thompson. New York: McGraw-Hill, 1993.

———. *Politics in the Twentieth Century*. Chicago: University of Chicago Press, 1971.

———. *Scientific Man versus Power Politics*. Chicago: University of Chicago Press, 1946.

Morley, Felix. *The Power in the People*. New Jersey: Transaction, 2010.

Morningstar, C., and F. Randall Farmer. "The Lessons of Lucasfilm's Habitat." In *The New Media Reader*, edited by Noah Wardrip-Fruin and Nick Montfort, 664–77. Cambridge: MIT, 2003.

Moutsopoulos, Evanghelos. "Kairos ou minimum critique dans les sciences de la nature selon Aristote." *Revue Philosophique* 124 (1999) 481–91.

Mussolini, Benito. *Fascism: Doctrine and Institutions*. Reprint. New York: Fertig, 1968.

Naulleau, É., and Alain Soral. *Dialogues Désaccordés: Combat de Blancs dans un Tunnel*. Paris: Éditions Blanche, 2013.

Nicholson, Michael. *Causes and Consequences in International Relations: A Conceptual Study*. London: Pinter, 1996.

Nicholson, M., and Peter Bennett. "The Epistemology of International Relations." In *Contemporary International Relations: A Guide to Theory*, edited by A. J. R. Groom and Margot Light, 197–205. London: Pinter, 1994.

Nietzsche, Friedrich W. *Beyond Good and Evil*. Translated by Judith Norman. Reprint. Cambridge: Cambridge University Press, 2002.

———. *The Birth of Tragedy*. Translated by Douglas Smith. Reprint. Oxford: Oxford University Press, 2000.

———. *The Gay Science*. Translated by Josefine Nauckhoff. Reprint. Cambridge: Cambridge University Press, 2001.

———. *The Genealogy of Morals*. Translated by Horace B. Samuel. Reprint. New York: Dover, 2003.

———. *Thus Spoke Zarathustra: A Book for Everyone and Nobody*. Translated by Graham Parkes. Oxford: Oxford University Press, 2005.

———. *The Will to Power*. Translated by Walter Kaufmann and R. J. Hollingdale. Reprint. New York: Vintage, 1968.

Nolte, Ernst. *Three Faces of Fascism*. Translated by Leila Vennewitz. Reprint. New York: Holt, Rinehart, and Winston, 1966.

Nye, Joseph S., Jr. *The Future of Power*. New York: Public Affairs, 2011.

———. *Understanding International Conflicts: An Introduction to Theory and History*. New York: HarperCollins, 1993.

O'Donnell, J., and Douwe Miedema. "Shadow Banking Hits $67 Trillion Globally: Task Force." *Reuters*, November 19, 2012. No pages. Online: http://www.reuters.com/article/2012/11/19/us-shadow-banking-regulation-idUSBRE8AI0SL20121119

Oldmeadow, Kenneth. *Traditionalism: Religion in the Light of Perennial Philosophy*. New York: Sophia Perennis, 2011.

Olivelle, Patrick. *Samnyasa Upanisads: Hindu Scriptures on Asceticism and Renunciation*. Oxford: Oxford University Press, 1992.

Osorio, Carlos et al., eds. "On 30th Anniversary of Argentine Coup: New Declassified Details on Repression and U.S. Support for Military Dictatorship." *The National*

Security Archive, March 23, 2006. No pages. Online: http://www2.gwu.edu/~nsarchiv/NSAEBB/NSAEBB185/index.htm

Overgaard, Søren. "Heidegger's Concept of Truth Revisited." *Nordic Journal of Philosophy*, 3 (2002) 73–90.

Pals, Daniel L. *Eight Theories of Religion*, 2nd ed. New York: Oxford University Press, 2006.

Pangle, Thomas L. *Montesquieu's Philosophy of Liberalism: A Commentary on 'The Spirit of the Laws'*. Chicago: University of Chicago Press, 1973.

Pangle, Thomas L., ed. *The Rebirth of Classical Political Rationalism: An Introduction to the Thought of Leo Strauss*. Chicago: University of Chicago Press, 1989.

Papandreou, Andreas G. *Democracy at Gunpoint*. London: Andre Deutsch, 1971.

Paton, Herbert J., ed. *The Moral Law: Kant's Groundwork of the Metaphysics of Morals*. London: Hutchinson University Library, 1948.

Patterson, John. "The Caring, Sharing CIA." *The Guardian*, October 5, 2001. No pages. Online: http://www.theguardian.com/film/2001/oct/05/artsfeatures

Pattison, William D. "The Four Traditions of Geography." *Journal of Geography* 89 (1990) 202–6.

Pelczynski, Zbigniew A., ed. *State and Civil Society: Studies in Hegel's Political Philosophy*. Cambridge: Cambridge University Press, 1984.

Peel, John D. Y. *Herbert Spencer: The Evolution of a Sociologist*. London: Heinemann, 1971.

Perkins, John. *Confessions of an Economic Hit Man*. New York: Plume (Penguin Group), 2004.

Perkins, Merle L. *The Moral and Political Philosophy of the Abbé de Saint-Pierre*. Paris: Minard, 1959.

Picavet, François. *Roscelin: Philosophe et théologien, d' après la légende et d' après l' histoire*. Paris: Félix Alcan, Éditeur, 1911.

Pipes, Daniel. *Friendly Tyrants: An American Dilemma*. New York: Palgrave Macmillan, 1991.

Pirenne, Henri. *Medieval Cities: Their Origins and the Revival of Trade*. Reprint. Princeton: Princeton University Press, 1969.

Plumb, John H. *England in the Eighteenth Century*. Harmondsworth, UK: Penguin, 1954.

Polanyi, Karl. *The Great Transformation: The Political and Economic Origins of Our Time*. Boston: Beacon, 2001.

Popper, Karl R. *The Open Society and Its Enemies*. 2 vols. London: Routledge & Kegan Paul, 1945.

Portal, Roger. *The Slavs*. London: Weidenfeld and Nicolson, 1965.

Preobrazhensky, Alexander. *The Russian Orthodox Church: 10th to 20th Centuries*. Moscow: Progress, 1988.

Pye, Lucian W. *Aspects of Political Development*. Boston: Little, Brown and Company, 1966.

Ratzel, Friedrich. *Politische Geographie*. München: Oldenburg, 1897.

Reanier, Patrick. "Geo-statistical Forecasting Using Attitudinal Survey Data in Afghanistan." *Military Intelligence Professional Bulletin* 37 (2011) 37–44.

Reeve, Simon. *The New Jackals: Ramzi Yousef, Osama bin Laden, and the Future of Terrorism*. London: Deutsch, 1999.

Reich, Robert B. *The Work of Nations: Preparing Ourselves for the 21st-Century Capitalism.* New York: Vintage, 1992.

Reiss, Hans S., ed. *Kant: Political Writings.* Cambridge: Cambridge University Press, 1970.

Reynolds, L. D., and Nigel G. Wilson. *Scribes and Scholars: A Guide to the Transmission of Greek and Latin Literature.* Oxford: Clarendon, 1991.

Ribe, Neil M. "Cartesian Optics and the Mastery of Nature." *Isis* 88 (1997) 42–61.

Richard, Carl J. *The Battle for the American Mind: A Brief History of a Nation's Thought.* Plymouth, UK: Rowman and Littlefield, 2006.

Romanides, John S. *The Ancestral Sin.* Ridgewood, NJ: Zephyr, 2002.

———. *Franks, Romans, Feudalism, and Doctrine.* Patriarch Athenagoras Memorial Lectures. Brookline, MA: Holy Cross Orthodox Press, 1981.

Romer, Paul M. "Endogenous Technological Change." *Journal of Political Economy* 98 (1990) 71–102.

Roosen, William. *Daniel Defoe and Diplomacy.* Selinsgrove, PA: Susquehanna University Press, 1986.

Rorty, Richard. "Postmodern Bourgeois Liberalism." *The Journal of Philosophy* 80 (1983) 583–89.

Rosa, Jean-Jacques. *Euro Exit: Why (and How) to Get Rid of the Monetary Union.* New York: Algora, 2012.

Rosenau, James N. *The Scientific Study of Foreign Policy.* London: Pinter, 1982.

Rosenberg, Alfred. *Race and Race History* (includes excerpts from *The Myth of the Twentieth Century*). London: Weidenfeld and Nicolson, 1970.

Roumeliotis, Greg. "Exclusive: U.S. Banking Regulator, Fearing Loan Bubble, Warns Funds." *Reuters*, January 29, 2014. No pages. Online: http://www.reuters.com/article/2014/01/29/us-banks-regulators-loans-idUSBREA0S0DG20140129

Rousseau, Jean-Jacques. *Émile.* Translated by Allan Bloom. Reprint. New York: Basic, 1978.

———. *First and Second Discourses.* Translated by Roger D. Masters and Judith R. Masters. Reprint. New York: St. Martin's Press, 1964.

———. *The Plan for Perpetual Peace, On the Government of Poland, and Other Writings on History and Politics.* Translated by Christopher Kelly and Judith Bush. Reprint. Lebanon, NH: University Press of New England, 2005.

———. *The Social Contract, with Geneva Manuscript and Political Economy.* Translated by Roger D. Masters and Judith R. Masters. Reprint. New York: St. Martin's Press, 1978.

Rowse, Arthur E. "The Secret U.S. War to Subvert Italian Democracy." *Covert Action Quarterly* 49 (1994) 20–27, 62–63.

Ruge, Wolfgang. *Novemberrevolution: Die Volkserhebung gegen den deutschen Imperialismus und Militarismus.* Berlin: Dietz Verlag, 1978.

———. *Weimar: Republik auf Zeit.* Berlin: Verlag das europäische Buch, 1977.

Ruggiero, Guido de. *The History of European Liberalism.* Boston: Beacon, 1959.

Sabine, G. H., and Thomas L. Thorson. *A History of Political Theory.* Fort Worth, TX: Holt, Rinehart and Winston, 1973.

Sachs, Carl B. "Nietzsche's *Daybreak*: Toward a Naturalized Theory of Autonomy." *Epoché* 13 (2008) 81–100.

Salem-Wiseman, Jonathan. "Heidegger's Dasein and the Liberal Conception of the Self." *Political Theory* 31 (2003) 533–57.

Samuelson, P. A., and William D. Nordhaus. *Economics*. 14th ed. New York: McGraw-Hill, 1992.

Sand, Shlomo. *The Invention of the Jewish People*. London: Verso, 2009.

Sartre, Jean-Paul. *Existentialism and Human Emotions*. Translated by Bernard Frechtman and Hazel E. Barnes. Reprint. New York: Citadel, 1957.

Scheuer, Michael. *Imperial Hubris: Why the West Is Losing the War on Terror*. Stirling, VA: Potomac, 2004.

———. *Osama Bin Laden*. Oxford: Oxford University Press, 2011.

Schopenhauer, Arthur. *The World as Will and Idea*. Edited and translated by David Berman. London: Orion, 1995.

Scott, Peter D. *The Road to 9/11: Wealth, Empire, and the Future of America*. Berkeley: University of California Press, 2007.

Scruton, Roger. *Spinoza: A Very Short Introduction*. Oxford: Oxford University Press, 2002.

Searle, John. *The Rediscovery of the Mind*. Cambridge: MIT, 1992.

Sedgwick, Mark. *Against the Modern World: Traditionalism and the Secret Intellectual History of the Twentieth Century*. New York: Oxford University Press, 2004.

Sengova, Joko. "Bilingual Data Collection and Research Protocols: Some Lessons Learned in Afghanistan." *Military Intelligence Professional Bulletin* 37 (2011) 45–51.

Sharp, Gene. *The Politics of Nonviolent Action*, 3 vols. Boston: Porter Sargent, 1973.

Sheehan, Thomas. "A Paradigm Shift in Heidegger Research." *Continental Philosophy Review* 34 (2001) 183–202.

Shestov, Lev. *Dostoevsky, Tolstoy, and Nietzsche*. Athens, OH: Ohio University Press, 1969.

Soral, Alain. *Chroniques d' Avant-Guerre*. Paris: Éditions Blanche, 2012.

———. *Reflections on Violence*. New York: Macmillan, 1950.

———. *Sociologie du Drageur: Le Livre sur l' Amour et la Femme*. Paris: Éditions Blanche, 2004.

Spykman, Nicholas J. *America's Strategy in World Politics: The United States and the Balance of Power*. Livingstone, NJ: Transaction, 2008.

———. *The Geography of the Peace*. Hamden, CT: Archon, 1969.

Stalder, Felix. *Manuel Castells*. Cambridge: Polity, 2006.

Story, Christopher, *The European Union Collective: Enemy of Its Member States*. London: Harle, 1997.

Strange, Susan. "The Name of the Game." In *Sea-Changes: American Foreign Policy in a World Transformed*, edited by Nicholas X. Rizopoulos, 238–73. New York: Council on Foreign Relations, 1990.

Strauss, Leo. *Natural Right and History*. Chicago: University of Chicago Press, 1953.

———. *What Is Political Philosophy and Other Studies*. Glencoe, IL: Free, 1959.

Tatakis, Basil. *Byzantine Philosophy*. Indianapolis: Hackett, 2003.

Tavakoli, Janet. "Fraud as a Business Model." *Huffpost Business*, September 6, 2011. No pages. Online: http://www.huffingtonpost.com/janet-tavakoli/fraud-as-a-business-model_b_950806.html

Taylor, Charles. *Hegel*. Cambridge: Cambridge University Press, 1975.

Teilhard de Chardin, Pierre. *The Future of Man*. Translated by Norman Denny. Reprint. New York: Harper and Row, 1964.

Thorne, John. "Local Conflict Assessment Framework: Analyzing Perceptions and Sources of Violence." *Military Intelligence Professional Bulletin* 37 (2011) 33–36.

Tilly, Charles. *Coercion, Capital and European States AD 990–1990.* Oxford: Blackwell, 1992.

Toland, John. *Adolf Hitler.* New York: Knopf Doubleday, 1976.

Tomlinson, John. *Cultural Imperialism.* London: Continuum, 1991.

United States Department of State. *Papers Relating to the Foreign Relations of the United States, 1918: Russia.* 3 vols. Washington, DC: U.S. Government Printing Office, 1931.

Van de Haar, Edwin. "David Hume and International Political Theory: A Reappraisal." *Review of International Studies* 34 (2008) 225–42.

Viotti, P. R., and Mark V. Kauppi. *International Relations Theory.* New York: Pearson Education, 2012.

Voltaire, François-Marie A. *Philosophical Dictionary.* Edited and translated by Theodore Besterman. Reprint. Harmondsworth, UK: Penguin, 1972.

Von Campenhausen, Hans. *Ecclesiastical Authority and Spiritual Power in the Church of the First Three Centuries.* Peabody, MA: Hendrickson, 1997.

Von Neumann, John. "The Mathematician." In *The Works of the Mind,* edited by Robert B. Heywood, 180–96. Chicago: University of Chicago Press, 1947.

Waltz, Kenneth N. "Reflections on *Theory of International Politics*: A Response to My Critics." In *Neorealism and Its Critics,* edited by Robert O. Keohane, 322–45. New York: Columbia University Press, 1986.

———. *Theory of International Politics.* New York: McGraw-Hill, 1979.

Warman, Matt. "Google Invites the Best and Brightest into Its Big Tent." *The Telegraph,* May 24, 2012. No pages. Online: http://www.telegraph.co.uk/technology/eric-schmidt/9285690/Google-invites-the-best-and-brightest-into-its-Big-Tent.html

Weber, Max. *The Protestant Ethic and the Spirit of Capitalism.* Translated by Talcott Parsons and Anthony Giddens. Reprint. London: Allen and Unwin, 1930.

Weigall, D., and Peter Stirk, eds. *The Origins and Development of the European Community.* Leicester, UK: Leicester University Press, 1992.

Willan, Philip. "US 'Supported Anti-Left Terror in Italy': Report Claims Washington Used a Strategy of Tension in the Cold War to Stabilise the Centre-Right." *The Guardian,* June 24, 2000. No pages. Online: http://www.cambridgeclarion.org/press_cuttings/us.terrorism_graun_24jun2000.html

Willan, Philip. *Puppetmasters: The Political Use of Terrorism in Italy.* Lincoln, NE: Constable, 2002.

Woessner, Martin. *Heidegger in America.* Cambridge: Cambridge University Press, 2011.

Wright, Moorhead, ed. *Theory and Practice of Balance of Power: 1486–1914.* London: Dent and Sons, 1975.

Zeller, Edward. *Outlines of the History of Greek Philosophy.* Translated by S. F. Alleyne and Evelyn Abbott. Reprint. London: Longmans, Green and Co., 1895.

Lightning Source UK Ltd.
Milton Keynes UK
UKHW022209060119
335118UK00016B/435/P